FEEL
GOOD
for
life

A recipe for great health and vitality

with NZ nutrition expert
Claire Turnbull

PENGUIN BOOKS

Contents

Preface

HOW THIS BOOK CAME ABOUT

Growing up, my mum and dad loved having people to come and stay. Close family, extended family, friends, friends of friends – you name it; they were welcomed with open arms.

Now, as an adult, I have inherited the 'open home' trait and just love having friends and family to come and stay for the weekend or a couple of weeks if they are in a transition phase in their lives or if they are travelling and need somewhere to base themselves. It is so nice to spend quality time with people who you love and treasure, to share meals with them and enjoy great conversations.

You might be wondering how this relates to building healthy habits and looking and feeling good. Well, when someone stays with me, they always seem to comment on how healthy they feel when they leave and how inspired they are to start eating healthier food, be more active, focus on getting good-quality sleep and generally, just start looking after themselves a little better.

A few years ago, I had family from around the world come to stay for the festive season and, without exception, they all said they had the best Christmas ever, loved every mouthful of the delicious healthy food they ate and, for the first time ever, actually lost weight rather than piling it on. They were all able to start the New Year feeling positive, healthy and energised rather than overfull and uncomfortable.

I also recently had some friends invite me over to their new pad where they delighted in showing me the contents of their healthy cupboards, a meal planning system they had and the new blackout curtains they had got to ensure they slept better! It was amazing to see how by staying with me for a while they had seen the value in making healthy their 'new normal' and that feeling good was totally achievable!

Over the years, my friends and family have said time and time again that I really needed to create some kind of checklist or resource that would help them to remember everything they had learnt during their stay and also to share my ideas about how to live a healthy life and feel good with the rest of the world. One friend even said she thought it was my duty to help people to make healthy living happen! I laughed at the time, but, I guess now I feel that is kind of true.

It was all those conversations that planted the seed for this book.

FROM FRIENDS AND FAMILY TO YOU!

I know it is not just my friends and family who want to have more energy and feel good. Whether I'm speaking at an event, running a cooking class or talking to my team at Mission Nutrition about what our clients want, it seems that most people are desperate to get their health in better shape and have more energy to live life to the full.

With life being so busy and tiredness being the norm, eating well, keeping active and taking the time to relax and unwind can feel like it is just too hard. Sound familiar?

Well, I am here to help. You don't have to live that crazy energy-draining life anymore. I want to show you that nourishing your body and generally taking better care of yourself doesn't have to be difficult and it really is possible to feel good for life!

As much as I would love to have you all round to stay at my house for a week at a time to help you on your way, I think my husband might struggle with the concept and sadly, as amazing as the little chickens in my backyard are, I don't think they could keep up with supply and demand for you all when it comes to eggs. So instead, I decided that the best way to help you on your own personal journey to look and feel better every day was to write a book that pulled all my ideas and inspiration together.

So, voilà – here it is. Your ultimate guide to living a healthy and happy life, where it is normal to have amazing energy and feel good!

Happy reading – I can't wait to hear what you think!

Claire
X

Introduction

My journey to a happier, healthier me and feeling good

I have certainly not always felt good. When I was growing up, I had a very unhappy time at school – especially in the early days. I was chubby, covered head to toe in eczema and got picked on for my looks and funny skin. Friends were few and far between.

Throughout my childhood and teenage years, I had a seriously dangerous, dysfunctional relationship with food – I would go from starving myself to binging and I had an incredibly distorted body image. I didn't sleep very well, found it impossible to relax and was either completely inactive or running obsessively. I also struggled with depression for years and the whole experience very nearly resulted in me ending my life.

At the time, I always used to wonder what all those annoying 'happy' people were going on about when they said you could live the life of your dreams. Other people's positivity and optimism made me even angrier. I used to think: *Lucky them. Their life is so perfect and easy – they have no idea.*

Over the years, through a lot of self-work, therapy to help me manage my dysfunctional eating patterns and a commitment to keeping active, I very luckily came out the other side of some extremely dark and terrifying times. I came to learn the real importance of eating well, sleeping well and generally taking care of myself in order to survive.

I started to understand that what you eat, how much you move your body and what you think make such a huge difference to every aspect of your life, from your relationships, to your work, inner peace and, of course, how you feel. Without good mental and physical health, life is much tougher than it needs to be.

From troubled times and difficult beginnings, things are now remarkably different. I qualified as a dietitian and personal trainer in the UK over 10 years ago and have been able to combine my knowledge and personal experience to help others live healthier, happier lives through the work I now do. I have also been able to create an awesome healthy, happy life for myself that is all about enjoying fabulous nourishing food and the odd glass of delicious Pinot Noir!

From my own journey I have learnt the tools and skills needed to make healthy happen and understand more than ever what it truly takes to feel good, and that is what this book is all about. I hope you find it to be a source of inspiration.

Your journey to feeling good

Regardless of what you have personally been through and where you are in your life right now, amazing health, happiness and feeling good are out there for you to find and keep, and I am here to help you do that.

My intention is that this book will help you get healthier and feel happier one step at a time. I know that many of you who are reading this will know at least the basics of eating well and the importance of moving your body, but what I also know is that many of you are likely to be struggling to apply what you know and make it all happen!

In my book *Lose Weight for Life*, I discussed concepts of making healthy happen, specifically in relation to losing weight and keeping it off. Here, whilst the things I will be going through will indeed help you get in great shape, I also want to help you develop the skills you need to eat well to help you feel good, look fabulous and get the most out of every day. Being slim is one thing, but what is not to be dismissed is the importance of how you feel when you wake up in the morning.

I want to help break down the barriers to eating well and living an active, healthy life – I know making it happen is often harder than it sounds. I want to make sure that you wake up in the morning ready to high-five the world – so full of energy that you can tackle anything. My intention is to help you shine and be your very best: the best version of yourself, inside and out.

This is a book to keep at your bedside, on your coffee table or close to hand so that you can dip in and out of it at any time to refresh yourself and try something new, and keep yourself heading in a healthy direction.

This book is to help you make changes that matter and actually make a difference. It does not mean that you have to give up everything you love and become boring – quite the opposite, in fact. I will show you that being healthy is fun and nothing to do with deprivation!

It is not a guide to living a 'perfect' life – I don't believe that notion exists, and who defines what is perfect anyway? It focuses instead on helping you do what feels right and is good for you as an individual.

It has been designed to help you make the proportion of days in your life that feel amazing, wonderful and happy more plentiful. Life is tough sometimes and you can be dealt some rough cards – I know that; it is the same for me, too. What I know though, is that by eating well, looking after yourself and committing to working through things one day at a time, you will get through and the days will be brighter again.

Feel Good for Life is a collation of what I have learnt through my studies, good-quality evidence-based research and my experiences. I am not going to try to be a nutrition encyclopedia or commit to being all things to all people, but my intention is that the collection of information and practical ideas this book contains will help you to feel amazing and wonderful as often as possible. I want to help you to eat food that nourishes your body, mind and soul more often than not and to feel that you have the tools you need to create a healthy life that you love.

Use this book however it works for you! You can read it cover to cover or dip in and out of it – but my one word of advice is to actually answer the questions I ask and do the exercises I have outlined. You have to do them if you want to make changes that last. If you find yourself saying 'I don't know' to any questions, then remember that is just your mind getting in the way – you do know. Somewhere inside of you, you do know the answer. You might just need to ask yourself, 'If I did know, what would I say?' You know more than you think.

THE RECIPE FOR FEELING GOOD

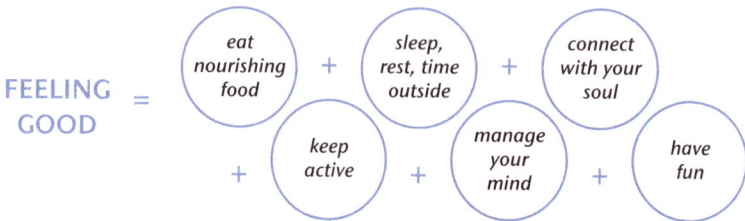

FEELING GOOD = eat nourishing food + sleep, rest, time outside + connect with your soul + keep active + manage your mind + have fun

This book covers all the aspects of the 'recipe' you need to feel good. Throughout the book I will be helping you to:

1. Eat nourishing food that makes you feel good
   - Enjoy nutrient-dense foods that your body loves
   - Understand your eating behaviour
   - Eat for the right reasons
   - Eat at the right time for you

2. Keep active and get results
   - Learn how to be fit and active each and every day – the easy way
   - Get the best results from your workout
   - Eat right around exercise

3. Sleep, rest and have time outside
   - Get a great night's sleep
   - Learn how to relax, unwind and disconnect
   - Understand the importance of time outside

4. Have fun – be an awesome kind of healthy!
   - Socialise the healthy way
   - Eat well when you are with friends and family
   - Manage your alcohol intake
   - Give healthy gifts

5. Manage your mind
   - Understand your thoughts
   - Learn to say 'no'
   - Feed your mind the right way

6. Connect with your soul
   - Get to know yourself
   - Be clear on what 'feeling good' really means
   - Use your soul as a compass
   - Surround yourself with amazing energy

Let's get to it!

1

Create your healthiest, happiest life

Our crazy, busy world

When you ask someone how they are, what is the most common reply you get? If it is a quick passing comment, then most often the response is 'fine thanks' because it is the easiest thing to say, even though sometimes the person you are asking doesn't really feel fine at all! If you are able to engage in a bit more conversation and know someone a little better, then you might get a slightly more honest answer, which nine times out of ten is more along the lines of 'I'm busy/flat out/full on' or 'I'm knackered/tired/exhausted/run-down/need a break' with the odd genuine positive reply thrown in there if they have just been on holiday, recently had a pay rise or moved into a new house. I bet you could count on one hand the number of times in the past few months that you have had someone say to you: 'You know what, life is really awesome right now and I am feeling really good'.

Our crazy, fast-paced, busy world means that most of us feel wired and tired much of the time. Having lots of energy and feeling genuinely healthy and happy from the inside out seems like a far-distant dream.

Many of us are accessible by phone or email day and night and it's all too easy to check our Inbox or Facebook timeline first thing in the morning before we have even acknowledged that a beautiful new day is here. There is a never-ending stream of information, ideas and 'things' stimulating our minds and there is always something we could be doing, achieving or worrying about – money, kids, marriage, not being married, work, wobbly thighs, arms, not feeling good enough – it doesn't stop. Our minds work overtime, all the time – it's no surprise we are all wired!

As for us all feeling tired – well, that's not rocket science either. So many of us find it hard to mentally switch off and rely on sugar or stimulants like caffeine to get us through the day. That, combined with poor-quality sleep, not being active enough (or training heaps but not recovering properly) as well as eating food that doesn't nourish our bodies from the inside out, is a recipe for burnout.

MANAGE THE MADNESS

The crazy busyness of our world isn't going to change anytime soon, so all you can do is look for ways to manage the madness and find strategies that help you to take better care of yourself so you can start feeling good and get the most out of your life without getting caught up in the rat race.

You need to make sure that you are choosing to eat healthy, nourishing foods that help your body work at its best. Food is, after all, the fuel for every cell in your body and determines how well your system can function. You also need to find ways to keep active, get outside more often and appreciate all the amazing things you already have, rather than always wanting more.

Your body needs time to unwind, too, even if you don't think it does. If you are anything like I used to be, swearing blind that 'chilling out' wasn't for me and telling people that I didn't need time out because I was much happier being 'busy', then it might be time to look at your life a little closer. 'Busy' is a smoke screen. If you can't sit and 'just be' for five minutes without needing to 'do something', I promise you there is something hiding that you need to deal with if you genuinely want to be healthier and happier. Being insanely 'busy' is a dangerous addiction in my opinion.

So, how are you?

Given that you are probably the one who always asks others how they are, it's time for me to ask you! Are you feeling a little (or very) wired and tired? Do you want to live a healthier life and feel happier when you wake up every morning but you are not sure how? Do you feel like you know what you 'need to do' to live a healthier life but just can't make it happen?

Getting to know and understand yourself, what you do and why you do what you do is the first stage in allowing you to make some changes. It is about creating awareness and being in tune with yourself – from here you can create a platform from which anything is possible.

The reason why generic rules, diet plans and guidelines about being 'healthy' and 'happy' often don't work or give you results that last is that they don't start with you and who you are. This step of clarity is absolutely vital. Here is how it is done . . .

STEP 1: WHAT NEEDS TO CHANGE FOR YOU TO BE HEALTHIER, HAPPIER AND FEEL GOOD?

When you move into a new house or flat you instantly see the things you would like to change. Maybe the curtains need to go, the garden needs a spruce up and the bathroom needs a lick of fresh paint. However, as soon as a few months have rolled by, if you haven't embraced your initial desire to redecorate, you kind of get used to the way the walls are and don't notice the brown curtains so much anymore – they become almost normal to you.

Life is much the same – when you are busy and don't ever make time to stop and think, you just do what you have always done and keep getting the same results over and over again.

If you want to build a healthy, happy life and start feeling really good, you need to look at the way things are for you now and identify what needs to change to help you step towards the life you really want and deserve.

Right now I want you to look at your life as if you had never seen it before, as if it was someone else's life. What is going on for you? What areas of your health and happiness need a bit of TLC?

Time to tune in!

Grab a cuppa, remove all distractions from around you and read through these questions. All you need to do is answer yes or no, but take the time to really think about your answers. Why do or don't you do these things? Feel free to write notes if any thoughts or ideas come up for you – the more time you give yourself to tune in, the better you will get to know yourself and the more likely you are to be able to shift the things that need attention.

What and when do you eat and drink?
Do you . . .
- Eat less than three handfuls of vegetables every day? Yes/No
- Opt for white bread over wholegrain? Yes/No
- Add sugar to your food/drinks? Yes/No
- Feel like you crave sugar a lot of the time? Yes/No
- Snack on muffins, cakes, biscuits and lollies at least a few times a week? Yes/No
- Rely on coffee/tea/energy drinks to help boost your energy levels? Yes/No

- Regularly grab food on the go? Maybe not always the healthy stuff. Yes/No
- Drink less than two litres of fluid each and every day? Yes/No
- Drink alcohol most nights of the week? Yes/No
- Often go 'past hungry' or go for a long time without eating? Yes/No

Your notes/thoughts/feelings:

_____
_____
_____
_____
_____
_____
_____
_____

Why and how do you eat and drink?

Do you:

- Rarely take a proper break for lunch – even if it is only a few minutes? Yes/No
- Sit down and eat with the TV on or eat when there are lots of distractions around you? Yes/No
- Not really plan your meals – just eat whatever is in the fridge or cupboard most of the time? Yes/No
- Feel like you always eat the same old things and are bored of what you eat? Yes/No
- Eat on the run – while you are walking/running around? Yes/No
- Eat when you are bored or tired? Yes/No
- Eat when you are angry, upset or feeling down? Yes/No
- Drink alcohol to help you unwind or cope with stress? Yes/No
- Eat more than you need sometimes? Yes/No

Your notes/thoughts/feelings:

_____
_____
_____
_____
_____
_____
_____
_____

How well is your body working?
Do you:
- Often get run-down? Sick? Feel like you have a poor immune system? Yes/No
- Pee and find that the colour is often dark yellow? Yes/No
- Find it difficult to do 'number twos' or feel bunged up? Yes/No
- Feel bloated after eating? Yes/No
- Have dry, cracked or tired-looking skin? Yes/No
- Find your nails always seem to break? Yes/No
- Have any health issues which are related or influenced by your lifestyle, e.g. heart disease or diabetes? Yes/No

Your notes/thoughts/feelings:

_____

_____

_____

Moving your body
Do you:
- Find it hard to move your body and do something physically active for at least 30 minutes every day? Yes/No
- Feel stuck in a rut with your exercise regimen? Yes/No
- Work out but don't feel like you are getting results? Yes/No
- Feel like exercise is a chore? Yes/No
- Find it takes a long time to recover from a workout? Yes/No
- Lose motivation quickly? Yes/No

Your notes/thoughts/feelings:

_____

_____

_____

Socialising and fun times
Do you:
- Feel being 'healthy' can sometimes be a bit boring? Yes/No
- Find it hard to eat well when social events often revolve around food and booze? Yes/No

- Struggle to make healthy choices when you eat out? Yes/No
- Find it hard to know what to make for people who come over for dinner that is healthy and still tastes amazing? Yes/No
- Feel it can be difficult to say 'no' to people when they offer you something to eat or drink? Yes/No
- Intend to eat well and not drink too much when you are being sociable but find more often than not that that just doesn't end up happening? Yes/No
- Feel like you need alcohol to have a good time? Yes/No

Your notes/thoughts/feelings:

_____

_____

_____

Balance of your body, mind and soul

Do you:
- Sometimes feel like you aren't good enough? Yes/No
- Often feel like life is too busy or there is not enough time to do everything? Yes/No
- Worry about what the future holds? What might go wrong? Yes/No
- Find it difficult to take any time for you each week? Even if it is just five minutes? Yes/No
- Sleep for less than seven hours a night? Yes/No
- Have broken sleep? Yes/No
- Struggle to relax? Feel anxious at the thought of doing nothing? Yes/No
- Find that you aren't getting outside for at least 20 minutes a day? (By getting outside, I mean time when you have your skin and eyes exposed to natural light, not through your car windscreen or a window – that doesn't count.) Yes/No
- Not get to spend much quality time each week with the people you love and care about? Yes/No

Your notes/thoughts/feelings:

_____

_____

_____

Time to add things up!

How many questions did you answer 'yes' to? These questions just give us a little snapshot into how things are for you when it comes to your health and happiness. Any question you answered 'yes' to could be an area where it might be time to focus your attention. Every 'yes' could potentially be affecting how wired and tired you feel as well as your health and happiness overall.

I used to answer 'yes' to nearly all these questions – but, over time, I have taught myself, as well as all those I work with and who have stayed with me, to manage things better so we can now all say 'no' to these questions – most of the time.

If you are able to sort through your answers and work on some small changes to each area of your health and wellbeing you will be amazed with the results and will look and feel so much better. The rest of this book is all about how to make this happen.

For a printable version of these questions go to: www.claireturnbull.co.nz/feelgood

Extreme tiredness and fatigue

Even though it isn't abnormal to feel tired and run-down sometimes (especially if you answered 'yes' to many of my questions), ongoing extreme tiredness and fatigue isn't normal and needs to be looked into further. If you genuinely eat quite well, try to be active and look after yourself pretty well most of the time and still feel super tired, it might be time to head to your GP to make sure there is nothing else going on. There are medical conditions, including coeliac disease, thyroid malfunction, hormonal imbalances, diabetes, iron-deficiency anaemia, B12 deficiency and chronic fatigue syndrome, which may need to be tested for. Depression and anxiety can also take their toll on the body and you may need additional support to help deal with these, so don't just leave it – please don't just have another coffee and try to push through. Instead, get help – there are some wonderful people out there.

My team at Mission Nutrition are amazing and will be able to help you manage any of these conditions or ongoing extreme tiredness, so do let us know if you need help; we understand.
www.missionnutrition.co.nz

STEP 2: DIG A LITTLE DEEPER – WHY DO YOU DO WHAT YOU DO?

Before we jump straight into the 'how to' and what exactly you need to be doing to get your health and happiness in a better place, we do need to dig a little deeper and get a little more clarity on your habits and behaviours to get to the bottom of why you do what you do. It is from here that we can make changes that will stick and help you feel good for life.

If you look back at the questions I just asked you and what you said 'yes' to, what I really want you to think about and reflect on is the 'why' behind what you do. Why do you not take a lunch break? Why don't you drink much water in the day time? Why don't you feel good enough? To be able to eventually say 'no' to these questions, you will need to understand the 'why' behind them first. Spend a little time getting clear if you can – it is really helpful.

How you learn to do what you do

When I moved in with my now husband we were constantly at loggerheads because I didn't do things the way he did them and he just couldn't understand it.

I always have multiples of everything in case we 'run out' – four packets of rice, three spare toothbrushes and about a thousand pens. My mum is exactly the same, if not worse actually. On my last visit home I found twelve cans of beans and six boxes of oats in the cupboard! My husband hates excess and prefers to just have one of everything – that's how things work in his family.

I also put things in drawers and cupboards wherever they fit and, admittedly, have a bit of a 'shoving them in' issue, and my mum, dad and brothers do the same. My husband on the other hand likes extreme order and organisation and things to have their place. His dad was in the military and his mum is naturally a wonderfully tidy person so it's really no surprise he feels that way.

Without boring you with my marital and family debates, the point I want to make is that we do what we do because it is normal for us and that can be influenced by many things, including our upbringing, experiences and the people around us – even though most of the time we don't consciously realise it. It wasn't until my husband spent two weeks with my parents in the UK that he said to me, 'Ah, now I totally understand why you do what you do.' He saw first-hand that I am just like the rest of my family! He might not like it, but he now sees that the way I do things is based on the way I have been hard-wired. My 'multiple purchasing' and 'shoving' issues are habits I spent more than thirty years learning.

It is my belief that for you to make positive changes in your life and step towards a happier and healthier way of living, the starting point is to understand the way you are hard-wired. By that I mean getting to know what your 'default settings' are or the habits you have that make you, well, you!

Some of your default settings or habits that you have learnt will be very helpful and we want to keep those – like looking before you cross the road, or brushing your teeth twice a day. However, there are some habits that you will have learnt that are leading you away from your healthiest, happiest life – like beating yourself up when you lose or fail at something, eating ice cream to cope with sadness or disappointment or skipping exercise because you are having a 'fat' day and it doesn't feel like it makes that much difference anyway.

When you are aware of your default settings – your default habits and behaviours – you can choose to change them to suit you and the life that you want to live. In my book *Lose Weight for Life*, I touched on this in relation to those habits and behaviours that lead you away from being slim and trim. In this book, I will be focusing more on you as a whole – all the habits and behaviours that affect your health and wellbeing, from food and exercise to sleep and managing what you think.

What influences your default settings?

There are many things that influence your default settings – the habits and behaviours that you feel are normal. Below are some of them.

YOUR THOUGHTS AND BELIEFS

Without even realising it, all day every day there are hundreds and thousands of thoughts going through your mind which completely control your life and the way you do things. When you come across a situation, read an email or talk to someone, your brain tries to interpret what you are seeing or going through and give it meaning. An example might be when you see someone in the street who you know and they walk straight past you without acknowledging you at all. It could simply have been that they didn't see you, but you might think: *She obviously doesn't like me. I must have offended her last time I saw her. She must be embarrassed to know me.* The list goes on. None of these things are necessarily true and you might not even realise that you are thinking them. It all happens by default.

Deep within us we also all hold beliefs about body image, weight, money, relationships, conflict, exercise and so on. These are influenced by your upbringing, experiences and environment and completely control your life whether you consciously know it or not.

Understanding your thoughts and beliefs and working on them is one of the most life-changing things you will ever do and is a vital part of the jigsaw when it comes to feeling good. You will read more on this in Chapter 9: Feed your mind and soul (see pages 196–207).

Managing your thoughts is essential for a healthy, happy life.

YOUR EXPERIENCES

The way you were brought up, the teachers you had at school, what someone said to you in the playground when you were five and your first job are all examples of things that have influenced who you are today, why you do things the way you do and why you think what you think. Your past experiences affect your thoughts and beliefs.

There are positives and negatives to this, of course. On the positive side, your experiences may have led you to know more about healthy food, exercise, sleeping and taking care of yourself, too, and that is all good news. On the negative side, an experience may have led you to lack confidence, to feel like you have to prove yourself all the time or that you need to look a certain way to be accepted.

YOUR ENVIRONMENT

Where you live and work, your local shops and facilities, and everything that surrounds you can influence your default settings. If you live in the country and spend a lot of time outside being active and in the sun, the way you eat and sleep will no doubt be very different from someone who has a corporate job, rarely sees the light of day and can only exercise if they can manage to get to the gym before work at some unearthly hour! You will know yourself, when your environment has changed in the past, be it with your job, the arrival of children or moving house, that your ability to live a healthy lifestyle will have changed – either for the better or for the worse.

THE PEOPLE YOU SPEND TIME WITH

It has been suggested that you become like the five people you spend the most time with, and, I guess, I have to agree. If you think about your life now and the people you spend the most time with, are you more like them now than when you first met them? Some people naturally make you feel good just by being with them; others, sadly, will bring you down.

If the people you surround yourself with most often make such a big difference, you need to consider who you want to be influencing your life in such a big way. More on this in Chapter 7: Have fun while keeping healthy (see pages 168–9).

You become like the people you spend the most time with, so choose carefully.

Time to tune in!

So, when you think about the way you eat, how active you are, how much you sleep and your general health and happiness right now, what thoughts and beliefs, previous experiences, environmental factors or people might be influencing why you do what you do?

Focus first on the things in your life that bother you the most or the things that you most want to change. Maybe it is that you can't get to sleep at night, or that you never stop eating when you are full. Write whatever comes to mind.

STEP 3: CHANGE YOUR DEFAULT SETTINGS – MAKE HEALTHY AND HAPPY YOUR 'NEW NORMAL'

I had the great fortune to visit Japan a few years ago and it was one of the most eye-opening experiences of my life. The Japanese are just so healthy and happy-looking – slim, trim and glowing, quite frankly! In Japan, being healthy is almost a social responsibility; it is part of the culture to take care of yourself and eat well – it is just what you do. In general, the Japanese don't eat on the run; they sit down for their meals and they certainly don't fill themselves up on sugary snacks like we do in New Zealand. They eat massive amounts of veggies, seafood and plain rice, and you know what? It works for them. There are even nutritionists in many Japanese primary schools, so the children learn to eat well from day one. How good is that? Overall, there is just this amazing sense of normality about having nourishing food, it is their society default. I loved it!

The Japanese have the longest life-expectancy in the world and, apart from needing to work on their salt intake with all their sauces and dressings (and they would probably be better off changing the type of rice they eat to a higher-fibre version), they are generally doing well. Sadly though, of course the Western influence is slowly creeping in. I just hope they can keep to their traditions for as long as possible and not allow their lives to be changed for the worse.

Having come from the UK, I have also been lucky enough to have had many trips to Europe in my early years – France, Italy, Spain and Greece, to name just a few. I just adore the beautiful fresh produce they so lovingly grow, the value they place on making things from scratch and making meal times an occasion to spend quality time with the people they love.

We need to learn from this and start to make healthy, happy and feeling good our 'new normal' like they do in other parts of the world.

Our 'normal' in New Zealand is often far from healthy and it is only getting worse. Morning tea now commonly means muffins and coffee, especially if you are at a meeting or function. Often the muffins and slices don't even taste that good – we end up eating them because everyone else is or because there are no other options. Eating unhealthily has become a bad habit for far too many of us.

I distinctly remember sitting with a group of children in Tokyo while they were eating their lunch of fish, cabbage and other green veggies with plain rice and thinking: *Wow – if you showed that meal to most children I know in New Zealand, they would turn their noses up and refuse to eat it.* Why? Because it is not normal for them. That is not to say, however, that they couldn't learn to like it.

Sugary milk drinks, sweetened breakfast cereals and processed food is what surrounds our kids today and it can easily seem normal to accept this because it is what our environment supports. As a new mum myself, this is very worrying. Jamie Oliver would agree, I am sure.

Another 'normal' habit many adults have is related to alcohol. For many people (and I used to be one of them), it seems perfectly normal to drink half to a bottle of wine a night or a few beers to unwind at the end of a day. It's just kind of what we have learnt to do. I'm not saying that enjoying the odd wine or beer is necessarily a bad thing, but it is a fact that some people have come to use alcohol as a coping mechanism for life and an easy way to unwind. There are better ways. If you choose to drink alcohol, then having it in small amounts and enjoying every mouthful is the way to go – knocking back several gin and tonics to cope with a job you hate or a difficult relationship is not the solution, it's merely a Band-Aid.

If you look around you and at the way you live, there are so many good, amazing and beautiful things, but there are also things that lead us off course, away from our dreams, and away from feeling and looking our best. We need to find those things – and change them.

STEP 4: BUILD NEW HEALTHY HABITS – ONE STEP AT A TIME

What follows are lots of ideas for different ways to adapt the way you currently do things in order to make yourself progressively healthier and happier. Ideas to help you eat well regardless how busy you are, keep active even on days when there is 'no time' and have fun while you get healthier, too.

Please don't be overwhelmed by all the ideas, just start somewhere and add to that. As you go through the book, highlight things you want to work on and look at integrating changes over time. Read this book as many times as you need and keep it close at hand so you are always reminded of the journey you have started and the reasons why you picked up this book in the first place.

Your journey to better health and happiness is not a race, it is not a competition and it is about no one else apart from you. There is no such thing as an overnight success in business and I absolutely believe the same when it comes to your health and happiness – it is a journey, and the journey is as important as the end result.

Like building a house, there is a process – first you need to understand the ground you are working with so you can build a solid foundation, and then you need to build the house, bit by bit. The same goes for building a healthy, happy life you love – you don't need to rush it – make sure you do it properly instead.

This process is all about adding more positive things to your life and making small daily improvements. One day at a time, become a winner, the best version of you.

Avoid the quick fix

When you are on a journey to look and feel good, there are any number of quick-fix options you can go for. Diet shakes, pills or doing some kind of intensive detox or fasting programme. Eliminating foods to the extreme seems to be the new normal in some parts of this country at the moment and is quite unnecessary in many cases.

Personally, I don't buy into the quick fixes – not because they don't work or get results, but because the results are often short-lived and the quick fix doesn't get to the root of why you are feeling unhealthy and/or unhappy in the first place. Why put yourself through the expense, hunger and deprivation when it is impossible to keep it up and there is a more fun way to achieve even better and lasting results?

The world of health, fitness and nutrition is more confusing than ever, I know that and I really feel for you. Two qualified professionals might give you completely opposing advice, depending on what and where they studied, what their beliefs are and what they find works for them.

My belief is that you need to find what works for you – but be sure to do what is safe, proven by good-quality research to be effective and will work for you in the long-term. The advice I give through this book is all of those things.

Another thing to be mindful of when it comes to any quick fixes and extreme approaches to overhauling your diet is that for any of you who have had a remotely dysfunctional relationship with food (which is over 90 per cent of all the women I have ever met), 'rules' and lists of 'good and bad' foods will only serve to enhance your unhealthy relationship with food because eating becomes about how disciplined you can be. We should be able to eat food and enjoy it, make choices that nourish our bodies and minds, eat for the right reasons and enjoy the odd treat without having to write a confession blog that you have 'broken' your diet and eaten something you should not have eaten – yes, people actually do that! It is so unnecessary. That is obsessive, unhealthy behaviour right there.

Please don't get bogged down in the hype – it's not helpful. Focus on making changes to your habits that help you enjoy the healthy, happy life you deserve.

STEP 5: BE AWARE OF THINGS THAT CAN TAKE YOU OFF COURSE

On the road to living a healthier, happier life, there will be things that will throw you off course, bad habits that creep back in and days when everything goes to custard.

What I want you to remember is that it is all part of the process. The best thing you can do is identify your excuses, tricky spots and things that lead you off course in advance so that when they come up you can see them for what they are! Don't judge them, these things are what they are – they are just unhelpful habits, thoughts and behaviours you have picked up on the way that you need to work on.

Time to tune in!

Spend 10 minutes now, just thinking about all the things that lead you astray when it comes to living a healthy life. Look back at the questions in Step 1 (pages 18–21) if you need some inspiration. As you are reading the rest of this book, if you find yourself coming up with excuses or barriers or becoming aware of things that take you off course, come back to this page and write those things down here.

Think about all the things you feel might get in the way of your success and take you off course, and how you could work to overcome those things so that when the situations or circumstances arise you are prepared to deal with them head-on – or at least have some idea of what you could do to help keep you on the right course and reach your goal of feeling good for life!

Here are a few examples of things that might lead you off course and ideas for how you could manage them a little better:

- Having one glass of wine with friends always seems to turn into drinking the whole bottle → I could offer to be the sober driver. I need to learn to say 'no' and be okay with that.
- When I skip yoga/the gym/my walk I feel bad and then eat more → I need to work on my thought process when this happens. I will seek professional advice on this.
- I don't like walking in the rain → I need to get a raincoat and get used to walking in the rain; it's just water and won't hurt me. I can have a warm shower as a reward when I get home!
- I don't have very good cooking skills, which makes it hard to eat healthily → I will book into a healthy cooking class, spend some time with friends learning how to cook and try one new healthy recipe from this book every week.

Your turn . . .

What might take me off course when it comes to eating well, exercising, sleeping and looking after myself?	How can I overcome this?

For a printable version of this table, head to:
www.claireturnbull.co.nz/feelgood

In my book *Lose Weight for Life*, I wrote all about overcoming excuses and managing difficult situations, so check it out if you want to know more details of how to put these things in their place.

The biggest hurdle, though, is overcoming the internal conversations you have about your life and why you can't do things which, really, you can do. You need to be able to let go of your excuses: they won't and can't help you. They are merely a blanket, holding you away from your healthiest, happiest life.

You need to let go of your excuses and your past to be able to live your healthiest, happiest life.

STEP 6: CREATE A SUPPORTIVE ENVIRONMENT – SURROUND YOURSELF WITH GREAT ENERGY

As well as understanding yourself and being clear on things you need to work on, you need to create an environment that will help support you to feel good for life and embrace a healthier, happier way of living that lasts!

The way to do this is to surround yourself with great energy and great people, and it doesn't have to cost a thing.

Here are some ideas to get you started:

- Create a vision board with images of how you want to look and feel, including role models who are doing it in a way you admire.
- Spend more time with people who lift your energy and less with those who bring you down.
- Unsubscribe from email newsletters or updates that make you feel anything other than fantastic when you read them, and do a Facebook friend cull if needed!
- Catch up with the friends who help you live a healthier life – those who will be keen to go to a yoga class, walk or have a cuppa rather than booze it up all weekend.
- Write positive quotes in your diary, a notebook or stick them on your wall.

STEP 7: MAKE IT HAPPEN

The final step in creating your happiest, healthiest life is to take action. It is time to find solutions to help you feel good and make healthy happen. In Chapters 2, 3 and 4, we will be focusing on the food side of things. Initially, we will be looking at understanding your eating behaviour in more detail and helping you to identify your 'eating type'. We will then be looking at exactly what you need to be eating to best fuel your fire, boost your nutrition and feel your best. Lastly, on the food side of things, in Chapter 5 we look at quick and easy meal ideas, food planning and how to stock your pantry to make sure you have everything you need to hand.

In Chapter 6 we will be looking at how you can move your body to help you feel good, and Chapter 7 is all about making sure you have fun on this journey to healthier, happier living.

Finally, we will be tying things together in Chapters 8 and 9, where we will work together to make sure you have the tools and skills you need to balance your body, mind and soul.

Onwards . . .

2

Understand your eating

When it comes to eating well and feeling good, knowing what to eat and when is hugely important and normally where you would expect a book like this to start. However, from my experience I honestly believe that you will benefit most from first looking at your default habits, behaviours and thoughts about food rather than getting bogged down in the 'what to eat' detail too soon.

So many of us eat for the wrong reasons in my opinion. We eat and drink out of habit when we aren't even hungry, we end up eating things because we can't say 'no' and we use food and/or booze to cope with our feelings. I honestly feel that this is one of the biggest reasons why so many people struggle with their weight, have low energy levels and, generally, are not living their healthiest, happiest life. It has very little to do with what you 'know' and more to do with what you actually 'do' when it comes to eating and drinking.

So, we are going to get the ball rolling in this chapter by focusing on understanding your eating and finding some answers to help make sure you are getting where you want to go and will feel good for life!

Why do you eat what you do?

It seems such a simple question, doesn't it? But, when you really think about it, there are a vast number of things that influence what you eat, when you eat and, overall, why you eat what you do. The relationship you have with food is unique to you and will have been shaped by your upbringing, your work, your hobbies, where you live as well as how you have learnt to think and feel about the food you eat. Much of this will have happened without you being aware of it at all.

If you can understand your eating behaviour and get into a space where most of the time you are making good choices for your body and eating for the right reasons, then I truly believe amazing things can happen for you.

The reality is that if you are reading this book, you are very likely to know that a salad is a better lunch option than pizza, right? And you probably know drinking half a bottle of wine a night to de-stress isn't actually going to lead you to a happier marriage/job/life overall – even if it temporarily might feel like it.

So many of us know what we need to do, but we just can't apply what we know, and that feeling of being powerless to manage our own behaviour is more frustrating than anything else. I know how you feel, I really do. I have totally lived that life. But it doesn't have to be that way. You just have to dig deeper and deal with the 'why' behind what you do.

Time to tune in!

Below are some questions to help you understand a little bit more about your eating behaviour. Read each question a few times and really think about it. Simply answer yes or no and write notes if you need to.

1. Are you able to stop eating when you are full, even if there is something on the plate? Or do you feel like you need to eat it all?

_____
_____

2. When you eat cake, chocolate or whatever you consider to be a treat food, how do you feel afterwards? Do you feel guilty? Wish you hadn't eaten it? Or do you feel totally fine – no negative emotions?

_____
_____

3. Do you tell yourself you are not going to eat chocolate, chips, cheese or whatever it might be, but find yourself buying it or still eating it anyway?

_____
_____

4. If it is someone's birthday or there is a celebration of some kind, do you find yourself overeating? How do you feel afterwards?

_____
_____

5. When you have achieved something, do you reward yourself by eating or drinking something? If so, what do you tend to eat or drink?

_____
_____

6. Do you eat when you are tired, bored, angry, upset or feeling down? What do you tend to eat? How do you feel afterwards?

_____
_____

For a printable copy of these questions, head to www.claireturnbull.co.nz/feelgood

How did you go? If you answered 'yes' to any of these questions, it may be that you are at times eating for the wrong reasons and using food or drink for things that it simply wasn't designed to be used for.

Did you know?

Most of us make over 200 food-related decisions a day yet less than 15 of those are conscious. So many of the decisions we make about food happen without us even realising![1]

What is your eating type?

I don't meet many people these days who can honestly tell me that they only eat because they have to – it would be the rarity for sure. In fact, in my whole nutrition career when I have asked this question in workshops and at events, I can remember only two women who ever put their hands up to say, yes, they just eat to survive. The others who said yes were all men.

The reality is that many of us eat food just because it is there. We eat to be sociable and because we feel like it is rude to say no. We eat food because it's free, because we don't like to waste things, because we have learnt to finish every scrap on our plate.

We use food as a reward, a treat and something to 'do' when we need a break in the day – have a coffee or a muffin and back to work we go. Food is used to ease pain, manage emotions, as a form of comfort and pleasure as well as punishment and escape. Food has become a drug of choice for many, but it's not a very good one.

The cycles that some people go through with eating are painful. I know that. I feel it and, as I have mentioned before, I have been there. The disappointment you feel from overeating and also having dessert at a dinner party when your goal was to lose 5kg by summer. The anger you feel towards yourself for having the cheese and crackers at your friend's place when you told yourself you wouldn't. The frustration on the drive home only makes you want to have a bar of chocolate when you get home to punish yourself more. It doesn't have to be this way; you just need to get to know why you do what you do and find solutions to help you manage better.

What you need to do first up is identify your 'Eating Type' at different times of the day and in different situations – this raises your awareness. From here, magic can happen.

There are several ways in which we could define eating types, but in this book I am dividing them into four different types:

- Fuelling the Fire
- Pleasure and Joy

- Habit and Haze
- Reactive Response

Let's look at these in a little more detail.

FUELLING THE FIRE

When you are eating to 'fuel your fire' you make conscious decisions about what to eat based on what you know your body needs. You choose foods that are nutrient-dense, healthy and delicious. This isn't just a case of eating because you have to for survival, but more that you feel in control of the choices you make around food. Eating when you are hungry, stopping when you are full. Saying 'yes' to food you want and need, and 'no' to food you know won't make you feel good in half an hour's time.

Fuelling the fire is nourishing your body from the inside out and is all about making choices that genuinely make you feel good – and that's our goal! When you sit down and eat to fuel your fire, you feel good before, during and after eating. You certainly get pleasure and joy from eating this food, but in a slightly different way from the treat food I outline in the next section.

Ideally, this is the way we should be eating most of the time. It doesn't mean just living off lettuce and sparkling water at all – this is eating a wide variety of delicious healthy foods that taste amazing but nourish your body, mind and soul at the same time.

Look back at what you ate yesterday and so far today. How many of your meals, snacks and anything else you nibbled on or drank were to help you fuel your fire?

PLEASURE AND JOY

This is fabulous eating – the times when you have a delicious slice of carrot cake at a café and you enjoy every single mouthful and feel zero guilt after it. It is the time when you are with your friends or family at an ice cream parlour and they have your favourite flavour, which no one seems to ever have – you have a single scoop, eat it slowly and every mouthful is sheer heaven.

When you are eating for true pleasure and joy as a treat and conscious indulgence, there is no guilt attached. You won't need to confess to your gym buddy that you were bad or 'failed' – you will have whole-heartedly enjoyed what you ate or drank, and here is the important part to reinforce: you *consciously* made the decision to eat or drink it. You made that decision based on wanting to feel good before, during and after –

not because you were 'treating yourself for being good', you 'deserved it' or you simply couldn't say 'no' because someone else was buying it for you – that is a totally different ball game and I would put that into the habit and haze or reactive response categories.

There is room in your life for delicious food that isn't always 100 per cent fuel for your body – some people might argue with me on that, but I think life without an ice cream in Italy, a homemade cookie from your grandma or a slice of cake on your birthday is pretty sad and unnecessary. These are real treats.

I don't think there is anything wrong with eating purely for joy and pleasure a couple of times a week – that is how I live. The thing is, though, that you really need to have worked a lot on getting over all of the eating-for-the-wrong-reasons stuff (I am coming to this next) before you can reach this point. So set this as your goal – you will get there, but it will take time.

Redefining 'treats'

Personally, I think the word 'treat' needs redefining. It is not an every night after dinner thing, or a Friday after work thing – those are habits. Because we are surrounded by doughnut stores, cupcake shops and takeaway bars, the problem now is that we have all become far too accustomed to the everyday eating of these foods.

If we are honest about it, most people eat treat foods not for true pleasure and joy as I have defined it, but more out of habit, lack of other options or the fact that they have developed a soft spot for a certain food.

HABIT AND HAZE

This is the type of eating many of us do, much of the time: eating unconsciously and mindlessly on autopilot.

When we are eating out of habit, because it is 'breakfast time', 12.30pm or mid-afternoon fatigue has hit us, chocolate or a biscuit seems to be the logical and habitual option. Do you have a coffee every morning because your friend buys you one on the way to work? Or maybe because you have a favourite coffee shop and love going in there and feel like it is a good mental start to your day? If so . . . is this a habit that is really helping you get where you want to go or is it just a quick fix?

I used to have six to eight black coffees a day, a habit for sure. Coffee was how I mentally started my day. Now I religiously start my day by reflecting on how I want to feel, writing down an intention of what I want to create in the day ahead or a goal of some kind and having a cup of herbal tea – I now find that much more awesome and helpful.

We really are creatures of habit, especially when it comes to food and drink. You might be a picker, nibble at food or graze; all of these are learnt habits. This was a chronic issue of mine for years. Having had a very dysfunctional relationship with food for so long, I never felt like I could commit to eating a proper meal and kind of felt that nibbling and picking at things didn't count! Eating half the cake mixture before it was baked, a handful of nuts here, half a packet of crackers there, you know the story – it used to drive my family mad. From a nutritional point of view I was falling so short and not getting what I needed at all.

Grazing isn't always a bad thing, but something to be aware of because these habits can lead you far away from a happy, healthy life if you are just eating mindlessly and picking at whatever is around you all day. If it is carrots and snow peas, rock on, but lollies, crackers or slices of cheese might be the more common culprits. For me, it was picking when I was cooking – a disaster. I probably had more than half my daily energy needs (kilojoules/calories) from food that I could hardly remember eating.

Do you eat food just because it is there? At a lunch do, a party or barbecue do you get stuck into the nuts, chips and dips? Were you even hungry, do you think? Try to remember the last time you were out and eating with other people: did you eat more than you needed or make choices that deep down you really didn't enjoy?

Sometimes a habit is simply that we can't say 'no', we feel that we will let someone down, disappoint or offend by not eating what we have been offered. Other people can lead you off course, too – your partner bringing home a king-sized chocolate bar when you have just started a new gym programme, your work mates who insist they can't have a wine if you're not having one or your friend who starts baking and bringing treats over the minute you declare you are on a health kick. Whether deliberate or not, other people can add to your challenges when it comes to eating for the right reasons. Blaming them and becoming the 'poor me' victim is no use, though – your job is to make decisions and choices about the way you think and act based on what is right for you and not fall into the traps.

If someone is offended by you saying 'no thanks' to a scone or a glass of wine, it is their problem to deal with, not yours. Provided you say it in a nice way, deliver your message confidently and swiftly move on, no issue should arise. If you have always been the person to say 'yes' to food/drink and a massive night out, it might take a while for people to get used to you changing, but you aren't becoming a different person – you are just developing into a happier, healthier version of yourself. Just remember, eating something to make someone else feel better is not going to help anyone and will make you feel worse.

If you eat when you are bored or have nothing else to do, you have just created another habit where food equals entertainment. Sure, it can do, but it certainly isn't helpful and long-term it doesn't help you look or feel good.

Haze eating (or mindless eating) is also a habit. Eating in front of the TV, whilst reading emails, when you aren't really consciously aware of what is going in your mouth and how much you are eating. This is a danger zone! Your brain will struggle to help you stop when you are full (if you even know what that is anymore) if it is distracted by other things. I am not suggesting eating in silence and having to worship every mouthful of food you eat, but sitting down, TV off, away from emails and looking at what you are eating, enjoying each mouthful slowly and chewing your food properly at every meal and snack is important.

REACTIVE RESPONSE

This is basically all the other types of eating that don't fit into the descriptions above, and this category is massive. For most women I have worked with who have ever struggled with their weight, it tends to be the root of most of their problems.

Reactive response eating is using food or drink to help manage or control a feeling that you have. It could be anger, frustration, disappointment or sadness. It could be self-doubt, lack of self-worth, self-hatred and not feeling good enough. This is where food can become a form of self-abuse, a form of self-sabotage, and can become a way to punish yourself. As I outlined in *Lose Weight for Life*, I think that emotional eating, which often seems to be linked to eating sweet foods as a form of comfort, is really less than half the picture. Most people I have ever worked with felt guilty, before, during and after eating and only felt about one minute of joy about their experience. Then they spent the rest of the day psychologically beating themselves up – that doesn't sound like comfort to me! That's punishment.

If you eat or drink to reward yourself or treat yourself for being 'good', you are having a reactive response. If you have had a bad day at work, don't have time to go to the gym and get angry at yourself for being hopeless so drive by a petrol station and grab a pie or cookie or even head to a drive-through for a burger, that is a reactive response.

We also have learnt as a society that overeating because it is a special occasion – be it a birthday, Christmas, Easter, anniversaries, engagements, reunions, parties or just because it is a long weekend – is to be expected and is all part of it. Feeling sick from overeating on Christmas day is almost part of the planning – it's madness! We are lucky enough to know that food will be there tonight, tomorrow and for the rest of our lives, so why do we want to eat until we feel sick? I am not being a party-pooper, I love food – but gorging because it is socially normal is crazy. I absolutely used to do it, but now have taught myself not to, and I feel so much better for it.

You are not bad, stupid or ridiculous for doing this, even if you know you are doing it, which a lot of people seem to; all that has happened is that you have learnt to use food and drink for something it was not designed to be used for. I know if you are eating like this most of the time, it can be a living hell!

Time to tune in and take action!

The first stage of change is awareness, so it is time to hand the reins over to you and ask you to tune in to what is going on for you.

Take a look at the questions I asked you on page 37 about your eating behaviour. Can you spot which of these are habit and haze eating, or a reactive response?

Keep a food diary for the next two weeks and next to each thing you eat, write down what 'type' of eating this was for you. It will soon become very clear if there are things you need to be working on to move towards mostly eating to fuel your fire. If most of your eating is haze, habit and reactive, there is work to be done.

For my food diary head to www.claireturnbull.co.nz/feelgood. You will also find a poster to print out and pop on your fridge to help remind you to tune into your eating type.

Tools to help you change your eating type

1. Notice patterns

Once you start to see the patterns in your behaviour and are able to notice the times, circumstances and situations in which they occur, you are then in a position to be able to make changes.

What you need to do is pick out and note down the patterns and the cycles that you see and get really clear on what is going on at that time. For each situation, look at where you are and what you are thinking at the time. You might not know right now, but when that situation next comes up, stop and just capture your thoughts. What is going on inside your mind? How do you feel at the time?

The next step is to work out what solution you can find to manage this situation better from here on. What can you think instead? Can you drive a different way home?

What is the specific situation?	Eating type	What am I thinking and feeling?	What could I do to manage the way I am feeling rather than eating?	What could I change my thoughts to?
When my husband and I have a fight or even just a heated discussion, I pick at everything in the cupboard until I feel sick	Reactive response	I am angry with him, angry with myself, feel like I am not good enough, feel lonely	Write a journal, call a friend, have a warm bath or shower	I am okay as I am . . .

To download a copy of this table for you to fill in, head to:
www.claireturnbull.co.nz/feelgood

2. Eat with awareness

As often as possible, eat without distraction. Sit down at a table with a knife and fork, TV off, emails far away from you (and no sneaky checking your phone). Just be present while you are eating. Commit to the experience. Be aware of what you are eating and how you feel before, during and after.

3. Start rating your hunger – use the hunger scale

How hungry are you – really? Most of us have completely lost touch with what it feels like to be hungry and what it feels like to be full. It can be really helpful to keep track of your 'hunger or fullness' before and after each meal for a few weeks to really tune in to how you feel. Aiming to eat when your hunger is between about −2 and −3 is about right, as is stopping at +2. You will notice that 20 minutes after eating you will often feel fuller than the moment you put your knife and fork down, so it is important to stop at +1 or +2 so you don't go above a +3 after 20 minutes. See how you go.

My hunger scale

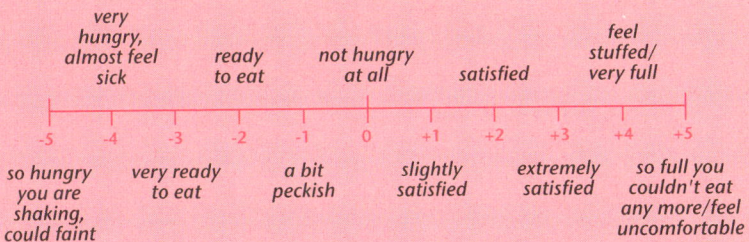

		very hungry, almost feel sick	ready to eat		not hungry at all		satisfied		feel stuffed/ very full	
-5	-4	-3	-2	-1	0	+1	+2	+3	+4	+5
so hungry you are shaking, could faint		very ready to eat		a bit peckish		slightly satisfied		extremely satisfied		so full you couldn't eat any more/feel uncomfortable

Head to www.claireturnbull.co.nz/feelgood for a printable version of the hunger scale.

3

Fuel your fire and up your energy

Right then, now that you have a bit more of an understanding about your eating habits and behaviours, we are ready to tackle the 'what to eat and when' side of things. We are going to be focusing on the foods you need to be eating each and every day to fuel your fire, up your energy and feel good for life. Let's get to it!

Eat what your body needs

THE ROLE OF FOOD FOR YOUR BODY

In the simplest terms your physical body is just like a car. Your car needs fuel in the form of petrol. It needs time out so it doesn't overheat and give up the ghost. It needs water to regulate its temperature, oil to keep things lubricated and regular servicing and checks to make sure all is well and nothing needs attention.

Your body needs fuel in the form of food, and the quality of that food, much like the quality of the petrol you put in a car, will determine how well it works. Your body also needs water, it needs to move, it needs rest and it needs check-ups, too, to make sure things are as they should be on the inside.

Your body is like the best car in the world. If you won a million-dollar car, would you put diesel in it instead of petrol? Forget to fill up the water tank? Never take it to the garage? Of course you wouldn't! You (or maybe more likely a man you know) would be buffing it, looking after it and making sure it was all safe and well. Why don't we do the same for our bodies?

Having two doctors, a pharmacist and a nurse in my immediate family, as well as having worked in hospitals since I was fifteen years old, means that I have a huge appreciation of how amazing the human body is and all that it can do. Also, I have seen first-hand how terrible the consequences are of not looking after our bodies properly. If you could sit in an anatomy and physiology lesson for an hour and start to understand how amazing the human body is, you might think differently about how you treat it.

I am amazed that people who don't take care of themselves – not eating well, not making time to be active and stressing all day every day – believe it won't somehow have an impact on them and are surprised when they get diabetes, high blood pressure or have a stroke! It saddens me that as a society we spend so much time 'chasing a better life' that we destroy ourselves, our health and happiness in the process. Sometimes we need to learn that less is more – chasing can be fatal.

We are not invincible and things catch up on us, so please, please I urge you, respect your body – it is a gift. There may be parts of it you don't like, but at least you have got them. Wobbly legs are better than no legs at all, and at least you can do something about making them less wobbly if you choose to.

THE BEAUTY OF EATING RIGHT

To get the most out of your body, your job is to work on eating the food it needs and loves. This has so many benefits:

- Helps you feel good when you wake up in the morning
- Gives you more energy
- Can help you keep slim and trim
- Ensures that you get the best results from exercise
- Gives you glowing skin, healthy hair and nails

Without being too scientific, your body needs a combination of things called macronutrients and micronutrients for it to work at its best, and getting the right amount of each of these things is the secret to a healthy body and mind and having great energy.

Macronutrients

- Carbohydrate
- Protein
- Fat
- Fibre

Micronutrients

- Vitamins, such as A, B group, C, D, E, K
- Minerals, such as calcium, zinc, iron, selenium, magnesium, iodine

In this book I will be helping you to get the right balance of these nutrients each and every day to ensure you feel fabulous!

If you do want to understand more about the specifics of the individual nutrients and a guide on how to read food labels, my book *Lose Weight for Life* would be really helpful for you to read alongside this book.

Getting in goodness

Over the years, I have studied dietary patterns from around the world with great interest. Through my investigations, I have discovered that despite the variation in the types of food that people eat in different parts of the world, there are common themes in the countries that have a higher proportion of healthy people.

These are a great basis for us to work on when it comes to working out what a healthy day looks like.

- Eat lots of fresh produce – fruits and vegetables, ideally locally grown and produced without the use of chemicals. (Read more on this on page 54.)
- Eat more seafood – all types and it doesn't just have to be the expensive stuff either. Mussels are as cheap as chips, and you can pick up a fresh mackerel for a couple of dollars.
- Use more pulses – lentils, chickpeas, black beans, kidney beans, soy beans – you name it, use them and more of them! (Check out pages 54–5 for tips.)
- Include grains (in particular whole grains) which have had as little processing as possible. (More on this on page 55.)
- Include healthy fats – olive oil, nuts, seeds and avocado. (Tips on this on page 56.)
- Where possible, make things yourself; don't rely on pre-packed, heavily processed food.
- Sit down to eat, eat slowly with awareness and enjoy your food.

HOW MUCH DO YOU NEED TO EAT?

One way to answer this question is to consider the amount of energy (kilojoules/calories) your body needs to think, breathe, digest your food, and move (and everything else it needs to do!), then try to match this to the amount of food you are eating.

The amount of energy you need each day varies depending on your age, stage, gender, how active you are, how much muscle you have and so on, but there are guidelines on roughly how much you will need, which we can use a starting point.

8700 kJ (which is just over 2000 kcals) is the average amount of energy an adult needs each day. I like to suggest that this is broken down to three meals of roughly 2000 kJ (500 kcals) each and a couple of snacks (healthy ones!) each at about 600–800 kJ (150–200 kcals).

If you know roughly what you are aiming for as a meal and snack you can then compare the kilojoules/calories in the food you are eating throughout the day and see how things match up, and if you are having more or less than you might need. It is important to point out though that these guidelines are only very rough and you will need to be advised on what is right for you specifically if you want to be more accurate.

Throughout this book I do mention kilojoules/calories from time to time, but it really isn't something I encourage people to get fixated on and certainly shouldn't be your only focus when you are trying to eat well – after all, you could have three pies a day and be on target for your 8700 kJ, yet be completely malnourished!

My goal with what follows in this book is to help you eat the right amount for you and be sure your diet is healthy, balanced and packed with the nutrients your body needs to look and feel good.

Note: 1 Kcal = 4 kilojoules. They mean the same thing; they are just different units, a bit like the difference between measuring in centimetres or inches.

ARE YOU GETTING THE NUTRITION YOU NEED?

Over the page, write down what you have eaten in the last two days. Include as much detail as possible about your serving sizes and types of food, e.g. write 1 cup of brown rice rather than just 'rice', or 2 slices of wholegrain bread rather than just 'bread'. It might also be helpful to write down why you ate what you did and the 'type' of eating it was – fuelling the fire, pleasure and joy, habit and haze, or reactive response?

We will review this in the next section and see how it stacks up against what your body needs.

Day 1

	Time	What did you have?	Why did you eat? What type of eating was this?	How hungry were you before and after? (Use hunger scale.)
Breakfast				
Morning tea				
Lunch				
Afternoon tea				
Dinner				
After dinner				
Hot drinks				
Cold drinks				
Alcohol				

Day 2

	Time	What did you have?	Why did you eat? What type of eating was this?	How hungry were you before and after? (Use hunger scale.)
Breakfast				
Morning tea				
Lunch				
Afternoon tea				
Dinner				
After dinner				
Hot drinks				
Cold drinks				
Alcohol				

Head to www.claireturnbull.co.nz/feelgood to download this food diary.

A GORGEOUS DAY FOR YOUR BODY

Here is what a healthy day looks like food-wise and how we try to eat in my house – seven days a week. This is the combination of foods you need to help you feel good! It might be a big change for you, depending on how you currently eat, but I promise you it is worth it.

Non-starchy veggies

Basically, these are all vegetables apart from potato, kumara, taro, green banana, yam and corn.

Aim for 3+ servings a day with 4–7 servings being the goal. A serving is a large handful, e.g. a large handful of salad greens or shredded cabbage (at least 1 cup), a handful of broccoli florets, ½ large capsicum, a large tomato, a medium carrot.

Top tips for healthy choices and balance:

- Try to eat a variety of different-coloured vegetables each week.
- Enjoy fresh, seasonal vegetables, including plenty of greens.
- Frozen vegetables are a great option.
- If you choose to use canned vegetables, go for those without added salt.

See pages 62–81 for more great info on veggies.

Fruit

Two servings a day is right for most people. A serving is what fits in the palm of your hand, e.g. a medium-sized apple or orange, 1 large or 2 small kiwifruit or plums, a large slice of pineapple, ½ cup chopped or canned/stewed fruit.

Top tips for healthy choices and balance:

- Try to eat a variety of different-coloured fruits each week.
- Enjoy fresh, seasonal fruit.
- Include frozen and canned fruit if you like for variety.

Lean meat, poultry, fish, seafood, eggs and pulses

Aim to include 1–2 servings a day of these protein-rich foods. A serving is a palm-sized portion of meat, chicken or fish (roughly 125–150 grams), 120 grams tofu, a small handful of prawns or mussels, 1 egg, ¾ cup cooked pulses.

Top tips for healthy choices and balance:

- Choose lean cuts of meats and skinless chicken.

- Ideally include 2–3 fish meals a week (at least 1–2 servings of oily fish).
- Enjoy vegetarian meals at least 1–2 times a week.
- Try including pulses as part of a meal or snack most days.

A quick note: pulses can be included in several of the different food groups. Sometimes you will see they are grouped in with vegetables and other times you might find them grouped with the starchy foods. There is no right or wrong, it just depends on how you look at it (as with so many things!).

Most commonly here in New Zealand you will see that they appear as I have listed them with other protein-rich foods. One thing to consider, however, is that there is a difference between pulses and the other protein-rich foods (meat, poultry, fish, seafood and eggs) and that difference is that pulses contain starch while the others don't.

All this means in practical terms is that if you include a significant amount of pulses in a meal (like a cup of chickpeas in your salad, a thick lentil soup or a chickpea casserole), you don't necessarily need to serve that meal with lots of extra starch. You will see more on this coming up throughout the book, but here I'm just giving you a heads up to avoid any confusion.

Milk, yoghurt and cheese

Most adults need 2–3 servings of dairy products a day, this increases to 3–4 servings for women after menopause. A serving is 1 pottle of yoghurt, 1 cup of milk, 2 small slices of cheese.

Top tips for healthy choices and balance:

- Opt for low-fat milk – ideally trim or trim with added calcium, or a similar alternative if you are unable to have cow's milk.
- Choose low-fat, unsweetened yoghurt.
- Use small amounts of high-fat cheeses.
- Enjoy cottage cheese and reduced-fat ricotta – do be aware, however, that these contain very little calcium compared with the other dairy foods so it's important not to rely solely on these as your dairy serves.

Starchy foods

These are cereals/grains (e.g. oats, quinoa, breakfast cereals), bread, pasta, rice, and starchy vegetables, such as potato and kumara.

Look to include small amounts at each meal and a little in some snacks – preferably minimally processed. How much you need will vary hugely depending on your weight goals and how active you are. As a rough guide, aim for no more than a small fist-sized serving of starchy foods at each meal and, ideally, healthy, wholegrain/high-fibre choices. You are likely to need more if you are very active.

Top tips for healthy choices and balance:

- Where you include grains, always choose whole grains (see pages 91–2).
- Enjoy starchy vegetables with their skin on for extra fibre.

See pages 90–8 for more info on grains.

Fats and oils

Examples of these are olive oil, spreads, avocado, nuts, seeds and nut butters.

Aim to include small amounts of healthy fats as part of your meals and snacks, e.g. a teaspoon of oil when cooking, a slice or two of avocado in a salad or a small handful of raw, unsalted nuts as a snack.

Top tips for healthy choices and balance:

- Choose the right oil for the job (see pages 107–9 for more information).
- Opt for raw, unsalted nuts and seeds.
- Try using avocado, nut or seeds butters as a spread.

Water

As a rough guide, aim to drink 2–3 litres – for more details, see pages 126–9.

For specific guidelines for weight loss, check out my book *Lose Weight for Life*.

Time to tune in!

So, how do you shape up? It is time to reflect on your food diary on pages 52–3. How did you compare to my suggested gorgeous day?

Day 1

	Gorgeous day guidelines	How much did you have?
Non-starchy veggies	3+ large handfuls	
Fruit	2 servings	
Lean meat, fish, eggs, etc.	1–2 servings	
Dairy	2–3 servings, ideally low fat	
Starch	Small fist-sized portions at meals and a little at some snacks	
Healthy fat	Small amounts at meals/snacks	
Water	2–3 litres	

What extras did you have to eat/drink that don't appear on the gorgeous day list, e.g. muffin, coffee, ice cream, juice, energy drink, wine.

Day 2

	Gorgeous day guidelines	How much did you have?
Non-starchy veggies	3+ large handfuls	
Fruit	2 servings	
Lean meat, fish, eggs, etc.	1–2 servings	
Dairy	2–3 servings, ideally low fat	
Starch	Small fist-sized portions at meals and a little at some snacks	
Healthy fat	Small amounts at meals/snacks	
Water	2–3 litres	

What extras did you have to eat/drink that don't appear on the gorgeous day list, e.g. muffin, coffee, ice cream, juice, energy drink, wine.

_____

_____

_____

_____

_____

_____

_____

_____

How does your food diary look?

What did you notice from reflecting on your food diary? Are there things you are missing? Areas where you are falling short? Was your 'extras' list longer than you realised? Despite good intentions, so many of us just don't get the balance right when it comes to the foods we eat day in day out. The most common patterns I see are the lack of vegetables (especially if you look at the weekend days!) and all plant foods in general; not enough dairy or only high-fat dairy choices when they are included; too much processed starch; and not enough water – all of which are areas that need addressing if you want to feel good!

Where do you need to improve? Write down 5 things.

1. _____

2. _____

3. _____

4. _____

5. _____

Overdoing the 'extras'

Did you notice there was no cake, wine or chippies on the gorgeous day list? That's not because you can never have them, but instead to point out that these types of treats are not what your body needs. Despite the fact that these days it has become 'normal' to include these types of foods every day, they really are best to be considered as treats and only include them occasionally.

Where next?

Now you are a little clearer on where you are tripping up, falling short and on what you need to focus your attention, we are going to work together to find easy, practical ways to make improvements to the way you eat which make a difference. Over the next sections we are going to look at the changes you need to make you feel good!

This includes:

- Increasing the amount of plant foods you eat – vegetables, fruits and pulses are all winners
- Opting for whole, real food that has been minimally processed as often as possible
- Including healthy fats every day
- Reducing the amount of added sugar you have in foods and drinks
- Keeping well hydrated
- Getting the overall balance of your diet right
- Helping you plan fabulous, healthy meals
- Sorting out your pantry, fridge and freezer so they are packed full of healthy foods
- Eating for the right reasons and eating with awareness
- Eating slowly and chewing your food properly

Let's get to it!

4

Boost your nutrition – nourish your body

Making adjustments to the way you eat doesn't have to be difficult or challenging, I promise. The advice that follows is certainly not about 'dieting' or enforcing restrictions – those approaches hardly ever work in the long-term and they just end up making you feel bad. I want to help you add more good-quality, nutrient-rich food to your life – that's what's needed to help you feel good!

Together we will go step-by-step through the things that really matter and make a difference, without getting bogged down in detail and jargon. This section of the book will provide you with the knowledge, tools and skills you need to make healthy eating happen.

We will be looking at easy ways to increase the amount of plant foods you eat, clearing up the confusion when it comes to fats and also sussing out whole grains. We will also be focusing on ways to eat less processed food and adapt to a life with less sugar.

STEP 1: ADD MORE VEGGIES, ESPECIALLY GREENS

I absolutely love vegetables, they rock my world. I love checking out my little veggie patch to see how well my spinach is growing, I can't wait to check out the fresh produce on offer when I go to a farmers' market or head overseas, and I enjoy finding new ways to get more veggies into my life every day.

I do understand this may sound a little like I have a very sad existence if the only thing that gets me up in the morning is the thought of broccoli – but fear not, that's not the reality! I still love shoes, a nice glass of vino and a good night out – I just know that eating veggies makes me feel amazing and I wouldn't ever give them up. I eat huge amounts of them each and every day and when people come to stay with me, one of the reasons they leave feeling fantastic is because they probably end up eating more than twice the amount of vegetables that they normally do.

My love for vegetables is, however, incredibly ironic. I was the fussiest child known to man, refusing anything green until my late teens and even then I wouldn't eat anything that was too raw or too well cooked. I used to hate vegetables, with a capital H. They seemed like some kind of torture and even ketchup didn't hide their evil taste in my eyes. Yet now, I grow them, prepare them in endless numbers of ways and enjoy them more than anything else. If you have kids who spit every vegetable back at you, there is hope! The fact is, though, I have learnt to love them. Eating vegetables makes me feel good, and that is the end game for me. I want to enjoy my life and feel fabulous in the process and I want the same for you.

I would love to help you eat a lot more veggies each and every day. I promise you, upping your veggie intake will massively affect how you look and feel. It is so worth it.

Suffer from veggie aversion?

If you have never been a lover of vegetables or if you have children who just can't abide them, the good news is this can change. Each of your taste buds is replaced about every two weeks and over time you can train them to accept new tastes if you are persistent.

Children

When it comes to kids, remember most of what they learn about food comes from you – not just what you say, but what you do, too. They can be influened by how many vegetables you eat and whether or not you appear to be enjoying them.

Because vegetables are 'good for us' and, of course, you really want your kids to eat them, what can end up happening is that children learn to associate vegetables with punishment, because they are something they 'have to have', rather than enjoy, because they are actually really nice if you get used to them.

I like to take the slow and steady approach to vegetable eating with kids who are super fussy. Simply try getting them to lick a vegetable, hold it and take one bite each and every day. Keep with the same vegetable for a while if you can, rather than mixing it up too quickly – introduce new ones over time. If possible avoid getting emotional, angry or frustrated – just as long as they take one bite and swallow, let it go. Then repeat – again and again and again and . . . yes again. In time (and it can be a long time), it will help them to accept the taste. This process can help them to build up an acceptance for a range of vegetables.

As I mentioned before in the story of my trip to Japan, the kids there were all eating vegetables without a hint of fuss. It was normal to them, they were never given other choices and all their friends ate vegetables, too. There is so much that needs to be done to get kids eating better in this country – but that's another story and another area for me to work on in years to come . . .

Adults

Adults, if I am honest, are probably a little trickier to manage than children when it comes to veggie aversion! Why? Because as adults we know we do have a choice, we have the option of making excuses and we also know that we won't go to bed hungry if we don't finish the broccoli on our plate.

If you swear that you just don't like salad, vegetables or anything green, well, you can learn to and you can change your taste buds – it is just a case of being persistent. You are not a child so no flapping your arms around – you can do it if you choose to. One bite at a time, then repeat, repeat, repeat. Take this on as a challenge and let me know how you go!

WHY VEGGIES ARE VITAL

I doubt that it will be news to you that vegetables are good for you. The age-old message to eat your greens has certainly stood the test of time and is probably one of the only consistent nutrition messages that you will get from people, regardless what else they believe about food and nutrition.

The World Cancer Research Fund report suggests that we should aim to be eating at least 600 grams of non-starchy vegetables and fruit every day to help keep our bodies in tip-top working order and healthy from the inside out. So, what is 600 grams? Well, it is around 7 or 8 servings (handfuls) a day. Ideally, I would suggest this to be 2–3 servings of fruit, and the rest, the extra five or so, the non-starchy veggies.

How many serves of veggies do you honestly have a day? Yes, take into account the weekend. And Friday night, too. Are you having anywhere near enough?

Currently, most of us know to aim for 5 + a day, and this is certainly a good starting point. However, given that 34 per cent of Kiwis aren't even getting three handfuls of veggies a day (and this figure actually includes the starchy veggies, too, so is an over-estimation when it comes to how many serves of non-starchy veggies we actually eat), there is work that needs to be done![2]

Upping your veggies can have so many positive effects. Not only can it reduce your risk of cancer and other diseases such as diabetes and heart disease, it also helps ensure that your digestive system stays healthy and that you don't get bunged up!

If keeping your body healthy for life and preventing nasty diseases isn't enough to encourage you to start chopping up carrots and plant a veggie patch immediately, then tune into the fact that eating lots of veggies will also help your skin look healthy and glow. Veggies are also vital to help you feel energised and they are super helpful when it comes to keeping you slim – surely that is enough encouragement?!

Eating heaps and heaps of veggies along with a balance of other nutrient-rich foods, a good night's sleep and keeping well hydrated will put you well on your way to looking and feeling your best every day.

VEGETABLE TYPES

Vegetables aren't all created equal. A potato is very different nutritionally from a spinach leaf and, let's be honest, celery and pumpkin aren't exactly the same, are they?

Vegetables can be classified in all sorts of ways – by their colour, whether they grow under the ground or on top, or if they are 'starchy' or 'non-starchy'.

The colour classification is an easy one to sort out, as is whether a vegetable likes to grow in a dark place or out in the sunshine, but the starchy verses non-starchy vegetable conversation is interesting and something that isn't very well understood. Let's see if I can help get some clarity on this one.

Most vegetables are predominately made up of carbohydrate (starch) and water. They do, of course, have tiny amounts of fat, protein, vitamins and minerals – but the bulk by far is the starch and water.

Whether a vegetable is classified as 'starchy' or 'non-starchy' is really dependent on just how much starch is in that vegetable. A potato is clearly very starchy and a cucumber is not – it is packed with water – but when it comes to veggies like pumpkin, corn, peas and carrots things can get a little hazy. Where do they fit in?

There is no official definition for a starchy or non-starchy vegetable, but dense vegetables like potato, kumara, yam, taro, green banana and corn sit at 15–30 per cent starch and I am comfortable for those to be classified as starchy. The rest are lower than this, peas 7 per cent, pumpkin 6 per cent, carrots 4 per cent and broccoli only 2 per cent, so these would be considered less starchy or 'non-starchy', but you can see that there can be room for different interpretations. Spinach, lettuce, mushrooms and all the rest of the vegetables are easier to clearly classify as they have very little starch so fit well into the 'non-starchy' camp.[3]

Why does this matter? Well, the vegetables with a higher starch component are much more energy-dense (have far more kilojoules per serve) than those with less starch and more water. A cup of cooked potato is 566 kilojoules (142 calories), for example, whereas a cup of cooked broccoli is 162 kilojoules (41 calories).

So, with my message to up your game on the vegetable front to help you look and feel your best, I am really asking you to focus on increasing the amount of the less starchy veggies rather than doubling your portion of mashed potato.

Including starchy veggies as part of a well-balanced, healthy diet is still fine and the amount you need will depend on how active you are and whether you are looking to trim down a little or not, but I personally put potato, kumara, yam, green banana, taro and corn into the same category as rice, pasta, bread, crackers and other well-known starchier foods (refer back to my 'A gorgeous day for your body' plan on pages 54–6 to see where they fit and how much to be aiming for).

I do completely realise that if you currently have one floret of broccoli a day and the odd carrot, the thought of upping your veggie serves to multiple handfuls a day might seem impossible – but you don't have to do it overnight. It is simply about finding ways to increase from one serve to two, then two to three, and so on, until you are really eating a lot more veggies than you used to. It has taken me a few years to nail this one consistently. I have lots and lots of ideas in the pages ahead and there are also heaps of veggie-packed recipes at the back of this book, as well as in *Lose Weight for Life*.

GO GREENS!

Eating a variety of different-coloured vegetables is important. Each vegetable has its own unique set of nutritional goodies and I certainly aim to include a mixture of colours every day. Personally though, I do have a soft spot for green veggies, and at least two of my servings of veggies most days would come from greens.

Leafy greens like spinach, silver beet (also known as Swiss chard) and kale are just absolutely packed with the nutritional goodness of fibre, vitamin C, B vitamins for energy, folate and non-haem iron (this is less well absorbed than the iron in meat, but certainly worthy of a mention), as well as an array of the vitamins and minerals that work together to help your body function well and you look your best. Broccoli, rocket and salad greens as well as all the herbs are winners, too – they just make you feel so good when you eat them regularly, and feeling good is the goal!

You can add greens to almost anything. Make totally green smoothies, add them to berry smoothies, omelettes, soups, mince dishes, serve them on the side – you name it, where there is a meal in my life, there is more often than not some green veg.

One of the reasons why I love them so much is that they are super easy to grow – and when you are trying to eat more veggies, if you want to avoid spending a small fortune, growing some greens in a pot, a half wine barrel or a little patch in your garden can be a life (and financial) saver. Growing a few of your own veggies, shopping at farmers' markets and local veggie stores and having some greens (like spinach) in your freezer makes upping your greens that little bit easier.

For those who are new to gardening or are looking for a few hints and tips, the wonderful gardening expert David Haynes has put together some advice for you, which you can download at www.claireturnbull.co.nz/feelgood.

B vitamins

There are a whole range of B vitamins (B1, B2, B3, B4, B5, B6, B7, B9 [folate] and B12) and they are a super-important group of vitamins that play a number of vital roles in the body, including helping to release energy from the food you eat.

What is essential to know about B vitamins is that they are water-soluble and most of them are unable to be stored in your body. In practical terms that means you need to eat foods packed with B vitamins every day if you want to feel good!

And, guess what is packed with B vitamins? Green vegetables! Yet another reason to pack in the greens.

To get a balance of all the B vitamins you need, other great foods to include are whole grains (see pages 91–2), lean meat, poultry, fish, eggs, nuts and fortified breakfast cereals.

MAKE IT AFFORDABLE

I appreciate that eating lots of vegetables could increase your food bill but, as this is something I'd like everyone to be able to do, I want to assure you there are ways to eat cheap when it comes to veggies and I certainly do this myself. Here are my tips:

- Reduce your meat/fish portion – you only need a small palm-sized amount, 100–120 grams per person is adequate. Cheaper cuts of meat can be used very successfully with the right recipe. Also, try the cheaper types of fish. You may need to find a new way of cooking them but you can pick up a whole mackerel, as an example, for a few dollars and it will serve two to three people. A few meat-free meals a week can also be good on so many levels – there are lots of recipe ideas in the back of this book to help you get started. The money you save from this approach can be used for you to spend on other things, like . . . veggies!
- Use frozen as well as fresh veggies – spinach, peas, broccoli, you name it, you can find it frozen these days and it can be a very cost-effective way of eating more vegetables. There is always a special on at least one of the frozen veggies, too.
- Use all your veggies – don't throw out those broccoli stalks; if you

take off the tough outer layer you can slice them and add them to a stir-fry, grate them into a salad or put them in a soup. Leave on the skins of potatoes and kumara, too – more fibre and goodness!

- Eat seasonally – it really is the only way to go when it comes to saving money.
- Compare prices – the cost of veggies varies hugely depending on which supermarket you shop at. If you go to a local fruit store or a farmers' market, look around. I certainly hunt out bargains and use what is cheap that week.
- Pack your own lunches – buying salads out can be pricey and it is much easier to have a healthy lunch when you make it yourself.
- Make soups – when the weather is cooler, this is such a fab way of getting 2–3 serves of veggies in each day without really trying. I do this in winter; then it is three servings down, only 2–3 to go! I always have a stock of single-serve portions of soup in my freezer, too, which I can quickly whip out for a light lunch or substantial snack.

How to make healthy happen!

Here are all the ways I get veggies into my day and these are things I have taught people who stay with me, too. Some of these ideas are great for beginners, others will require a little more thought and open-mindedness – so start where it feels right for you and, over time, try some new things.

HOW TO ADD MORE VEGGIES TO YOUR BREAKFAST (1–2 HANDFULS)

1. Add spinach to a breakfast smoothie
Blend a handful or two of thoroughly washed spinach with ½ cup of water. To this you can add:

- A handful of frozen berries, a cup of low-fat milk, a tablespoon or two of vanilla yoghurt and a few teaspoons of ground LSA (linseeds, sunflower seeds and almonds) or any seeds of your choice.
- 1 small frozen banana, blended (peel it before you freeze it – I didn't the first time and it got very messy!), 1 cup of low-fat milk and a few teaspoons of ground LSA or, again, any seeds of your choice.

There are more recipes for smoothies with greens on pages 216, 217 and 220.

2. Have veggies with your eggs

When you say 'eggs' to most people at breakfast time, the logical addition is bacon. But there is no reason why you can't have veggies at breakfast.

- If you are having poached or scrambled eggs, why not add some mushrooms and tomatoes on the side? Either grill or lightly fry them in a tiny bit of oil in a pan. Spinach is also a great accompaniment to eggs, just pop some in the microwave (without water) for 30 seconds to wilt it or add it to the pan with your mushrooms and tomatoes to soften.
- Omelettes are a winner for breakfast or a light meal option – I have chickens so eggs are always on tap and, wow, what a quick and easy meal they make. I use about 1–2 handfuls of veggies and 2 eggs per person. Onion (white, red or spring onion), mushrooms, tomatoes, leafy greens (I often use frozen free-flow spinach), capsicum and courgette all work super well – you can even add peas (with a little chopped mint – mmm, so good!). It might be more of a weekend thing if your week is super busy, but that's fine.

Lose Weight for Life **has some great omelette recipes; be sure to check them out.**

Time to tune in and take action!

Which of these ideas are you going to try? And when? Get your diary out right now and over the next month plan in a few days when you commit to trying these ideas. You will need to make sure that you add the ingredients you need to your shopping list and have the recipe handy on the day, too.

HOW TO ADD MORE VEGGIES TO YOUR LUNCH (2+ HANDFULS)

IDEA 1: Have salad veggies as your 'base'

In the warmer months, most days my lunch has two handfuls of non-starchy veggies as the starting point and to that I will add some protein, a little healthy starch and some healthy fats. I know that most people plan their meals around the protein or starch part, but I like to start the other way around – the veggies are just as important. This is a mind-set shift, but something people who have stayed with me have learnt to do as have all of our clients at Mission Nutrition.

Here are some of the combos I enjoy:

COLESLAW

Lettuce can be pricey, but cabbage and carrots are often cheap. I will prepare coleslaw as the veggie component of my dinner one night a week (served with some baked chicken or fish, for example) and I always make extra so that I have enough coleslaw to last me for 2–3 lunch meals on the following days.

Half a white or red cabbage, finely shredded (you need a good knife or mandolin, ideally), plus 3–4 large carrots, grated, will make about 8–10 handfuls of veggies. I add herbs to mine (mint and parsley), some fresh chilli or chilli flakes and I would add a little dressing just before I eat it. (See dressing recipes on pages 248–9).

You can also add capsicum, edamame beans and some spring onions along with an Asian-style dressing to mix things up (see my recipe on page 226).

GRATED VEGGIES

Grated beetroot and carrot with some chopped parsley is just magic – I often use a food processor with a grater blade to make it all less messy and again, I make enough for several dinner meals and/or lunches. I add a dressing just before I eat it most of the time (or in the morning before work when I take it out of the fridge, or I keep some dressing at work) and then just add some protein, healthy fat and possibly some starch.

Grated carrot with chopped veggies like celery, baby spinach, spring onion, capsicum and sliced snow peas along with some nuts and seeds also make a great combo.

My carrot and currant salad recipe on page 231 of *Lose Weight for Life* is still one of my all-time favourites.

Grated courgette is a wonderful base or addition to a salad, too, and when they are in season this is a genius use of courgettes – check out my recipe on page 228 – you will be amazed!

MIXED SALAD COMBOS

It is easy to make a delicious salad by mixing and matching whatever ingredients you have at hand using this magic formula:

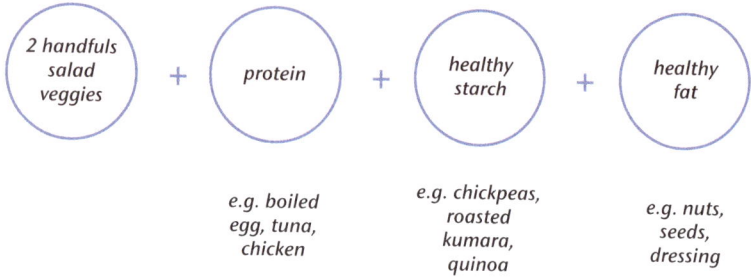

```
( 2 handfuls     ( protein )     ( healthy     ( healthy
  salad      +               +     starch  )  +    fat  )
  veggies )
```

| | e.g. boiled egg, tuna, chicken | e.g. chickpeas, roasted kumara, quinoa | e.g. nuts, seeds, dressing |

Salad veggies

A good starting point is to put a handful of salad leaves like lettuce, mesclun, rocket, shredded cabbage or baby kale into a bowl or container and then add a combination of other veggies depending on what you find works well for you. Veggies can be added when they are raw, roasted, grilled or steamed and cooled, depending on your preference. I always just go with what is in season when it comes to making salad combos.

These veggies are all wonderful in a salad: capsicum, cabbage (red or white), cucumber, tomatoes, mushrooms, alfalfa sprouts, bean sprouts (mung beans), grated courgette, carrot, fennel, snow peas, beetroot, spring onion, red onion, asparagus, broccoli, green beans, radish, artichokes, eggplant (pre-roasted or grilled is best), corn, baby corn and peas.

Protein

If you are making a salad that is going to be a complete meal, it is really important to make sure you include some protein-rich foods to help keep you full and provide your body with the goodness it needs. Canned fish like tuna, salmon, mackerel or sardines are great choices. Fresh cooked New Zealand king salmon or smoked salmon are also good, and are a great way to get some omega-3 as well as protein. A boiled egg, shredded skinless chicken, cottage cheese, cold roasted meat or tofu are other ideas.

Chickpeas, lentils or other pulses also count as a source of protein, but it would be best to make sure you are also adding some nuts and seeds to your salad to boost the protein content a bit if pulses are the only thing in your salad other than veggies and a little fat.

Healthy starch

Although pulses do fall under the same category as lean meat, poultry, fish and alternatives, they also have a good amount of starch in them so, personally, I use them in salads as a source of both starch and protein.

I am a big fan of using chickpeas, kidney beans or butter beans and if they are the only starch source I am having in that meal, I will be sure to have a good handful to fill me up. Brown rice, quinoa and bulgar wheat are good, too.

A little roasted or steamed kumara can work well as a source of starch and boiled potatoes are also lovely. I often add these to a tuna Niçoise salad to make it a little more filling.

There is a great tuna Niçoise recipe on page 236 of *Lose Weight for Life.*

Healthy fat
Be sure to add a little healthy fat to your salad for a dose of fat-soluble vitamins and essential fatty acids. A sprinkle of nuts and/or seeds or a few slices of avocado are easy ways to include healthy fats. If you are watching your waistline, be mindful of the amount you add because fats are very energy dense (high in kilojoules/calories).

Protein power
The current recommendations from the Ministry of Health suggest that the average amount of protein needed by an adult is 82–135 grams per day. This serves only as a rough guide because the exact amount of protein you need varies from person to person. If you want to know exactly how much you need, it is best to seek individual advice.

The good news is that most people in New Zealand get an adequate amount of protein overall each day, but the mistake many of us tend to make is that we don't eat enough protein-rich foods during the day and then have heaps with our dinner meal at night. It is much better to try to spread this out a little more if you can. Aim to include protein-rich meals and snacks throughout the day rather than waiting until dinner time.

A protein-packed meal will help stabilise your blood sugar levels, which is really helpful for managing your energy levels throughout the day – a vital part of feeling good! Protein also helps you feel full, so if you don't have enough protein at a meal (say you just have a big bowl of salad veggies and a little roasted kumara), you are much more likely to feel hungry soon after compared to if you have had a boiled egg, some tuna or cottage cheese with it, too.

There is also a theory that your body will keep telling you to eat until it has had its protein needs satisfied. For example, let's say you eat a pizza with lots of carbohydrate and fat but little protein – your body would not send the 'full message' as quickly as if there had been a decent amount of protein in that meal. The net result is that you end up eating more.

Now, this is not the time to start gobbling down protein bars; you can meet your protein needs with normal everyday foods.

Here is a list of protein-rich foods and the amount of protein per serve so that you can figure out whether you are getting enough in your meals and snacks, and if you are overdoing it at your evening meal!

Serving size	Grams protein/serve
1 cup trim milk	9
150g unsweetened yoghurt	6
40g Edam cheese (2 slices)	11
100g cottage cheese	11
1 egg	6
100g chicken breast (raw weight)	22
100g lean beef (raw weight)	23
100g white fish	20
100g canned tuna	22
100g NZ king salmon	18
100g canned salmon	20
1 cup chickpeas/lentils/kidney beans	12
¾ cup cooked white rice	4
¾ cup cooked brown rice	10
100g tofu	8
¼ cup nuts	8
¼ cup seeds	10
1 slice wholegrain bread	4
¾ cup cooked quinoa	6
¾ cup cooked pasta	5

Note: The exact amount of protein may vary depending on the product you buy.

IDEA 2: Stuff your sandwiches/wraps/pita bread

If you are a sandwich fan, it can be very easy to fall short on veggies at your lunch meal as there is only so much salad a couple of slices of bread will accommodate. So, we need to find a way to help you fit more in! You can either try to double the amount of lettuce, cucumber, grated carrot or seed sprouts that you pop in there, or simply take some extra veggies to snack on the side. Carrots, tomatoes, capsicum, mushrooms, snow peas, courgette, broccoli and cauliflower are all good alongside sandwiches.

Wraps and pita bread (wholemeal, of course) are easier to pack with heaps of veggies – aim to get 2 handfuls in there if you can. If you can't manage it without it all falling apart, just add the extra veggies on the side.

This might all sound a bit 'hard' and time-consuming, but I simply prepare my veggies to eat the next day as I am preparing veggies for dinner. I just chop or wash a few extra things and it takes less than two minutes to sort. Two minutes out of 24 hours to feel good is an investment that's worth it.

'Making healthy happen' is all about moving towards this way of living one step at a time. Like I have said before, it has taken me years to learn to eat like this – a journey of discovery, trying new things and making a plan that works for me and my very full-on life. So, it is just about taking your time, and at least starting to shift things day by day. Remember: you are worth it and so are the results!

IDEA 3: Make soups

Anyone who follows me on Facebook or has checked out my blog (find it at www.claireturnbull.co.nz) will know that I am a massive soup fan – it is such an easy and cheap way to get goodness in. As soon as the cooler months arrive I am right into it. I try new recipes every couple of weeks and basically make one batch at the weekend to last the week for lunches and snacks – how easy is that?

Soups are a great way to use up less-than-awesome-looking vegetables, broccoli and cauliflower stalks and you can also add frozen vegetables – whatever works for you. When you make your own soups, use homemade stock if you can or buy reduced-salt stock.

To make a soup more filling and a complete meal, you can add lentils, split peas, barley, quinoa and all sorts of other things.

IDEA 4: Veggie-packed frittatas

Eggs and veggies are such a great combo and a frittata makes a quick and easy meal, a perfect packed lunchbox item and can be as simple or as fancy as you like, depending on what you choose to put in it. Check out my recipe on page 227 for a delicious example of a veggie-packed frittata.

Time to tune in and take action!

How are you going to make sure that you are having more veggies at
lunchtime? Which of these ideas are you going to try? Put a star by them,
put a bookmark in this page or create a meal planner and shopping list for
next week that will help to make this happen!

HOW TO ADD MORE VEGGIES TO YOUR DINNER (2+ HANDFULS)

Your evening meal is probably the easiest place to start increasing your
veggie quota. Ideally, aim to have half your plate covered with veggies.
Two handfuls of veggies can either be served separately with a meal like
baked fish, roasted kumara and then broccoli/peas and carrots, let's say,
or those two handfuls of veggies (per person) can be added into the dish –
or do a combination of the two!

A healthy dinner plate

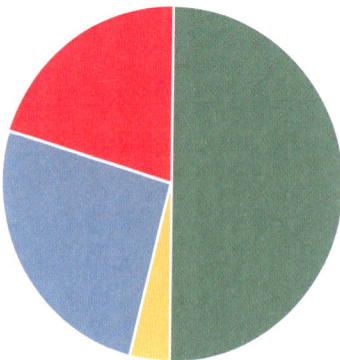

- Plant food (non-starchy veggies)
- Healthy fat (oil, nuts, seeds, avocado)
- Protein rich foods (fish, seafood, meat, legumes, dairy)
- Healthy starch e.g. brown rice, kumara

1. Adapt your recipes to add more veggies

- Mince – it is very easy to add extra veggies to mince dishes. When I make a Bolognese, chilli or meatballs, for example, I will use more onion than the recipe says, and often add some very finely grated carrot, courgette, chopped capsicum or mushroom.
- Casseroles/stews – there is no easier meal to add veggies to. I tend to double the amount of veggies suggested in most recipes – 2 onions, more carrots, and an extra can of tomatoes – this means I get away with using less meat. (See my casserole recipe on pages 242–3.)
- Curries – I love curry, but I make an effort to make healthier versions. I will either add veggies to a meat/chicken/fish curry – carrots, cauliflower, broccoli and greens beans can work well – or I will make a totally vegetable-based side dish to go with a meat/chicken/fish curry. Curry recipes freeze well so if time is an issue for you, you can make double and freeze half. Often I will make, say, a double batch of chicken curry one week and eat half and freeze half. I will serve this with a spinach saag which I will have made a double batch of the previous week (see recipe on page 246). Then I will just keep repeating this so I only have to make one dish at a time, and have the other dish in the freezer ready to go.
- Overhaul your pizza – homemade pizza made on a wholemeal pita or pizza base can be a quick and easy meal. It is easy to add a lot more veggies to the top of your pizza and serve it with a salad. If you want to be more adventurous, you can actually overhaul it one step further and make the base from veggies, too. Now, you may not believe this works (and I can assure you I was equally sceptical the first time I tried this), but you can use grated cauliflower as the base – mixed with an egg and a little cheese, it is seriously amazing and great if you have anyone who needs to be gluten free in your family. Honestly, try it (see recipe on page 240) and let me know how you go, I am a total convert.
- Wrap your burger, falafels, meatballs, lamb koftas or mince dishes in lettuce. Lettuce? Yes, you read it right! I know . . . it is not the same as a bread bun or wrap, I get that, but it is an option! You will need a sturdy leaf like iceberg or cos lettuce (also very easy to grow), or you could use spinach or blanched silver beet (with the stem removed) – it is worth a try.

2. Try some vegetable-packed meat-free meals

I was brought up as a vegetarian because of the whole BSE (mad cow disease) drama in the UK, so for 14 years I didn't have a scrap of meat, chicken, fish, any cheese that wasn't vegetarian or anything with gelatine anywhere near it because that was what my whole family were doing and, at age four, I didn't really have much say in the matter.

I guess because my family decided to become vegetarian when I was so little, I was brought up knowing nothing about meat and, let me tell you, we had some amazing meals – my mum became very creative!

Like many children, as I mentioned before, I was fussy – to the extreme actually (sorry, Mum). I have since found out, however, that even though I thought I was dodging vegetables, my mum was a master at hiding them in meals so I actually ate far more than I realised. Veggies can go into anything and be hidden where need be. I have included a great lentil bake recipe (see page 239) which my mum conjured up to get some goodness into me and my little brother (who was equally difficult when it came to veggies).

I am definitely no longer a total vegetarian and I even prefer my steak rare rather than well cooked – a far cry from the old me, that's for sure. But, to be honest, we still certainly enjoy our fair share of meat-free meals in our house and when we do have meat it really isn't that much.

Here are some great ideas for meat-free, veggie-packed meals:

- Chickpea curry
- Tofu stir-fry
- Lentil bake (page 239)
- Chickpea patties (page 238)

3. Serve more on the side

Adding extra veggies on the side of your meals is a great idea – but I know that peas and carrots day in, day out won't fill you with joy, so here are some ideas for interesting combinations, which are quick and easy to throw together.

STIR-FRY VEGGIE COMBOS

You can use any combination of veggies you like. Here are some of my favourites as an example.

- Shredded Brussels sprouts with chopped hazelnuts
- Asparagus and green beans
- Capsicum, red onion and shredded cabbage
- Broccoli, bean sprouts and finely sliced carrot sticks
- Courgette and mushrooms with garlic
- Silver beet, spinach and kale

Garlic, fresh ginger, chilli, spring onion, herbs, nuts and seeds are all perfect additions to any stir-fry veggie mix, too.

HEALTHY MASH MIXES

- Potato, kumara and parsnip
- Potato and cauliflower
- Pure cauliflower mash
- Peas and potato mash
- Smashed swede and carrot (see recipe on page 245)

Time to tune in and take action!

What will you do this week to boost your veggies at dinner time? How will you make sure you have half a plate of veggies? Make a plan – write down the things you are going to try, schedule them in, add to your meal planner. Make it happen!

VEGGIE SNACKS (1–2 HANDFULS)

When the word 'snack' comes to mind, most people will think of a biscuit or cereal bar before the image of veggies comes up – but I am here to challenge that. Veggies make an awesome snack. A snack in my mind is a healthy addition to the day that helps your body work better. For me, treats like muffins, cakes and biscuits aren't to be put in the same category as a snack – they are occasional extras to be enjoyed and appreciated, not wolfed down for lack of a better option.

Veggie snack ideas

- The veggie box – I have a snack box with chopped up veggies at the front of the fridge at all times. If I am out all day I take my veggie box with me. The veggies I mentioned in the 'Stuff your sandwich' section on page 75 all work well.
- Celery filled with a little peanut or almond butter – you can even top it with a few raisins or sultanas; ants on a log, I believe this is called in children's land. I never had this as a child but think it is a very good idea! You can also add a few raw almonds on top to give extra crunch.
- Corn on the cob – when in season you can have cooked fresh or frozen mini cobs.
- Edamame beans – technically they are a pulse, but I will let them stay in this section; they are still green and a great choice! You can buy them from the frozen section of the supermarket or Asian food stores. Pop them in the microwave for a minute or steam them and there you have it, a healthy snack.
- Vegetable-based dip with wholegrain crackers (see the healthy dips on pages 252–6 for my fabulous recipes).
- The ultimate green smoothie snack – blend 1 cup of well-washed spinach (baby spinach is ideal as it is softer) with 1 cup chilled water (or you can use coconut water) and ½ apple and/or ½ frozen or fresh banana. You can add a good squeeze of lemon, too, for a really fresh taste and parsley if you are feeling game – it is all extra goodness to help you look and feel good. A good blender is vital for this – if you end up with a chunky mess, you might need to invest in a new blender.

VEGGIE-PACKED DAY

Here is an example of a veggie-packed day:

- Breakfast – berry smoothie with greens, 3 brazil nuts (1 serving vegetables, 1 serving fruit)
- Morning tea – fresh fruit and low-fat yoghurt (1 serving fruit)
- Lunch – coleslaw with chickpeas, chicken and seeds (2 servings vegetables)
- Afternoon tea – 1 cup homemade veggie soup and 2 wholegrain crackers with cottage cheese (1 serving vegetables)
- Dinner – casserole with veggies galore in it and peas (2 servings vegetables – one in the casserole, one with peas on the side)

TOTAL = 2 fruit and 6 vegetables. See – it's easy when you know how!

WHAT ABOUT FRUIT?

The main focus of this section is on upping your veggies because that is the area most of us need to work on, but remember fruit is still good for you, too. Two servings a day is a good guide for most people, maybe three servings a day for those who are more active. A serving is a cupped hand-sized portion like an apple, orange or large kiwifruit, for example. When it comes to fresh fruit, the fresher the better. Frozen fruit is also super handy and useful in so many ways.

Canned fruit in juice can be a good standby option and dried fruit is great to add sweetness to breakfast and healthy home baking, but do be mindful that a serving of dried fruit is much smaller than fresh fruit given that the water has been removed and it is a much more concentrated source of sugar. If 2 small apricots or 12 grapes is a serving when fresh, then 2 dried apricots and 12 raisins is a serving when dry. I'm not suggesting you need to start counting your raisins, this is just to give you a rough idea!

Juicing fruit isn't ideal, as you end up with a very concentrated source of sugar in a glass and if you are only going to be having two or three servings a day, then it is better to enjoy most of your fruit whole, in my opinion. Adding a little fruit (½ apple or pear, for example) to veggie juice would be enough to add a little sweetness without going overboard.

STEP 2: EMBRACE PULSE POWER

When anyone looks through my pantry they are always amazed at just how many packets of lentils and other dried pulses I have, as well as plenty of canned varieties like black beans and kidney beans. They are just so fantastic and I use them most days in one way or another.

Using more pulses is another fantastic way to increase the amount of plant-based food you are eating, which is important to help reduce the risk of many diseases They can also help to save you money.

Let's be honest, though: pulses like lentils, chickpeas and split peas are a little on the ugly side and for many people will be associated with a hippy vegan lifestyle, and they certainly aren't something many men like to venture near.

Sadly, I feel that pulses are very misunderstood – they really are fabulous on so many levels and certainly aren't just for non-meat-eaters. I can also vouch for the fact that men can learn to love them, too. In my days working as a nutritionist in professional rugby, I managed to get my whole team of big muscley men enjoying pulses every week without any complaints – so, if that is possible, anything is, right?! It is time to make pulses cool.

ABOUT PULSES

Stripping right back to basics, pulses (also known as legumes) are the seeds of a particular family of plants. The most common types of pulses include:

- Chickpeas, kidney beans, butter beans, soy beans (one way you might eat soy beans is as edamame)
- Haricot beans, black beans, navy beans (the beans commonly used in baked beans)
- Lentils (brown, green, red, Puy/French)
- Split peas (yellow, green)

You can buy pulses dried (these need to be cooked before eating; some will need to be pre-soaked, too) or you can buy them pre-cooked and canned.

WHY PULSES ARE AWESOME

Nutrition powerhouse
Nutrition-wise they are:

- packed with fibre – great to keep things 'moving through' your body and also helpful to reduce your risk of cancer, heart disease and diabetes[4]
- able to release their energy slowly (they are low GI) and help keep you feeling full and stabilise your blood sugar levels

- a great way to get protein into your diet
- a good way to add extra B-group vitamins (especially folate), iron, calcium, phosphorus, zinc and magnesium to your day
- low in saturated fat.

What more could you want?! Including pulses every day is a great idea, and having several cups (cooked volume) throughout the week is a really good goal.

Pulses are perfect nutrition-wise to add to your diet, but also a great way to help you rely less on meat. Many of us here in New Zealand eat too much meat. The World Cancer Research Fund research suggests that we limit our meat to less than 750 grams (raw weight, which is about 500 grams cooked) per week[5] to reduce our cancer risk, and pulses are a great way to help you do that.

Super cheap

Pulses are a great way to make cost-effective meals and snacks. A can of chickpeas (which you could make into a dip, falafels or add to a curry) can cost less than $1.80. Half a cup of dried red lentils (which you could add to a mince dish and use less meat) will cost you less than 50 cents.

Seriously, if you are trying to slash your food bill, you may have just stumbled on the answer here. I am committed to keeping my weekly shop to a minimum and helping others to do the same. Pulses for me are part of that picture.

Super versatile

Having been brought up as a vegetarian, with 14 years of meat-free living, I have had a lot of experience with pulses and, boy, are they versatile – you can use them in almost anything. They can be made into dips, added to soups, casseroles and salads. I have included a whole heap of ideas over the page to help you make healthy happen and use more pulses every day.

HOW TO USE DRIED AND CANNED PULSES

Dried pulses

Here is some guidance on preparing some of the most common pulses.

Pulse	How to prepare
Chickpeas	Cook 1 cup chickpeas in 3 cups water (or use the 1:3 ratio to cook however much you need).
	Quick-cook method: Rinse, bring chickpeas and water to the boil in a large pan, simmer for 45–60 minutes until soft. Rinse again and then they are ready to eat.
	Traditional preparation method: Soak chickpeas in a large bowl of water for 6–8 hours or overnight, drain and rinse. Add chickpeas to fresh water and boil/simmer for 20–30 minutes. Rinse again and then they are ready to eat.
Kidney beans	Cook 1 cup kidney beans in 3 cups water (or use the 1:3 ratio to cook however much you need).
	Quick-cook method: Rinse, bring kidney beans and water to the boil in a large pan and simmer for 55–70 minutes until soft. Rinse again and then they are ready to eat.
	Traditional preparation method: Soak kidney beans in a large bowl of water for 6–8 hours or overnight, drain and rinse. Add kidney beans to fresh water and boil/simmer for 30–40 minutes. Rinse again and then they are ready to eat.
	Note: It is super important to discard the water you soak the kidney beans in before you cook them. It can be dangerous to use this water as it can be considered toxic. Don't use dried kidney beans in a casserole or slow-cooker without soaking and cooking them first.
Lentils	These do not need to be pre-soaked, but dried lentils will need to be rinsed and cooked before eating. Some recipes will call for them to be pre-cooked and then added, others will call for them to just be rinsed and then cooked as part of the dish. Check the recipe you are using for further guidance on this one.
	Brown lentils – to pre-cook these, simply rinse thoroughly and cook in plenty of boiling water (1 cup lentils to 4 cups water) for about 20 minutes or until soft, then drain and rinse if needed. Overcooking brown lentils will cause them to go mushy so be sure you watch them.

Pulse	How to prepare
Lentils *continued*	Red lentils – if you do need or want to pre-cook them (you can do this before adding to a mince dish, for example), then simply rinse and cook 1 cup lentils in 3 cups water. Bring to a boil and simmer for about 20–30 minutes – be sure to keep an eye on them so they don't stick to the bottom of the pan. Drain off any excess liquid.
	French green/Puy lentils – these delicious lentils are meant to stay firm and not break down when you cook them. Simply rinse them, cover with plenty of boiling water (1 cup lentils to 4 cups water) and cook for 20–25 minutes until they are soft and tender but not falling apart. Drain and rinse with hot water.
Split peas	Again, these often only need rinsing before adding to a recipe to be cooked. Check the recipe you are using for guidance on how long to cook them; it will vary from recipe to recipe.

Canned pulses

With canned pulses, just rinse and drain and you are good to go! This is a more expensive way of using pulses, and you do need to consider that some of the pulses will be canned with salt, so do be sure to rinse them well to remove as much of the salt as possible. Canned pulses are a great option for those new to them or short on time, and there are some brands that pack their pulses in spring water so they are a great choice.

WHY DO PULSES MAKE YOU GASSY?

Excuse the frankness here, but I know it's what some of you might be thinking: *Nice idea Claire to up the lentils, but my house will start to smell like a farm if everyone gets into that!*

Pulses contain short-chain carbohydrates (called galactans) which the human body struggles to break down completely. What ends up happening is that these end up in your bowel and the bacteria that live in there have a little party because they love using them as a source of food. This isn't a bad thing, as you need to feed the bacteria in your bowel (well, the good ones anyway), but the end result is that the bacteria do make gas when they are eating away on these carbohydrate chains.

For most people, I suggest that you slowly increase the amount of pulses you have over time rather than having them at every meal straight away – this can be helpful to allow your body to adjust! A little extra gas when you eat pulses is totally normal.

However, if you have been diagnosed with Irritable Bowel Syndrome

(IBS) or have another gut-related disorder, you may find that pulses just aren't for you or that you can only tolerate them in very small amounts. If that is you, then you may have to skip over this section and focus on other areas of your life where you really can make a difference because, realistically, upping your pulse intake is only likely to cause you grief.

If you do have IBS, you are very gassy after eating, your bowel habits are all over the place or you look six months pregnant after eating, please contact your GP or come and see one of my amazing team at Mission Nutrition (www.missionnutrition.co.nz) who will be able to help you get to the bottom of things – pardon the pun!

Go low GI and stabilise your energy

Carbohydrate-containing foods can all be rated on what is called the 'glycemic index' (GI) scale. This is basically the rate at which food is broken down by your body and how quickly it will raise your blood sugar levels. It can be really helpful to have meals and snacks which have a low GI overall to help stabilise your blood sugar levels and, ultimately, help you feel better.

Here are some quick and easy ways to use more low GI foods every day:

- Use more pulses – they are low GI, which is great news.
- Oats are a great low GI option – good for breakfast made into porridge or Bircher muesli. You can also add a tablespoon or two to a smoothie. Blend them up and use instead of breadcrumbs. They are good in my savoury oaty loaf recipe, too (see page 232).
- Milk, yoghurt and cottage cheese are all low GI and awesome to include every day.
  - A glass of milk can be a good snack, ideal to add into smoothies as well as with breakfast cereal.
  - Yoghurt is perfect as part of a healthy breakfast, as a snack or added to a smoothie.
  - Cottage cheese with raw veggies or wholegrain crackers is a winner, too. I also have cottage cheese with salad at lunchtime.
- When you eat bread, always opt for a dense wholegrain variety.
- Quinoa, barley and buckwheat are some great low GI grains you can try.

For more on this, check out www.glycemicindex.com

Time to tune in and take action!

How to use more pulses every week

1. Healthy dips and spreads

Hummus is the most widely available pulse-based dip and it is made from chickpeas. You can also make some delicious dips with other pulses, too – check out my recipes on pages 252, 253, 255 and 256. These dips or spreads are great as an everyday snack on crackers or with chopped up fruit or veggies – they are perfect for entertaining, too.

2. Delicious snacks

Did you know you can roast pulses in the oven and eat them as a snack? Well, you can! Pre-cooked chickpeas and butter beans work the best if you are new to this. All you do is flavour them with some herbs and spices, spray with a little oil and bake.

3. Soups

Pulses absorb flavours very well and are a fantastic way to add texture and interest to a soup recipe. There are a huge number of soup recipes that have pulses in them, so look out for those – they can make a healthy, filling lunch or light meal in the cooler months.

Red lentils and split peas are best suited to thick-style soups and they break down quickly when you cook them. French/Puy lentils are more suitable if you want the lentils to stay whole.

Large pulses like chickpeas and butter beans are best added to a soup when they are cooked.

4. Salads

As I mentioned before, I pretty much add pulses to all my salads – it is a great way to make a salad a complete meal and more filling, as they are packed with both protein and starch.

- Chickpeas work really well in a light, leafy salad.
- Kidney beans are fabulous in a Mexican salad (see recipe on page 230).
- Puy lentils are fabulous in a salad.
  (See *Lose Weight for Life* for a wonderful Puy lentil salad recipe on page 229.)
- Edamame beans and chickpeas make a great combo. See page 231 for a recipe you will love.
- When I have leftover meat or chicken and maybe some roasted veggies, I will mix them with salad leaves and some butter beans, chickpeas or haricot beans and add a nice dressing.

5. Meat-free meals

Make amazing meat-free culinary masterpiece meals using pulses. Here are some ideas:

- Chickpea curry
- Falafels – you can buy a mix from the supermarket or make your own from scratch
- Curried chickpea patties (see recipe on page 238)
- Lentil bake (see recipe on page 239)
- Dhal – curry made with yellow split peas
- Chilli – made with vegetables and kidney beans

6. Bulk out dishes

You can add a can or cup of pulses to many dishes to bulk them out and you will end up using less meat/chicken/seafood in the long run, saving money and adding goodness.

- Mince – add ½–1 cup cooked red or brown lentils to 300–400 grams of mince (this will serve approximately four people); you won't even notice they are in there! You can use this to make spaghetti Bolognese, chilli, lasagne or any other mince-based dish.
  (See *Lose Weight for Life* recipe on page 246.)
- Casseroles/stews – as well as adding extra vegetables as I suggested in the last section, you can bulk out a casserole or stew by adding a can or cup of cooked pulses like kidney beans, chickpeas or butter beans. The pulses take on the flavour of the dish really well, and with extra veggies, too, you will have a fantastic, nutrition-packed meal right there.
- Stir-fry – add a cup of edamame beans (in the frozen veggie section of the supermarket) to a stir-fry. They are already in some frozen pre-mixes of stir-fry veggies, too.

7. Mash them

Butter beans and haricot beans work best and are a great alternative to mashed potatoes (with more fibre and goodness). They must be well cooked and very soft to be able to mash them (see recipe on page 244). Try mashing potato or kumara half and half with pulses for a mixed mash.

Inside your body

Like it or not, you are covered in bacteria, inside and out. Surprisingly, though, it's not a bad thing! There are trillions of different types of bacteria, some of them helpful, some of them harmful, but when you get the balance right and have lots of the good ones, it is all round good news for your health!

Your digestive system is like a large hose pipe that travels from your mouth to, well, your bum. The tube starts off at the back of your mouth and takes food to the stomach; here it is all churned up and mixed with lots of different things to help break down your food.

From your stomach, the mashed-up food heads into your small intestine where much of the goodness from your food is absorbed and heads into your blood stream. From here, what is left passes into your large intestine where more water is absorbed and the bacteria that live there work on fermenting parts of your food to produce short-chain fatty acids and other things that are important for good health and wellbeing. What remains, the poo, then comes out the other end.

What you need to know is that the inside of this tube (your digestive system) is like a living ecosystem – think of it like a rainforest. There are lots of things living in there and the health and wellbeing of the inside of your gut (much like a rainforest) depends on things working in balance and harmony. If you cut down all the trees in a rainforest, the wildlife would die. If you wiped out all the insects, there would be a knock-on effect and other things would suffer – your 'internal ecosystem' is much the same.

There is a huge variety of different types of bacteria that live throughout your gut, with most being found in the small and large intestines. The problem is, when you don't eat well, you have a lot of stress in your life, you drink a lot of alcohol or you generally don't take good care of yourself, the health of your internal ecosystem suffers. If things aren't healthy on the inside, your body isn't able to absorb nutrients properly. You might be shoving in the vitamin pills to make up for your mad, crazy, busy stressful life where eating well is just too hard, but they won't be working if your inside isn't able to absorb any of the goodies because it is so unhealthy.

So, as well as focusing on eating well to look and feel good, remember that at the same time you are helping maintain a healthy internal ecosystem, too! This will give your body the best chance to absorb the goodness from your food as well as helping you keep your immune system healthy. Start looking after yourself from the inside out.

Here are a few tips on how to do it:
- Eat plenty of foods packed with healthy bacteria, for example live yoghurt and other dairy foods with added probiotics.
- Have plenty of fibre, particularly soluble fibre and resistant starch – the bacteria in your gut feed on this and need it as fuel. More on fibre on page 99.
- If you go on antibiotics you will need to take a course of probiotics afterwards. Antibiotics can strip the good as well as bad bacteria out of the gut; this can be a big issue if you have had several doses of treatment. Talk to your pharmacist about it.
- Keep well hydrated (see pages 126–9).

STEP 3: GO WHOLEGRAIN

We are surrounded by super-processed, grain-based foods everywhere we look. Fluffy white bread, bagels, highly processed breakfast cereals, white burger buns and pizza bases, which are not only made with white flour but often have added sugar and salt in them, too.

It has become normal to eat highly processed foods and they can be hard to avoid. There are white bread sandwiches at every lunch bar and café as well as mega muffins and cookies wherever you turn. It certainly isn't helpful when it comes to looking and feeling good.

As you know, I am no extremist and certainly have the occasional crumpet and wrap as well as enjoying white rice from time to time, but in my house we certainly don't use a lot of highly processed grains at all. We opt for less-processed, wholegrain options as our staples which are much higher in fibre, generally low GI and have a lot more vitamins and minerals remaining in them than more-processed grains. I would like to help you do the same.

WHAT ARE GRAINS?

Grains are the edible seeds of specific grasses which are grown all over the world as a source of food. The most common grains you may be aware of are wheat, rye, oats, rice, barley and corn (maize).

When the 'grain' is removed from the plant from which it grows it is 'whole', which is where the term 'wholegrain' comes from. To get the best from grains nutrition-wise, and to help you look and feel your best, it really is better to have most of your grains whole rather than heavily processed and all ground up.

To help make sense of all this, it is time for a mini grain anatomy lesson.

Whole grains

A whole grain has three parts to it, a bit like an egg really. The outside layer is the bran layer (like the egg shell), the middle part (like the white of an egg) is called the endosperm, and at the centre of the grain (much like an egg yolk) there is the germ.

If we look at the wheat grain for example, here is how it looks:

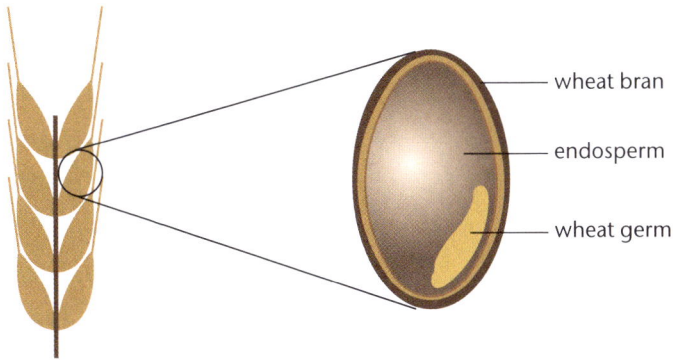

When you eat the 'whole grain' you are eating all three parts of the grain, and as I mentioned before, nutrition-wise this is by far the best thing for you.

The bran layer is where a lot of the fibre is. It also contains B vitamins (which you need to help your body convert food into energy), and a whole host of other vitamins, minerals and phytonutrients that play an important role in protecting your body from cancer and other diseases.

The germ part is where you will find essential fatty acids, vitamin E as well as B vitamins, minerals and phytonutrients, too.

The endosperm is the food supply for the germ (if the seed was to be planted and grow), and is a dense source of carbohydrate and protein.

How 'whole' are your grains?

You can eat a 'whole grain' in one of two ways. First, literally eating the whole grain as it is, with very minimal processing, e.g. eating porridge made from chunky wholegrain oats. Here you are eating the entire oat (it has just been squashed, as oats start off oval-shaped). The wholegrain oat hasn't been chopped or ground and nothing apart from the inedible outer husk has been removed.

The other way you may encounter whole grains is when they have been ground, milled, cracked or flaked. If the ratio of the bran, endosperm and germ are kept the same as in the original grain, all these can still be called 'wholegrain'. You commonly find these in things like breakfast cereals, breads and crackers. Eating wholegrain this way isn't quite as good.

Be sure when you buy a product that says 'contains whole grain' or 'the goodness of whole grains' that you look at the ingredients list and see how much whole grain is actually in there – some might only have a minor scattering of whole grains.

The processing of grains

Most of the grains that you eat will be processed in some way before you eat them as I have described below. The best thing to do is opt for the less-processed versions of each of the grains where possible for maximum nutrition and goodness.

OATS

Oat groats will be cleaned, have the inedible outer husk removed, then steamed and squashed to make them into the chunky oats you will be familiar with. This level of processing is relatively small. Oats are also sometimes cut up to make smaller flakes and rolled super thin to allow them to cook more quickly.

RICE

Brown rice is the 'whole grain' whereas white rice has had the bran layer removed (so has less fibre and B vitamins). This doesn't make white rice 'bad' – as you will hopefully realise by now, I don't believe that food needs to be looked at like that – but it simply means from a nutritional point of view, brown rice has a little extra goodness. Rice can be ground into flour and this can be used in cooking or made into rice noodles. Rice is also puffed to make Ricies.

WHEAT

Wheat can be parboiled, dried and cracked to make bulgar wheat, which is probably most well known here as the main ingredient in the salad tabbouleh. A small amount of the bran is removed in this process but much of the wholegrain goodness is retained.

Wheat is also commonly ground into flours which are then used to make breads, breakfast cereals, noodles, crackers, cakes, muffins, biscuits, pastry and so on. Wholemeal flour is not the whole grain but does have a little of the germ and bran remaining. White flour, however, doesn't have the goodness of the bran or the germ and is simply a highly refined source of carbohydrate that lacks fibre.

Durum wheat is a species of wheat with a high protein content and is used to make pasta, couscous, puddings, breakfast cereals and some breads. Wheat can also be puffed to make a breakfast cereal.

RYE
Often eaten as a whole grain as rye flakes in something like muesli or can be ground into flour and used as an ingredient in baking.

BARLEY
Most commonly you will find this as pearl barley, which is barley that has had its outer husk and the bran layer removed. You can also get barley flakes, which can be used as a breakfast cereal or in cooking. You can buy barley flour, too.

CORN
The wholegrain version of corn is, of course, corn on the cob! When the kernels are dried and then popped, you get popcorn. How good is it, to know that popcorn is a wholegrain?! It is best to have it without added sugar, fat and salt, though, and, of course, caramel-coated popcorn isn't on my list of recommended everyday eating, that's for sure. Corn can also be ground into cornmeal (polenta) or very finely ground to make cornflour.

NEW GRAINS ON THE BLOCK
As well as these more well-known grains, in recent years you may have seen the rise in the availability of other grains, sometimes called 'ancient grains', which include quinoa, amaranth, millet and buckwheat. These aren't really true 'grains', but their nutritional value is similar to that of the other grains and they can be used in a similar way, so it is good to mention them here. Nor are they really 'new' actually – they have been used in other parts of the world for donkey years, but they are new to a lot of us.

These 'new grains' are helpful for a number of reasons. First, they are gluten free, which is great for those who need to follow a gluten-free diet, and also they are such a fabulous way to add interest and variety to the way you eat. When eaten whole, most will have had only a minimal amount of processing, too, which is more good news. Like other grains they can also be ground to make flours, puffed to make cereals and rolled to make flakes which can be used in a variety of ways. As with the other grains, opting for the least processed version of each is best.

Depending on where you shop, you might be able to find these 'ancient grains' in your local supermarket; if not, health food shops and some bulk bin stores will have them.

Gluten

Gluten is a protein that occurs naturally in the grains of wheat (including spelt), rye, barley and oats*.

People who are diagnosed with coeliac disease have a permanent lifelong intolerance to gluten and they must avoid all traces or they are at risk of causing serious damage to the inside of their gut.

In recent years there has been a huge trend for people without coeliac disease moving to a gluten-free diet; it has almost become fashionable! While it is certainly true that some people have a gluten intolerance (without having coeliac disease), there are a huge number of people who are removing gluten unnecessarily. A gluten-free diet isn't automatically a healthy diet by any means, especially if it includes lots of highly processed gluten-free bread, gluten-free cookies and other treats.

Is gluten really the issue?

Self-diagnosing gluten intolerance or an 'issue with gluten' is not a good idea. If you have bloating, pain after eating or think that any of the grains or gluten may be an issue for you – please, please, please seek individual advice from a qualified professional – and no, that is not Doctor Google, Facebook or a trainer who has just done a bit of 'reading'. Why? Because in more than 10 years working in this field I have seen far too many people who try eliminating things from their diet without good advice and have ended up missing a much bigger issue or just, quite frankly, making their lives far more difficult than they need to be, creating unnecessary drama.

Irritable Bowel Syndrome (IBS) – If you have IBS then gluten isn't necessarily the issue. It is more likely that the whole wheat grain, certain fruits and vegetables, pulses and a multitude of other foods and drinks will be affecting you and you will need to get some advice from a qualified health professional who knows all about managing IBS to get the best results.

Coeliac disease – This cannot be confirmed by your doctor if you have already been following a gluten-free diet. To be able to check whether you have it or not, you need to have been eating gluten for several weeks so that the doctor can check your blood and the inside of your bowel to see if it is actually gluten that is causing your issues. If you go to your doctor having already tried lots of different diets and exclusions yourself, it can make things a lot more difficult.

Gynaecological problems – One of the most common things

I see being missed when people self-diagnose a 'gluten issue' because of gut problems is endometriosis or another 'downstairs ladies problem'. One in 10 women have endometriosis so, if you do have pain that you are putting down to what you eat or a gut-related issue, make sure you have endometriosis excluded as a cause before you just assume it is something you are eating.

Anaemia – If you are tired and fatigued, it could be that you are anaemic or short on other vital nutrients, or it could be that you're actually just tired and run-down and it has nothing to do with gluten.

I don't want you to miss these potentially serious problems so make sure that you get good advice. The biggest problem with taking advice from non-professionals who don't have good knowledge, qualifications and experience and who just tell you to try and go 'gluten free' to solve your issues is that they don't know what they don't know, and this can lead to greater problems in the long-term.

If you do feel tired or bloated then going gluten free (which can often make you feel better purely because you are cutting out a lot of processed foods from your diet and eating healthier overall) may seem to solve some of your problems – but is it the real answer? What is really going on with you? That's what I would want to know!

As well as those who just focus on removing gluten, it seems to have become increasingly common to find people who reportedly feel better eating very few grains altogether, particularly wheat. If that is you and that is your personal choice I respect that. However, please be mindful that if you do have a limited amount of grains in your diet you really need to make sure you are getting adequate carbohydrate, fibre and B vitamins from other sources. You may find that cutting back on certain grains and moving towards the alternative grains that I have discussed is the way that works for you, but complete exclusion is very rarely necessary.

*Note on oats: Oats are also considered alongside other gluten-containing grains for two reasons. First, they contain a protein called Avenin that some people with coeliac diesease can react to. Second, in New Zealand many of the oats we purchase and eat will be grown near other gluten-containing crops, or processed with or near other grains. As such, they can't be considered gluten free because of cross contamination. The current advice at the time of publication for people in New Zealand who have coeliac disease is to avoid oats unless your specialist advises otherwise. Oats are fine for everyone else though.

NEW WAYS TO GO WHOLEGRAIN IN YOUR EVERYDAY EATING

Changing the way you eat takes time and effort, I really do understand that. Here are some suggestions for quick and easy ways you can regularly include more of the wholegrain versions of the grains I have been talking about, so you can reap the nutritional benefits and feel amazing as a result!

Oats

Oats are a great way to get into whole grains if you aren't eating them already. They are packed with fibre, which is great for keeping things 'flowing' nicely through you, as well as having a positive impact on cholesterol levels and they are certainly great at helping you feel full.

I love oats and have them several times a week – normally I go for the big chunky ones. The little ones are okay but they will be broken down more quickly in your body (they have just been chopped up to make them cook quicker).

- Oats make a great breakfast – make them into porridge, Bircher muesli or make your own cereal from them. There are also many types of muesli you can buy in the shops. Look for one without added sugar – the sweetness of dried fruit will be enough.
- Add a tablespoon of oats to a smoothie to thicken it up.
- As I mentioned before, you can make a delicious vegetarian 'meatless' loaf with oats (see recipe on page 232).

Brown rice

This delicious nutty rice is very versatile – it might take longer to cook than white rice, but it is well worth including where you can. To speed up the cooking time, you can soak it in the morning before you leave the house, then when you come to cook it at night, it cooks more quickly.

- Eat rice for breakfast – cook it up with milk (like you would rice pudding) and sweeten with dried fruit, fresh fruit or berries. Try adding spices like cinnamon, nutmeg, mixed spice, cardamom or vanilla extract.
- Rice is perfect with a stir-fry, chilli con carne or curry. Wherever you normally have white rice, try brown for a change. All you need to learn to do is start cooking it before you start preparing the food for the rest of your meal – I cook it in the microwave and it takes about 20–25 minutes. ½ cup rice to 1 cup water is the ratio that works.
- Have you tried wild rice? Black in colour and quite pricey, but a little can go a long way. I mix a little in with my basmati rice to make a fabulous black and white rice mix.

Corn

Even though corn can be classified as a vegetable, it is actually a cereal grain so we can talk about it here, too.

You can buy corn kernels ready to pop from the supermarket and they are super cheap. I bought a popcorn machine for about $40 from one of the big kitchen-homeware stores when it was on special and I use it all the time.

Quinoa

Quinoa is a light 'grain' with a nutty flavour and it has a low GI, meaning it is slowly absorbed by the body.[6] It also has a high protein content compared with many other grains. It contains all the essential amino acids (that is basically all the amino acids your body is unable to make itself), which is actually unusual for a plant food and really good news. Meat, fish, eggs and dairy foods are known to have all the essential amino acids, but as quinoa does, too, it makes it a really helpful additional source of protein if you are vegetarian and vegan.

Quinoa comes in several colours. The most common is white, but you can also get red and black varieties and it needs to be cooked before eating. Quinoa can be substituted for any grain in almost any style of recipe.

- You can make porridge with quinoa.
- You can cook it in water or stock and make it into a salad much like you would with couscous, bulgar wheat or rice. Check out my recipe for tabbouleh (see page 225) where I have suggested this as an alternative.
- Quinoa can be added to soups and casseroles for a great taste and texture.
- Cooked quinoa can be used to make sushi instead of using rice.

Buckwheat

Despite its name, this grain has nothing to do with wheat (it is actually related to the rhubarb, sorrel and knotweed family) and is fine for those who can't have wheat or gluten. These little pyramid-shaped bluey-grey grains are really quite delicious! It is now gradually being added to a few mueslis on the market. My first introduction to this grain was buckwheat pancakes which my mum used to make as she can't eat wheat. I now use buckwheat all the time; it is great and adds texture and flavour to heaps of dishes.

- Add it to your homemade raw muesli mix (see my recipe on page 214).

- You can make it into porridge. I often mix it 50:50 with oats, and this makes a really nice change from just plain oats.
- Cook it instead of couscous or rice. It is really good in salads, too.

Amaranth

Amaranth is a tiny little 'grain' that will stay quite crunchy even when cooked, so it is best used in combination with other grains like oats, rye and millet in homemade mueslis or cereal bars.

You can make it into porridge or add it to soups or slow-cooker meals, but it won't fluff up nicely like couscous or quinoa so it doesn't work well in salads. Puffed amaranth is also available and can be used in homemade breakfast cereal mixes or in baking. Like most of the grains you can get a flour version, too, but it is well worth finding a recipe where the experimenting has been done because these different types of flour certainly don't behave like wheat flour.

Millet

When I was little I had two budgerigars, Sabrina and Buttercup. How kids come up with names for pets I have no idea! Anyway, I used to feed them millet and now I can't believe that I eat it myself and actually really like it! In some parts of the world this is a staple grain, much like wheat is to us in New Zealand. Millet can be made into porridge; it can also be boiled and cooked and served much like rice or couscous.

Personally, my main use for millet, much like amaranth, is in my Bircher muesli mix, which I soak before eating so I don't break my teeth. I will endeavour to be more creative with millet as time goes by.

Wheat

The easiest way to include more 'wholegrain' wheat is to opt for dense wholegrain breads, breakfast cereals made with wholegrain wheat, wholegrain crackers and wholemeal pasta. The amount of wholegrain you will get from these products will, however, vary depending on what you buy so it really pays to check. Also, give bulgar wheat a go.

Rye

I grew up eating a lot of rye with my mum being intolerant to wheat – rye is delicious! Rye flakes are a wonderful addition to cereal mixes and rye flour can make nice bread. Pumpernickel is a delicious, very dense bread made from rye – a little goes a long way, but it is well worth trying.

Time to tune in and take action!

What can you do to make sure you are upping your whole grains and relying less on highly processed grains?

What new grains are you going to try? Write a few ideas down and then plan to make it happen!

Up the fibre

I am the biggest fan of fibre but most of us don't get enough and it is a real issue. Fibre is so important to keep things moving through your digestive system, and certain types of fibre are also vital to feed the healthy bacteria that live in your gut and do amazing things for you without you even noticing.

Having fibre-rich meals and snacks also helps stabilise your blood sugar levels so, all round, fibre is king.

Up your fibre today by:

- Adding a tablespoon of wheat bran, oat bran or ground LSA (linseed, sunflower and almond) to your cereal and smoothies.
- Having at least 4–7 handfuls of veggies every day (there are endless ideas on pages 69–81).
- Using more pulses – yes, another reason!
- Choosing wholegrain breads, cereals and crackers – the less processed, the better.
- Keeping the skin on your fruits and veggies.
- Enjoying cold potato salad, rice salads and bananas that aren't too ripe – they are packed with a type of fibre called 'resistant starch' which is vital to keep those bacteria in your gut healthy.
- Trying chia seeds – you can add them to a homemade muesli or you can soak them in milk or yoghurt with the added sweetness of fruit and enjoy as a dessert or snack.

STEP 4: SAY HELLO TO HEALTHY FATS

Now we have got the plant food side of things sorted, it is time to move our attention to fats. Advice on fats has changed over the years and it can be a bit of a minefield, so we need to make sure that you are getting things right in that department. Here goes . . .

PAST TO PRESENT

In days gone by, low-fat diets were all the rage. As fat is the most energy-dense of all of our nutrients (fat has 39 kilojoules/gram [9 kcal] as opposed to carbohydrate and protein which have 17 kilojoules/gram [4 kcal]), reducing the amount of fat in your diet to a bare minimum seemed to be the logical answer to slash your calorie intake and in turn help you lose weight. I remember reading diet books of my mum's when I was younger where the total focus was on having low-fat everything. No oil, no spreads and certainly no cheese. Nuts and seeds were also off the list. What a miserable existence!

With the low-fat food craze there was also an emergence of an endless array of adapted food products which you will no doubt still see today – low-fat biscuits, cakes and lollies with big 'fat free' labels on them. The problem is that the 'eat me, I am guilt free because I am fat free' health halo that surrounds these types of products only encourages you to overindulge. Fat free or not, cookies are still cookies, loaded with sugar and not something any of us need when it comes to looking and feeling good.

At university, I did my thesis on the effect of low-fat food claims on both men and women. My research showed that men tended to steer clear of low-fat products more often than not as they believed they would taste inferior. Women, on the other hand, said that when they saw a food labelled 'low fat' they would eat the same amount as (and often more than) they would of the standard product because they felt like it was 'guilt free' or 'better for them' and it was therefore okay to have a bigger serving. They believed that little bit extra wouldn't hurt! No wonder the low-fat everything approach didn't really work at getting us any slimmer.

When you solely focus on following a super-low-fat diet, it also means that you end up removing a lot of the healthy fats as well as the unhealthy ones and that is not a good thing! Having good fat is vital to help you look and feel good, keep your skin glowing and your hair and nails looking amazing, not to mention the fact that fat makes you feel full. So we need to strike a balance.

WHY FAT IS VITAL

As you now know, some fat is vital for good health and wellbeing – I certainly don't follow a fat-free diet by any means. Here are just some of the super-important roles that fat plays in your body:

- Foods containing fat carry the fat-soluble vitamins A, D, E and K which are incredibly important to help your body work well and will help to make sure you look and feel your best. Vitamin A keeps your skin and eyes healthy. Vitamin D helps keep your bones strong. Vitamin E keeps your cell membranes healthy and acts as an antioxidant. Vitamin K helps make sure your blood can clot when it needs to.
- There are certain types of fats that our bodies are unable to make by themselves. These are known as essential fatty acids and include omega-3 and omega-6, without which you will be unable to look and feel your best and your health will be compromised. Omega-3, for example, is vital for keeping your brain and eyes healthy as well as playing a role in managing your mood and how you feel.
- Fat can also help the absorption of other nutrients, therefore including a little fat in your meals and snacks helps ensure that you get all the goodness from the food you eat.

HOW MUCH FAT DO YOU NEED?

The exact amount of fat you need in a day is highly individual. However, to give you a starting point, the nutritional guidelines for New Zealand released by the Ministry of Health recommend that we have around 20–35 per cent of our total energy needs from fat, which works out to be around 45–80 grams in total of fat per day.

In real terms, this is equivalent to 9–16 teaspoons of fat (with 5 grams being 1 teaspoon worth, just to save you having to do the maths). To help you look and feel good, the best thing to do is make sure the fat you eat comes from healthy sources (nuts, seeds, avocado and healthy oils) rather than cream buns and chocolate biscuits.

Even though there are some 'low fat' products that can be a trap, such as the low-fat biscuits I mentioned before, there are still many cases where I do suggest you opt for the lower-fat versions of food. This includes low-fat dairy products like milk and yoghurt, choosing lean cuts of meat and grilled options over deep-fried, for example. You simply do not need the extra fat in the higher-fat versions of these foods and you are much better to make sure that the 45–80 grams of fat you are having each day come from healthy oils, nuts/seeds and avocado rather than from fatty meat and creamy sauces.

The 45–80 grams a day does sound like quite a lot, but this also includes all the fat that you naturally find in foods, it isn't just the amount you add to your food. For example, ¼ cup of almonds has 22 grams of fat and ¼ large avocado has 12 grams of fat, so it is very easy to get to the 45–80 grams without drizzling oil on everything left right and centre.

As this book is all about making healthy happen, rather than blinding you with science, I'll give you a rough guideline of what might work fat-wise for you in meals and snacks. This is not a 'set in stone' kind of guideline as that simply doesn't work; it is more of a helpful tool for you to use as part of everything I am teaching you. It is important to remember that it all depends on who you are individually and what your goals are.

Meals = 10–20 grams of fat

Snacks = 5–10 grams of fat

There will be times when you will have less and times when you have slightly more; we are looking for an overall balance, not some kind of obsessive military operation. As I have said before and I will say again, obsessing over food and being anxious about everything you eat is as unhealthy as being too relaxed about it.

HIGHER-FAT DIETS

Despite the guidelines I have mentioned regarding the upper level of fat, I have worked with some people who successfully follow diets that are much higher in fat than I have suggested and they report looking and feeling good.

These individuals are simply spending more of their daily kilojoule/calorie intake on fat (that being healthy types of fat) and less on other nutrients. To get results however, they are strict on including very little processed food, particularly starchy foods, little to no added sugar, limiting or not drinking any alcohol and eating massive amounts of veggies.

It is best to seek individual advice from a qualified dietitian or nutritionist is this is something that interests you.

If you want detailed information or individualised nutrition advice on any matter, head to see one of my team at Mission Nutrition – they will be able to work out exactly what is right for you. www.missionnutrition.co.nz

Time to tune in!

How much fat do you have in a day?

Keep a record of what you eat for a day or two, check out your food labels and see for yourself. Even if you consider yourself a healthy person, you might be having far more than you think! Use the space below to jot down your notes and total up how much fat you really have. Be realistic, too. Choose a few days that genuinely reflect what you eat rather than your healthiest day ever. Include a weekend day and any treats or snacks you have. It is just good to start raising awareness for what is in your food.

Day 1

Food eaten	How many grams of fat?

Day 2

Food eaten	How many grams of fat?

To download a food record diary to check your fat intake, go to www.claireturnbull.co.nz/feelgood.

FAT TYPES

Fats are not all created equal. There are lots of different types and, as with so many things in nutrition these days, lots of different opinions on which are best. My thoughts are based on the most current, up-to-date credible research and this is exactly what I apply to my own life and those who I love and cook for.

One thing to consider is that despite the fact we can separate fats out into different types, depending on their chemical structure, in reality the majority of foods we eat will actually have a mixture of fat types. So, after my mini lesson on fat, I will follow up with the practical part and let you know what food choices to make to ensure that, overall, you are getting more of the good and less of the not-so-good fats.

Now, for a little background, let the mini lesson on fats begin.

Saturated fat

Saturated fat always used to be labelled the 'bad fat', no questions asked. Now, though, new research is suggesting that not all types of saturated fat affect our body in the same way. However, at the time that this book was published, the jury was still out on the effects of each type of saturated fat and while that is the case, my opinion is that it's not the time to start increasing saturated fat of any type until we know much more. I personally feel that there are enough other great fat choices (like those in nuts, seeds and avocado, for example) which have been proven to be ideal for your health and wellbeing, so at this stage they remain the best option and are what I feed my family.

My recommendation is to reduce the amount of saturated fat you have by trimming all the white fat off your meat, removing chicken skin before cooking and opting for an alternative to butter as your primary spread or baking ingredient. Choosing reduced-fat dairy products can also be a helpful step in reducing the amount of saturated fat you have.

Trans fats

These are very much like saturated fats and are dealt with in the body in a similar way, and there is no doubt that these are definitely not good for you! There are all sorts of horror stories from overseas (particularly the US) of how much trans fat is hiding in food. Luckily, here in New Zealand, it is not nearly as bad as in other countries. The foods to watch out for are pastries, cakes and biscuits, which, let's be fair, aren't exactly health foods anyway. With trans fats, less is definitely best.

Keep your heart healthy!

When it comes to keeping your heart healthy, fat isn't the only thing to focus on. There are some other really vital things to know which can help strike a healthier balance.

1. Increase your fibre – this helps things move through your bowel and prevents re-absorption of cholesterol in the bowel. Upping your whole grains and pulses, and including psyllium husks every day, is a good way to go.
2. Keeping active is also an important part of the picture. This can help increase the good type of cholesterol (HDL) and can help strengthen your heart and improve your blood pressure.

Unsaturated fat

Unsaturated fats are a really important part of a healthy diet and you won't want to be doing without these. Foods packed with these healthy fats include avocado, nuts, seeds, oily fish and oils such as olive, flaxseed and canola.

Unsaturated fats fall into one of two camps: either they are monounsaturated or they are polyunsaturated, and all of the foods mentioned above contain a combination of these two in different proportions. The difference between mono- and polyunsaturated fat is simply in their structure.

When it comes to looking and feeling good, including unsaturated fats rather than saturated or trans fats is the way to go. There are some types of unsaturated fats that are worthy of an extra-special mention and these are a type of polyunsaturated fat called omega-3.

OMEGA-3

Long-chain omega-3 fats are known as 'essential fats' because your body is unable to make them itself so it is 'essential' that you eat them!

Omega-3 is important on so many levels at all stages of your life. It is vitally important to help with the growth and development of a baby's brain, eyes and nervous system during pregnancy. Through childhood and into adulthood and old age, omega-3 helps keep the brain functioning at its best as well as working to keep the heart, bones and joints healthy. It also helps your skin to look good as well as improving your mood and playing a role in the prevention and management of depression.

There are two types of long-chain omega-3: DHA (docosahexaenoic acid) and EPA (eicosapentaenoic acid). For good health and the prevention of chronic diseases it is suggested that the total amount of these you have each day (when you add DHA and EPA together) is 610 milligrams for men and 430 milligrams for women. The best food source of these long-chain healthy fats is oily fish, particularly salmon. More on this on page 110.

You might also see the letters DHA and EPA if you pick up a bottle of omega-3 capsules from the pharmacy and, occasionally, they might be listed on food labels – at least you now know what it means.

As well as the long-chain omega-3 fats, there is also a shorter-chain variety (these are called ALA [alpha-linolenic acid] in case you ever see that listed on a food packet). These shorter-chain omega-3 fats are most commonly found in flaxseeds (linseeds), chia seeds, walnuts and canola oil. They are good for your health, but only very small amounts can be converted into long-chain omega-3, which are the ones you really need for heart health and most of the other positive health-related factors that are linked to these great fats. It is still excellent to include foods packed with these shorter chains (ALA) but you need to have foods with the long-chain omega-3, too. If you don't eat any seafood at all, it may be that you need to look at supplementation to make sure you are getting enough omega-3.

For more on this, head to www.omega-3centre.com

OMEGA-6

Omega-6 is another type of polyunsaturated fat found in a variety of foods, including some nuts, seeds and oils. While a little is needed by the body, most of us eat too much omega-6 relative to omega-3, which is not ideal when it comes to your health. Too much omega-6 can lead to the formation of pro-inflammatory substances which could lead to inflammation-related diseases.

OMEGA 3:6 BALANCE

To get the balance right when it comes to omega-3 and -6, my advice to you is to increase the amount of omega-3-rich foods in your diet and limit your use of oils that are high in omega-6 – more on this coming up soon.

Make healthy happen!

Right, it's time to get down to the nuts and bolts of it. When it comes to fats, what do you need to do on a daily basis to make healthy happen and get things right? Here are some great choices to tip the balance:

- Trim the white fat from your meat and keep your portion sizes of meat to palm-sized servings.
- Opt for lower-fat dairy products and go for unsweetened where possible – that means choosing products without added sugar. Sugar does naturally occur in milk products (lactose = milk sugar), so you will see that there will be some sugar on the nutritional information panel of these items – that type of sugar is fine. What I would like you to avoid, however, are products that contain lots of added sugar. Check the ingredients list on dairy products to see whether sugar has been added.
- For cooking and salads use good oils (see the lists below and over the page), and not too much of them.
- My choices for a spread on bread or crackers are avocado, nut spreads, tahini, hummus or mayonnaise made with a healthy oil. When I was a child, this was all we ever had, so that is what I am used to. I have never used butter or a spread on my bread simply because I never have. You may also choose to use a spread based on one of the healthier types of oil; it's up to you.
- Increase your oily fish intake (see my suggestions on page 110).
- Include more nuts and seeds – see pages 113–18 for some great ideas on this.

1. CHOOSE THE RIGHT OIL

The oil section in food stores seems to be ever growing with new varieties – from oils that we are more familiar with, such as canola (from the rapeseed plant) and olive, to those made from different nuts, seeds and avocado. It is so exciting, really. Each type of oil has its own unique flavour and different oils are useful for different things – it is all about choosing the right oil for the job.

Whichever oil you use, do remember that all oil is very energy-dense and 1 tablespoon (3 teaspoons) is roughly 480 kilojoules (120 kcal) which is a huge contribution to the 8700 kilojoules (2175 kcal) it is suggested we eat a day (this varies, of course, from person to person, but you get the point, right?).

Here is what I suggest using to help you look and feel fabulous as well as make your food taste great:

Salad/Dressings (for cold use)

When I use oil to make dressings for salads, rather than the more traditional 50:50 or 75:25 oil to vinegar ratio, I flip the balance, using 25 per cent oil to 75 per cent vinegar to keep the energy (calories) down.

- New Zealand extra virgin olive oil – this is a great first choice given its great health track record, high levels of antioxidants, wonderful flavour and its stability.
- Flaxseed oil – high in omega-3 and a really good choice. It must be kept in a dark bottle in the fridge.
- Avocado oil – New Zealand has an amazing variety of delicious avocado oils.
- Sesame oil – use a few drops for a little flavour.
- New Zealand nut oils – I love macadamia and peanut oil when it comes to flavour; good-quality walnut and hazelnut oils are also a great choice.
- Canola oil – ideally an extra virgin or cold-pressed variety.
- Rice bran oil – this is, however, more heavily processed and refined than other oils mentioned in this section.

Cooking

Good-quality New Zealand olive oils with a low acidity and high smoke point are a good choice for cooking. There is a misconception that olive oil can't be used for high-heat cooking – that is only really true when you are talking about imported olive oils which have higher acidity and a lower smoke point. Overall, if you choose to use olive oil for cooking, you are best to opt for a Kiwi-made option that you know is suitable for the purpose.

Canola oil, peanut oil, sesame oil, macadamia oil and rice bran oil are other options – the degree of processing of each type of oil will vary depending on the brand you buy.

Remember that 10–20 grams of fat per meal I mentioned earlier? 1 tablespoon of oil is 15 grams – so think about how much you are using when you are cooking: less is often more, especially as there will be fat coming from other parts of your meal, too.

Baking

If I get in the kitchen and do some baking, I often use recipes (or make up my own) that allow me to use oil as the fat in the recipe. I use a variety of different oils depending on what I have to hand and what will work for each particular recipe. Using olive oil in a healthy slice, for example, will add a strong flavour and, unless that is what you are looking for, is not really ideal. Slightly more-neutral-tasting oils would be a better option, like canola, rice bran or the nut and seed oils previously mentioned. Olive oil works better in savoury baking or in recipes where you don't mind the taste coming through.

You may also choose to use spreads made from these oils, if you like, rather than butter. It is important to understand that you will need to find recipes or play around with them if you plan to use oil rather than a solid spread or butter for baking as it will change the consistency of the recipe.

Oils to watch out for

Whether you are cooking, baking, making dressings with oil, or oil is an ingredient in a product you are buying, there are some that are best to reduce in your diet.

Sunflower, safflower and soybean oil are all high in omega-6, making them less favourable options across the board.

Palm oil is also not a good option. Firstly because of its high saturated fat content and secondly because in sourcing the oil, huge areas of forest are often destroyed. This is putting the lives of the animals that live there at huge risk, particularly orangutans. Currently, palm oil often hides behind the ingredient 'vegetable oil' on food labels so do be mindful of that when you are purchasing foods. I am hugely in support of mandatory labelling of foods which have palm oil in them so that as consumers we can make informed choices.[7]

Tips for keeping oil fresh

- Buy the best quality you can afford – the cost of an oil is likely to reflect the quality. Cold-pressed extra virgin olive oil, for example, is extracted from the first press of the olives and is produced without adding heat or excessive pressure. This results in a high-quality product that has been minimally processed. Less expensive oils are likely to have been made using high temperatures and processing chemicals to extract more oil from the olives. This doesn't make them 'bad' per se, but it just means they aren't quite as good.
- Buy oils in a dark bottle or can that doesn't let any light through and keep them in a dark place – light can spoil oil and make it go rancid.
- Keep the lid on your oil – exposure to air can cause oxidisation which can also make it go rancid.
- Avoid reheating oil. Reheating and pressure can create trans fats. This is more likely to happen in food manufacturing and in fast food outlets than in your own home, but still, it's best to avoid reusing oil.

Overall, the message is to buy the best you can afford, store it correctly, choose the right oil for the job and use an appropriate amount.[8]

2. EAT MORE OILY FISH

The easiest way for you to get the dose of long-chain omega-3 that your body needs is by eating oily fish. Fresh or smoked salmon is the richest in these fats by far, with New Zealand king salmon being the salmon of choice. In New Zealand, we only farm king salmon (this is the species name) – which is great news for Kiwis – but do be aware that in other parts of the world other salmon species are farmed and these can be lower in omega-3. This means that if you eat imported salmon products, the amount of omega-3 will vary. One example of this is canned salmon. While it is a good way to get omega-3 into your diet, as it won't be New Zealand king salmon in the can it won't have as much omega-3 as the fresh salmon you would buy over the counter, or smoked salmon either.

Other oily fish to include are mackerel, sardines, trout and tuna. Fresh tuna has much more omega-3 than canned varieties, but if you cannot get fresh, canned is still a good choice. Mixing it up is a good way to go. White fish and other seafood, such as oysters, scallops and prawns, also have a little omega-3 so are good to include for variety.

Try to include a fish meal at least two or three times a week if you can, and if one or two of these can be oily fish that would be fantastic! Below are some quick and easy ways to help you include more oily fish meals each week.

For breakfast
- Add smoked salmon to an omelette or have smoked salmon alongside your eggs on toast.
- Sardines on toast – choose sardines in spring water, mash with a little lemon and black pepper – a great breakfast or healthy snack!

As a snack
- Sardines, salmon or tuna on wholegrain crackers or with some raw chopped veggies.
- Sushi made with salmon, or sashimi.

For a meal
- Grilled salmon with steamed greens and brown rice.
- Fresh mackerel grilled on the barbecue with a delicious salad.
- Fish pie made with white fish, salmon and prawns served with lots of greens.
- See pages 236–7 for my salmon salad cups recipe.

On a non-nutrition note (this is more of a personal passion of mine), do what you can to opt for fish that have been fished in a sustainable way. Some of the fishing practices that happen around the world are simply unacceptable, in my opinion, and should not be supported.

Head to the Forest & Bird website (www.forestandbird.org.nz) for more information about buying sustainable seafood. Their *Best Fish Guide* is a great resource.

Time to tune in and take action!

How can you include more oily fish in your diet? From the previous suggestions, what can you do to make this happen?

Iodine

Iodine is a mineral that is vital for your body to work well. It is used by the thyroid gland to regulate metabolism and is required for growth and development – you can't do without it. Your body cannot make it by itself, so you have to get it in your food. It is essential for normal brain development and so it is particularly important for pregnant women to get plenty for the sake of their unborn baby. Also, it is vital that young kids get enough.

Iodine occurs naturally in fish, shellfish and seaweed. It is also found in eggs, milk (but far less than there used to be due to a change in processing), seameal custard (which has seaweed in it – not that you would ever know!), bread (as iodised salt is used) and, of course, iodised salt itself.

The amount of iodine in your fruit, veggies and grains very much reflects the soil in which it is grown and, as you may know, here in New Zealand our soil doesn't have much in it at all, so our fruit and veggies as well as other crops grown here don't have much iodine in them either. The same goes for the iodine content of meat, fish, chicken and milk – it all depends on whether the animal feed used has iodine in it or not.

How much do you need?

For an adult, the recommended daily intake (and this is to prevent deficiency) is 150 micrograms (μg) per day. For optimal health and wellbeing, more may be helpful. The upper limit is 1110μg per day, so you can see there is a lot of room for flexibility here. Given that in New Zealand the entire adult population is now considered to be mildly iodine deficient, we have work to do!

How to up the ante on iodine

- Limit the amount of processed food you eat. Over 75 per cent of the salt New Zealanders eat comes from processed food and it is not iodised.[9] Soups, sauces, packet flavouring mixes and instant noodles are a good place to start cutting back.
- The trend towards using 'fancy' salts that aren't iodised has affected our intake of iodine. Opt for an iodised salt to use in cooking and at the table. Remember, though, most of us have far too much salt overall, so this isn't a time to start going mad with the salt shaker just because it's iodised.
- Increase the amount of iodine-rich foods you eat – this is by far the best option.

Everyday foods that contain iodine

- 1 cup of trim milk = 17 micrograms (μg) (trim has more than lite blue or blue)
- 1 egg = 23 μg
- 2 slices of wholegrain bread = 28 μg
- 4 mussels = 74 μg
- 2 oysters = 30 μg
- 100 grams canned tuna = 13 μg
- 100 grams canned sardines = 23 μg
- 100 grams canned salmon = 27 μg
- Nori sheet (seaweed) = 68 μg

How to include more seafood and seaweed

- Nori (the seaweed sheets that are used to make sushi) is probably one of the easiest ways to increase iodine. You can tear up a sheet of it and add it to a salad, put some into a soup or use them like wraps – fill with salad, hummus or

avocado and some protein like chicken, salmon or tuna, for example, then wrap and eat!
- When it comes to barbecue season, don't just rely on meat – try seafood! Mussels are super cheap, too.
- Canned fish makes a good option for lunch with a big salad or on a slice of wholegrain toast (which, of course, has iodised salt in it).

If you think you might be very low on iodine, come and see one of my team at Mission Nutrition and we can help make sure you are getting all the nutrition you need and address the other vital vitamins and minerals at the same time. You may need to consider taking a supplement. An iodine supplement is absolutely required in pregnancy in New Zealand.

3. OPT FOR AVOCADO

I hang out for avocado season. I love stopping at a stand on the side of the road and picking up a monster bag of avocados. When they are in season, I use them as a spread, as a base of several desserts (yes, you did read that right) and in salsas and dips.

Avocados are technically a fruit because they have a stone in them, but I have put them in this section of the book because they are actually 50 per cent fat. Luckily though, they are jam-packed with healthy fat!

The thing to remember is that fat is high in energy, so avocados are a high-calorie food. One medium avocado has around 1600 kilojoules (400 calories) and 42 grams of fat. So, if you are looking to have avocado as a snack on crackers, one-eighth would be a sensible portion, possibly up to one-quarter.

Avocados are also packed with vitamin E and folate, and are, surprisingly, a source of fibre. They are fabulous for your skin and hair and overall a winning food to help you look and feel good.

How to include avocado in your diet
- Try it as a spread on bread, crackers or wraps.
- Use in salads.
- Chop finely and make into a salsa with tomato, red onion and chilli.
- Mash or chop up to make a guacamole (see recipe on page 254).
- Use as the base for chocolate desserts. (See recipe on page 261 for chocolate mousse.)
- You can mash and freeze avocados if you buy them in bulk, too.

4. INCLUDE NUTS AND SEEDS

What I love about nuts

Nuts are fantastic! They are nutritional awesomeness all packaged up. Healthy fats, fibre and protein – what more could you want? They are also a great way to get a dose of vitamins and minerals, including folate, calcium, magnesium and potassium.[10]

Nuts are commonly classified as a 'protein food' and while they sure do contain a good amount of protein and are really helpful, particularly for vegetarians and vegans, nuts also contain 40–80 per cent fat and are very high in energy which is why I have decided to put them here in the fat section. I personally think of nuts as a healthy fat source with bonus protein rather than the other way round – purely because I am then more mindful about my portion rather than digging in and polishing off a whole bag.

Some great ways to include nuts every day

ALMONDS
- Eat whole with fresh or dried fruit for a healthy snack.
- Sliced or whole almonds are perfect to sprinkle over salads or on top of yoghurt.
- Ground almonds can be used in healthy baking.

CASHEWS
- Add cashews to hot breakfasts, sautéed vegetables and curries.
- Raw cashews are really nice in salads.
- Blend cashews and use them to make a sauce instead of using cream (you soak them, then blend them).

HAZELNUTS
- Roasted hazelnuts are great in salads made with couscous, quinoa or buckwheat.
- Perfect to sprinkle on roasted vegetables.
- Chop hazelnuts and add to stir-fried green vegetables, great with Brussels sprouts, too.

BRAZIL NUTS
- Eat them raw or chopped up with breakfast for your daily dose of selenium.
- A perfect addition to homemade, healthy cereal bars or nut/seed balls.

PEANUTS
- Make Asian-inspired satay dishes and stir-fries.
- Sprinkle onto salads or add to sautéed vegetables (whole or chopped).
- Make into your own peanut butter by blending peanuts in a food processor, adding a little oil if needed. No added salt or sugar required – super easy and delicious. (See recipe on page 250.)

PECANS
- Fantastic in salads.
- An excellent addition to homemade muesli or chopped on top of porridge.
- I love using pecans in healthy baking.

WALNUTS
- Great in almost any salad – an easy way to add a dose of ALA omega-3.
- Lovely addition to steamed green vegetables and perfect in healthy baking or as a snack.
- Fantastic blended with dried fruit to make healthy snacks (see recipe on page 258. You can use any kind of nuts to make these, too).

PINE NUTS
- Throw on a healthy homemade pizza or salad.
- Ideal to grind and make sauces such as pesto.

MACADAMIA NUTS
- Great in muesli or healthy desserts.
- Delicious crushed and used to crumb fish before cooking.

PISTACHIOS
- Perfect tossed into salads.
- Great with fruit-based desserts.
- Wonderful with brown rice dishes.

People often ask me, which nuts are best? Well . . . they all have their own unique benefits so my advice is to have a mixture.

Having previously been addicted to the salted variety, I have since adapted my taste buds to the raw unsalted versions. At first, I thought *These aren't the nuts I am used to, they are awful and don't taste of anything*, but that was purely because the salty hit was all I was used to. Now, though, I love raw unsalted nuts and would choose them over salted any day and that is all because my taste buds have adapted – I encourage you to do the same. You don't need the extra salt and the taste of the nuts themselves (especially when they are fresh) is a winner.

Do it yourself!

Make your own snack mix
You can make your own healthy snack mix by mixing nuts, seeds and a little dried fruit together – check out page 149 for my favourite mixes.

Selenium
Selenium is a mineral which is also involved in thyroid metabolism and it is important for keeping your immune system healthy. It is known as an essential trace element, which means it is essential to include selenium in your diet as your body can't make it on its own. If you don't have enough selenium, it may mean that you have reduced protection from cancer and heart disease as well as compromised thyroid function – now that's not good at all!

In New Zealand, there are many of us who just don't get enough selenium. This is because our soils are generally very low in the mineral, and that in turn means that the food we eat that has been grown in New Zealand is likely to be very low in selenium.

It is suggested that women have at least 60 micrograms (µg) per day and men 70 micrograms per day but, as with many things, more isn't necessarily better, and it's important to know that more than 400 micrograms per day can be toxic.

By far the easiest way to get the dose of selenium you need each day is to have 2–3 Brazil nuts every day. I have mine every morning with my breakfast. It is a healthy habit I have created – try doing the same.

If you don't hugely like the taste, just chop them up in your cereal or add to a smoothie and blend them up.

If you are allergic to them, then other sources of selenium are seafood, poultry, eggs, and some other nuts do have small amounts. Here is the comparison:
- 2 Brazil nuts = 100 micrograms (µg)
- 2 boiled eggs = 25 µg
- 150 grams grilled chicken = 25 µg
- 150 grams cooked white fish = 54 µg
- 100 grams canned tuna, drained = 63 µg
- 6 mussels = 75 µg

What I love about seeds

Seeds are just as nutritionally fabulous as nuts but often don't get much of a mention – so it is time for me to change that. Seeds, it is your time to shine.

Seeds are to plants what eggs are to chickens – their future generation. In an ideal world, seeds would like to grow into plants one day, but we are very lucky and can enjoy eating them, too. Seeds, much like nuts, are packed full of healthy fats and an array of different vitamins and minerals. They also have a fantastic amount of fibre and are so good to keep things going in the gut department, if you know what I mean. All round, seeds are total winners when it comes to helping you look and feel fabulous.

As it is my job to help you feel good for life, I have come up with some super-easy ways to use more seeds in your everyday life. Remember, though, like nuts, they are high in energy, so it is important to be mindful of your portion size. For example, 1 tablespoon of ground flaxseed is 3356 kilojoules (84 kcal) and has 6.5 grams of fat, so for most people, 1 tablespoon a day is a good starting point portion-wise. Below is the lowdown on seeds and how to use them.

SESAME SEEDS

- Make your own tahini by dry-roasting sesame seeds in the oven at around 180°C for 10–15 minutes (keep an eye on them) and then blend with a little oil. Seriously good.
- Nice raw or toasted on salads, in hummus and sprinkled over steamed green veggies.
- I love adding these seeds to homemade wholegrain bread along with other seeds like sunflower and flaxseed.
- You can now get black sesame seeds, too. They look so good sprinkled on rice or mixed into rice when you make sushi. Also, they are good on salads and in baking (that being the healthier baking recipes, of course).

CHIA SEEDS

These are small and very hard and they go 'gummy' when you soak them – try putting a teaspoon in a few tablespoons of water and wait – it is like magic! I really enjoy using chia seeds in my homemade muesli mix (see recipe on page 214).

- Soak 1–2 tablespoons of the seeds overnight in water or milk and then add to a smoothie in the morning, or you can just add them straight into a smoothie – they will be crunchy to start with, but will soften up if you leave them for a few minutes.
- Add to homemade muesli.

PUMPKIN SEEDS

Beautiful green seeds packed with flavour and nutrition. They are one of my favourite seeds and are certainly very versatile.

- Great to add to homemade muesli, cereal mixes or porridge.
- Add to any salad.
- Sprinkle on top of an omelette just before serving.
- Add them to homemade bran muffins and other baking recipes.

SUNFLOWER SEEDS

Light grey in colour and not that pretty, but still so delicious!

- Lovely on salads and added to stir-fries – check out a fabulous salad recipe packed with sunflower seeds on page 222.
- A perfect addition to homemade cereal mixes as well as porridge.
- Lovely as a snack along with other nuts and seeds.
- Sunflower seeds make a great seed butter; you just make it in the same way as the nut butter and tahini. Check out the recipe on page 250.

FLAXSEED

Also known as linseed, flaxseed comes in a variety of colours, but you will most commonly see the dark brown variety. This is most well known for its omega-3 content (ALA), and like all seeds is a good way to get a little dose of fibre in your day.

- Brilliant added to smoothies (you can grind it first if you like or use pre-ground flaxseed).
- As with all the other seeds, it is great on salads, in cereals and with porridge.

Top tips

- To make nuts and seeds taste fresher for longer, keep them in your fridge. If this isn't practical, a dark cupboard or an airtight container is ideal.
- Store any ground nuts or seeds in the fridge as they go rancid super fast.
- You can also freeze nuts and seeds.
- LSA – you can buy a ready-made mix of ground linseed (flaxseed), sunflower seeds and almonds. This is a really easy and tasty way to use a delicious nut and seed combo. It is great in smoothies and baking, on cereal or in porridge.

Do it yourself!

Make your own seedy cereal. I mix chunky oats, rye flakes, buckwheat (all grains so far), then add sesame seeds, linseeds, pumpkin seeds, sunflower seeds and chia seeds. I often add a few chopped dates, sultanas or cranberries, too.

Soak a few tablespoons overnight in milk and then in the morning you'll have a winning breakfast . . . YUM! Alternatively, you can just eat it as is with milk or yoghurt (if you like a super-crunchy breakfast). Sometimes I will cook this mix and make it into a porridge, too.

Time to tune in and take action!

How can you include more nuts and seeds in your diet? From my ideas, what can you do to make sure you are regularly having nuts and seeds?

STEP 5: CUT THROUGH THE SWEETNESS

Do you find yourself craving sugar sometimes? Have you noticed how much sugar is in our food these days? It is time to talk sugar and look at how you can reduce sugar in your diet on your journey to looking and feeling your best.

Coming up I will be helping you understand more about sugar and give you some quick and easy solutions to help you get used to having less sugar every day. It can make all the difference.

In New Zealand, around 47 per cent of our energy comes from carbohydrate and about half of this comes from sugar, with your average adult having 108 grams per day[11] – that's 27 teaspoons worth!

ALL ABOUT SUGAR

Sugar has never been called a health food, but in recent times people have really been getting their knickers in a twist about it. Sugar has been demonised, referred to as 'toxic' and some are blaming it single-handedly as the cause of all our health problems. You have seen the books, read the blogs and no doubt heard people talking about doing 'sugar detoxes' and all sorts. But is sugar really the source of all evil?

There is no doubt that removing sugar from your diet can help you feel better and lose weight. Certainly I have met a huge number of people who have successfully slashed their sugar intake and are looking better for it, but there is a balance to strike here.

By eliminating much of the sugar from your diet, you are likely to focus more on what you are eating, which means that you will be eating less junk food overall, eating more veggies, having less salty, fatty processed foods and having more natural fresh produce. So far so good, but there is a line that needs to be drawn. That line is between actively looking to remove much of the added sugar from your diet for good health, with the added bonus of helping you look and feel better (I am totally on board with that and do it myself), and becoming obsessive, preachy and judgemental in the attempt to remove all sugar from all sources vowing never to have a slice of birthday cake again!

In my line of work, I have met too many people who decide to put themselves on a very restrictive diet or take an extremist approach to nutrition and they are, quite frankly, often unhealthy on many other levels. Some people get so caught up and obsessed by what they eat that I swear they will die from anxiety rather than any issue that could have been related to their nutrition. I personally don't feel that's what being fit and healthy is about.

For sure, sugar is part of the issue we have with obesity, it is part of many of our health problems including dental health issues and diabetes, but it is not the only issue. There are still other things we are having too much of: unhealthy fats and salt for example, and just too much food altogether. Other things we fall short on have a big impact on our health, too – vegetables, vitamin D, iodine, selenium, sufficient sleep and regular exercise. We need to consider all these things in context.

Okay, now back to sugar! I think the key thing to understand is that there are different types of sugar. I am all for slashing back on as much of the 'added' sugars in your day-to-day eating as possible. Adding sugar to your tea, having sugar on your breakfast cereal and eating biscuits after dinner every night, for example, are just unhealthy habits and you can adapt and learn new healthier ones. However, cutting out fruit to avoid sugar and not allowing yourself any dairy products because they have naturally occurring lactose (milk sugar) is taking it too far, in my opinion.

We really need to focus on cutting down on the types of sugar that our body simply doesn't need.

WHAT IS SUGAR?

Sugars are a type of carbohydrate and exist either as single sugars, known by their technical name of 'monosaccharides', or two sugars joined together to form double sugars, which are called 'disaccharides'.

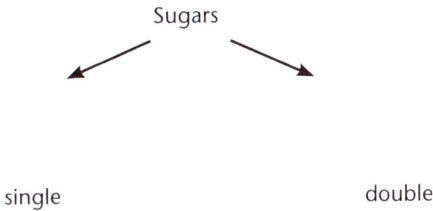

Sugars

single   double

Single sugars
- Fructose (most commonly known for being in fruit)
- Glucose (fruit also contains glucose)
- Galactose (part of the sugar that is in milk)

Double sugars
- Sucrose = glucose + fructose (this is table sugar, the most common type of sugar you will find)
- Maltose = glucose + glucose (this is found in some drinks and processed foods)
- Lactose = galactose + fructose (the sugar found in milk products)

Sugars can also join together to form medium chains (oligosaccharides) and long chains (polysaccharides). In plants, these long chains exist as starch and cellulose which we then eat in foods such as vegetables, seeds and grains. In the human body, we store long chains of carbohydrate in our liver and muscles as something called glycogen.

WHERE IS SUGAR FOUND?

Naturally occurring sugars
Sugar occurs naturally in some foods. Where you do include sugar, it is best for it to come from foods that are naturally sweet and that also have other nutritional benefits – fruit and milk products are two examples.

Fruit has a combination of both glucose and fructose. As well as the naturally occurring sugars it contains, fruit is packed with fibre, antioxidants, phytonutrients, vitamins and minerals, making fruit a great healthy choice. It is much better to eat your fruit whole rather than as juice though as juicing fruit concentrates the sugar and removes the fibre.

Milk products naturally contain lactose but also have the goodness of protein, calcium and other vitamins and minerals. Do be mindful, however, that many milk products also have a lot of added sugar so you want to look for those that are unsweetened or have no added sugar (which you can tell by looking at the ingredients list).

Sugar also naturally occurs in honey and maple syrup, which are both intensely sweet because a high proportion of the sugar in them is fructose, which is 'sweeter tasting' than sucrose, i.e. table sugar.

Added sugars

There are so many types of sugar that are added to food it is unreal. In this country, the most common types originate from sugar cane which is processed and made into a variety of sugars, including raw, brown, Demerara, white and icing. Syrups are also made from sugar cane, including golden syrup, treacle and molasses. It is a common misconception that brown sugar is better for you than white, but it really isn't – it is still sugar, still 68 kilojoules (17 kcal) per teaspoon and provides no nutritional value other than energy (calories).

Unless you are running a marathon or doing an extreme amount of exercise where added sugars can be very helpful to provide fuel during training or to assist with recovery, then you are best to try to use less – you are sweet enough.

As well as the 'sugar' you may be more familiar with on a day-to-day basis, there are a whole host of other sweeteners that are added to our food and drinks, most which provide kilojoules/calories just like the 'added sugars' mentioned above. This includes dextrose, glucose syrup and maltodextrin.

High-fructose corn syrup is another example of a sweetener which over the years has certainly received its fair share of bad press. It is heavily used in the USA but luckily this is not the case in New Zealand. Let's hope it stays that way.

New sugars on the market

In the last few years, with the growing interest in banishing white table sugar and all its varieties from foods, there have been some different types of sugar appearing on the market. These include coconut sugar, brown rice syrup and agave.

Coconut sugar is all the rage in some health food stores as it is believed to have a low GI and therefore be more slowly absorbed; this, however, hasn't been tested by official methods so it cannot be confirmed. It may indeed have a slightly lower GI than normal white sugar and if you are paying a premium price for an organic version, you will be getting something that is likely to be less 'processed' than white sugar – but, it is still sugar at the end of the day, still high in energy, not good for your teeth, and less is best. There's also a lot of hype about the vitamins and minerals it contains, but there are much better ways to get goodness without needing to turn to a sugar! If you want to spend the money, the choice is yours, but don't be getting into daily baking with it or sprinkling it on everything, thinking, *Hey, I can have as much as I like of this, it is a 'healthy sugar' and 'good for me'*, which is a trap I am seeing people fall into.

Brown rice syrup and agave nectar (syrup) are another couple of examples of new sweeteners on the market. While they aren't white sugar, they are still a type of sugar and I won't be converting anytime soon. In my day-to-day life I don't use much of any sugar – when I bake (I don't bake much anyway), I use adapted recipes with less sugar, or sweetness that comes mostly from fruit, or, as you will see in my recipes, occasionally I use a little honey as it goes a long way. To be honest, when you have a wonderful selection of the healthy foods, there isn't really a need to have much added sugar, whatever the type.

Sugar alternatives

As well as the new sugars that are hitting the shops these days, there are a variety of sweeteners on the market that can be used to sweeten foods without 'sugar'.

The man-made varieties include sweeteners like aspartame (which is found in many of the diet drinks), ace-K (acesulfame potassium), saccharin and cyclamate.

There are also natural sweeteners available which are being increasingly used as an alternative to sugar, the most common one being stevia. This is extracted from a plant (*Stevia rebaudiana*) and is intensely sweet, so if you are looking for an alternative to sugar, it can be a good option. It is increasingly being used in foods and drinks to add sweetness without sugar.

While stevia may be a good choice if you are wanting to use less sugar, I don't personally use a lot (or really any) of it or any other sweeteners as over the years I have just adapted my taste buds to enjoy less-sweet foods which, long-term, I feel is a better option. My overall goal is to help you get used to less-sweet foods rather than just swapping one sweet taste for another.

Where I used to literally gag at the thought of unsweetened, low-fat live yoghurt on its own, now I like it and think sweetened yoghurt tastes awful. I never thought I would be able to have porridge without brown sugar but now, honestly, I don't miss it at all. I personally feel getting used to less-sweet food over time and cutting right back on added sugar while still enjoying the natural sweetness of fruits and other nutritious foods is the way to go – no detox needed, no obsessive tendency, just a positive, healthy approach. That is the best way to look and feel good!

I could write a whole book on sugar, debating the different effects on your body and the pros and cons of all the alternatives, but as I want to get you eating real, less-processed food and adapting to eating less-sweet food, I will focus my efforts on helping you make this happen.

How to have less added sugar

- If you add sugar to tea or coffee, it's time to break the habit – cut back to half, then a quarter, then stop. It may take you a few weeks, but it can be done if you allow your taste buds the opportunity to recalibrate. You could use a sweetener but in my personal opinion, as I have previously mentioned, it is better if you get used to less-sweet tasting food and drinks.
- Check your drinks. My drinks of choice are water, sparkling water, soda water and coconut water with the occasional diet tonic to go with a splash of gin for that healthy balance. I would drink fruit juice a couple of times a year if that, but I do make my own veggie juice from time to time with lots of high-water-containing veggies like celery and cucumber, maybe with a bit of carrot, beetroot and ginger – at most I would put in half an apple per serve for sweetness. If I am out, I might have a tomato juice (if I am not drinking alcohol on that occasion), often with lots of black pepper and chilli – I love it hot! If you check the back of the drinks you have, 4 grams of sugar on the nutritional information panel is 1 teaspoon, so it is time to do some maths. A 250ml carton of fruit juice has around 6–7 teaspoons of sugar (even though it is fruit sugar), 750ml of sports drink has around 14 teaspoons of sugar and 600ml of fizzy drink has around 16 teaspoons. Be warned, normal tonic water is similar to other fizzy drinks like cola or lemonade – it is bitter because of the quinine, not a lack of sugar.
- Snack smarter – it will be no surprise to you if you have ever done any baking that cakes, biscuits and slices are packed with sugar. Reflect on how much sugar goes into the mixture. Find healthier snack options – pages 148–9 are packed with them.
- Adapt your recipes – one thing we do at *Healthy Food Guide* (where

I work as one of their nutritionists) is spend a lot of time working out how to change recipes to work with less sugar. You can just use less, but it can affect the texture of the finished product so it is important to find a recipe where someone has done the experimenting for you or use substitutes like dried or sweetened fruit or yoghurt. You will see in the recipes in the back of this book that I have frequently opted for honey as a little goes a long way – it is still sugar, though.

- Be aware of what you buy – as I mentioned before, 4 grams is 1 teaspoon of sugar: you can use this to work out the amount of sugar in your food as well as in drinks. Remember, though, that just because something is lower in sugar, that doesn't make it automatically healthy – it is all a balancing act.

Your guide to enjoying foods that are naturally sweet

- Aim to have two serves of fruit per day and enjoy this as your main source of 'sweetness'. You can use grated apple or pear or maybe some blueberries on top of your porridge or muesli to sweeten it, or add a little dried fruit like raisins, cranberries or apricots instead. I am aware this isn't the same taste as brown sugar and for the first few weeks I was in mourning, too, but now, as I said before, I don't miss the sugar and feel so much better for it.
- Use fresh or frozen fruit in a smoothie to add sweetness without using syrups or sugary mixes.
- Try adding fresh, stewed, frozen or canned fruit (in juice) to unsweetened low-fat yoghurt – delicious.
- Make your own cereal mixes, and, if you purchase ready-made ones, be sure to check the sugar content.
- Choose canned fruit packed in fruit juice rather than in syrup.
- Be aware of how much sugar is in sauces. Go for the lower sugar options, use less and/or make your own or use alternatives to flavour your food like fresh herbs, lemon juice or real chilli.
- Make your own 'ice cream' by blending frozen bananas and berries – seriously amazing and no added sugar needed!

Time to tune in and take action!

What can you do to cut through your sweetness? Maybe it is walking away from your sugary drink fix? Or stopping adding sugar to your tea? Or could it be going for unsweetened yoghurt? Write your goals and ideas down here. Commit to making a change and building healthier habits.

STEP 6: HELLO HYDRATION!

Now we have the food side of things sussed, it is time to check in with the drink side – an essential thing to consider if you want to look and feel your best.

HOW IS YOUR HYDRATION?

Keeping well hydrated is really important to help your body work at its best, and I find it can make a big difference to the way people feel. If you don't get enough fluid you may feel tired, get headaches and not perform at your best – none of us need that. Dehydration isn't good for your skin either, so if you want to look good it's time to drink up!

The exact amount you need to drink varies from person to person. It is influenced by how much you sweat, whether you work outdoors or in an air-conditioned office as well as the time of year. Two litres a day tends to be suggested as a rough guide, but it really is only rough – some of you will need far more.

A quick and easy way to work out whether you are well hydrated and drinking enough is to become a 'pee watcher'. Yes, that is exactly what it sounds like – looking at your pee. The goal is that over time you will become aware of how the colour of your pee varies at different times of the day. You will also notice that it will change depending on whether you have done exercise (and sweated a lot) or if you have been chugging down water all day.

The colour of your pee can tell you a lot. If it is dark yellow and concentrated, you are likely to be dehydrated. If you are passing large volumes of pale, straw-coloured pee, then you are likely to be closer to being well hydrated which is the goal. First thing in the morning when you wake up, your pee will probably be more yellow and darker than throughout the day and that is normal. What I would love you to do, though, is aim to have pale pee throughout the rest of the day by ensuring that you are drinking regularly and making an effort to stay well hydrated.

Just a side note – if you take a B-vitamin supplement or a multivitamin with B vitamins in it, this is likely to affect the colour of your pee and make it fluorescent yellow, so this means the pee watching won't be accurate.

Time to tune in – it's challenge time!

Head to www.claireturnbull.co.nz/feelgood and download the pee chart and hydration calendar. Stick it on the back of your toilet door at home and if possible at work, too. For two weeks keep track of how much you are drinking each day on the calendar and also the colour of your pee at different times of the day. See if you can work out roughly how much you need to be drinking to be passing pale pee. It is a good idea to repeat this at different times of year, too. Get your family, kids or flatmates involved if they are game – keeping well hydrated can be a team effort!

WHAT TO DRINK

It will be no surprise to you that good old water is the best drink for the bulk of the two or so litres you need each day. If you 'don't like it' you can learn to if you want to. Trust me, if all cordial, sweetened drinks, juice and other options were taken away from you and you had no other choices, you would drink water and, after a while, you would learn to love it. It is the same principle as we applied to vegetables – you just need to train your taste buds to accept it. You can always flavour it up with a squeeze of lemon, fresh mint, a slice of ginger or cucumber. Herbal teas are also a great way to get warm water in during the cooler months.

I never used to like water because in the UK everyone drinks 'squash' (cordial in Kiwi terminology) as their standard drink and I never got used to drinking plain water. Over the years, I have just weaned myself off it and now don't miss it at all. Water to me tastes amazing.

Low-fat milk can be a good alternative to water sometimes and it is particularly good after exercise – it will rehydrate you and provide protein at the same time. Fruit juice is not for everyday drinking unless you are super sporty and need the extra carbohydrate and calories. As I have mentioned before, you are much better eating your fruit whole rather than drinking it. For some alternative drink ideas for social occasions see page 184.

Are you relying too much on caffeine and other stimulants?

Coffee, tea and other caffeinated drinks have become embedded into our culture. They can help increase alertness and boost your energy before a workout and for most people, in moderate amounts cause no issues.

However, with coffee shops everywhere you look and new energy drinks on the market seemingly almost every day, moderation seems to be a thing of the past and I am now seeing a huge number of people who have a whole raft of health issues that are a result of overuse of and reliance on these caffeinated drinks.

Caffeine has a long half-life, meaning once you have had food or drink containing caffeine, it stays in your system for a long time. In fact, for the average person, roughly six hours after you have (say) a coffee, you will still have about half the amount of caffeine from that coffee in your system![11]

In practical terms, what this means is that when you go to bed, even if it has been hours since you had caffeine, there can still be some hanging around in your body. This won't necessarily stop you from going to sleep, but it can affect the quality of your sleep. It can prevent you from getting the deep sleep you need to feel rested and recover adequately. The end result is that you wake up feeling tired and need – oh, a coffee!

For most people, it is better not to become reliant on caffeine and where possible to have it in the earlier part of the day. This will allow most of the caffeine to be cleared from the system by the time you head to bed. Otherwise, you can end up with a vicious cycle of needing coffee/tea/stimulants to stay awake because you are tired, then not sleeping well, and so on. If you are really struggling with tiredness and fatigue yet still drink large amounts of tea, coffee and other caffeine/stimulant drinks, try weaning yourself off them over a couple of weeks and see how you feel.

Before I understood about the impact of caffeine on sleep and other hormonal processes, I used to drink a huge amount of black coffee. Now, I drink Swiss Water® decaffeinated coffee (it is decaffeinated without the use of chemicals – you can get it in supermarkets) and very occasionally real coffee. I do have the odd cup of English breakfast tea (you will never part me from my roots), but I keep it to the morning and really only one a day.

Overall, my message is that if you are wanting to look and feel your best and you are currently feeling tired and low in energy, look to cut back on your caffeine (and even try to go without when you get down to 1 cup per day) and see how you feel. The first week or two you are likely to be missing the buzz – but increase your water, have a green smoothie first thing in the morning and give it a month – see how you feel then. That's the way I did it and I am so happy I did.

Time to tune in and take action!

Get into a routine

Keeping well hydrated isn't exactly a new health message, but so many of us struggle to make it happen because we simply don't have a routine around drinking water. It is time to change that.

Making healthy the 'new normal' is just about re-programming yourself to make healthy habits so easy you don't even think about them. Over time, they just happen. The routine you create around drinking will very much depend on the nature of your life, your work and whether you are in or out a lot, or at home all day.

Below I have suggested some different strategies you can apply to help make sure you are drinking enough each day. Tick the one or two that you think will work for you and start putting them into practice. Put notes in your diary to remind you and, even better, get someone else to do this with you or a few people, in fact. The more the merrier.

- ☐ Set yourself a target for how many litres of water you plan to drink in a day and keep track of it in your diary.
- ☐ Aim to drink a glass of water first thing in the morning, mid-morning, at lunchtime, mid-afternoon, early evening and late evening – you can put times on it if that works for you.
- ☐ Fill up 2–3 bottles of water at the start of the day and make it your aim to get through those during the day. You can also just have 1 water bottle and aim to refill it 2–4 times depending on the size of the bottle and how much you need to be passing pale pee.

Don't forget – weekends count, too! If you work Monday to Friday it can be easy to get into a routine that fits alongside your work, but when it comes to the weekend, days off or if your days are always all over the place with no structure, it can be a little trickier to create a routine – but it can be done. At the weekend, when we go out (say food shopping or to the dreaded homeware/DIY stores) I always take a bottle of water with me because if I don't, I often end up having to buy a bottle of water at some ridiculous expense anyway.

5

Boost your nutrition – action time!

Now you have a good idea about what you need to be doing to boost your nutrition and get yourself healthy. To tie everything you have learnt together, here are some more practical hints, tips and ideas to make sure that getting healthy can happen. Below is how to apply what you have learnt and how to eat what you need.

Stock up your kitchen

Having the right food in your cupboards, fridge and freezer is the perfect place to start building healthier meals and snacks. Here are some of the key things I have to hand in my kitchen all the time. It is not a complete list, but these are things that I would use every week in my everyday eating.

KITCHEN BENCH

- Lemons and any in-season fruit (either from your garden, from a fabulous farmers' market or your local fruit and veggie store)
- Garlic and ginger – I use a huge amount of these

FRIDGE GOODIES

- Low-fat milk – on cereal, in smoothies and a great refreshing post-workout drink
- Unsweetened natural yoghurt – for breakfast with muesli and fruit, in smoothies, added to curries or made into a dip with chopped mint, grated cucumber, garlic and lemon
- Homemade vegetable chutneys
- Olives, gherkins, sundried tomatoes, capers – great in salads
- Cheese – I tend to have Parmesan as a little goes a long way, a reduced-fat hard cheese, cottage cheese, ricotta and extra-light cream cheese for dips or as a spread
- Hummus and other dips made from pulses – normally homemade
- Lean red meat, SPCA-approved lean pork, free-range skinless chicken, fish or other seafood
- Free-range eggs
- Tahini (sesame seed paste) – again, normally homemade but you can easily buy this
- Wasabi, mustard and hot chilli sauce – for flavour punches
- Fresh seasonal veggies of all kinds
- Ground LSA – I sprinkle it on salads, add it to smoothies, cereal and, really – everything!

FREEZER STORES

I currently only have a tiny two-drawer freezer under my fridge, but a little space can go a long way.

- Frozen veggies – I always have peas, beans, corn and spinach
- Edamame beans – they make a great snack or a fantastic addition to salads
- Lean red meat, SPCA-approved lean pork, free-range skinless chicken, fish, prawns
- Homemade chicken stock – I freeze the bones every time I roast a chicken and put them in a bag or box in the freezer, then when I have three or four lots, I take the bones out and make my own stock
- Stewed fruit – when there is excess fruit on my trees at home or something on special in the fruit shop or on a stall on the side of the road, I will often cook the fruit and then serve it with low-fat yoghurt or make a healthy homemade crumble in winter
- Soups – when I make a batch of soup, I will portion it out into individual servings and freeze in little zip-lock bags – I lie them flat so they stack nicely and don't take up too much space
- Homemade meals – I will sometimes have a lasagne, chilli or casserole in the freezer if I have made a double amount and this is fantastic when I am short of time; it is great to have a homemade dinner ready to go
- Frozen fruit – most commonly berries which go into smoothies, or bananas which I eat frozen as a snack or whip up into a banana ice cream by simply blending them
- Chillies – I grow chillies and have so many I always end up freezing them; they can be chopped straight from the freezer
- Ginger – yes, more ginger. I thoroughly wash a root and then pop it in the freezer. You can then just grate it frozen and pop it back in the freezer until next time. Great if you find you don't use your fresh ginger up in time and a hundred times better than using ginger from a jar which just will never taste the same!

DRY ITEMS

- Whole grains – brown rice, oats, quinoa, buckwheat, millet, amaranth, corn kernels
- Other grains – bulgar wheat (to make tabbouleh and other wonderful salads), couscous, polenta, pearl barley
- Pasta, udon/hokkien noodles, rice noodles – for soups and fresh Vietnamese spring rolls
- Dried lentils (red, green, brown, French), split peas (yellow, green), chickpeas, kidney beans, black beans

- Nuts and seeds – I must have almost every type; I am possibly a little obsessed! Raw unsalted almonds, Brazils, cashews and peanuts are probably the most commonly featured along with flaxseed (linseed), sunflower seeds, pumpkin seeds and chia seeds
- Wholegrain crackers
- Dutch cocoa – dark, rich and delicious! I use it in smoothies and sweet treats (see recipes on pages 218, 256 and 261)
- Wheat bran and oat bran – these are such a wonderful way to add fibre; I add wheat bran to my porridge sometimes or to homemade bran muffins
- Dried fruit – cranberries, sultanas, dates, apricots; I add these to my homemade cereal and use them in healthy baking
- Cornflour – to thicken sauces
- Every kind of herbal tea known to man . . . mostly loose leaf. My husband has to fight through the cupboard to find the food!

CANS AND JARS

- Tomatoes – I have so many cans and use them in almost everything; soups, casseroles, curries, mince dishes
- Pulses – chickpeas, butter beans, kidney beans, black beans for soups, casseroles, salads and dips
- Peanut butter and other nut/seed butters made from almonds, cashew nuts, sunflower seeds and pumpkin seeds – mostly homemade
- Canned fish – salmon, tuna, sardines
- Honey and maple syrup
- Mayonnaise – I use one made with real eggs and oil, but I make a very little amount go a long way and mostly use other things to dress salads; this ends up being used more as a spread

CONDIMENTS AND FLAVOURS

- Dried spices – I have them all really! Good ones to start off with if you are new to spices are ground cumin, ground coriander, curry power, turmeric and chilli flakes – those are what I would use most often
- Dried herbs – I mostly use fresh herbs, but I do have a stock of dried oregano (great in Italian dishes or on homemade pizza, pasta or mince dishes), and dried sage is also good
- Oils – I have a range of oils, including extra virgin olive oil and oils made from avocado, nuts and seeds which I mostly use for salads
- Vinegars – balsamic, white and red wine are the winners, and I have

white vinegar for when I poach eggs and sushi vinegar for, well, for when I make sushi!
- Curry pastes – most of the time, I will make spice pastes myself, but I do always have tandoori and Thai green curry paste on standby
- Reduced-salt soy sauce

Plan, plan, plan

You can know everything there is to know about eating well and making good choices – but at the end of the day, in my experience, if you have a busy life with lots going on, without some kind of plan of what you are going to cook for dinner and make for lunches, you can end up going for less-healthy food options. It will be too easy to grab a takeaway (even if it is 'healthy' it is still probably more expensive than what you could make yourself), and if you do manage to make something healthy under these circumstances, it probably won't be very inspiring.

More than anyone, I know exactly what I need to/want to/should be eating, but if I come home late super hungry, have nothing in the fridge and no ideas about what I could make, I wouldn't promise that I would be able to make good choices every time, particularly if I had unhealthy options in my home or a takeaway shop on speed dial (but luckily I don't!). There is nothing worse than staring into the fridge with zero inspiration when you have a family to feed or are super hungry yourself and it all starts to feel a bit too hard.

I plan, and I always will. I encourage you to do the same. This doesn't mean that you can never be spontaneous or eat what you feel like on the night. It just gives you a framework to help you work out roughly what you will eat for the week, what you need to buy, and then you can eat what you have bought in whatever order works for you. For anyone who says they don't have time to plan, well, if you have time to stare hopelessly into the fridge or to go to the supermarket more than once a week, you have time to plan. It takes 10 minutes a week and is an investment worth making.

To plan, simply grab a piece of paper, fold it in half and on one side make yourself a little table with the headings lunch and dinner at the top, and the day of the week down the side. You can buy yourself a fancy planner if you like, but a piece of scrap paper is fine.

Start by working out what dinners you will have each night of the coming week. You don't have to eat them in the order you write down, but at least you know what you will need to buy. The first couple of weeks may take you a little longer if you need to have a flick through some magazines, recipes books or look online for inspiration, but even if you just start with the meals you make at the moment and add one new recipe to your list each week, that is a good place to begin. I tend to make Saturday night 'new recipe night' – a chance to try something new, see if it works and if it will be something I can add to my general repertoire.

When I have tried a recipe that works, everyone likes it and it allows me to use part of the meal to make a lunch for the next day, I add the recipe to a folder I keep in the kitchen which I call 'recipes that work'.

Once you have your dinners listed, work out what you can have for lunch the following day by using part of the dinner meal you have cooked (if there are leftovers) or, say you are having fish and salad for dinner, by making yourself a nice salad that you can pop into a lunch box along with a boiled egg. If there is nothing you can use from your meal the night before, then just work out what else you can take for lunch – a salad, some soup from the freezer, a wrap or sandwich filled with salad galore.

The next step is to write yourself a shopping list on the other side of the piece of paper – have a look at what you have in your pantry, fridge and freezer already and then just write down what you need to get. After you have done your shopping, stick your planner up on the fridge and then everyone knows what is on the menu this week.

There are so many other ways to do this, too. I was speaking at an event recently and a gentleman came up to me and said he plans the family meals for the week with his kids on a blackboard which is on the kitchen wall – they do it together and then everyone knows what is coming up and there are no fights at the dinner table. How awesome!

Find a method that works for you. If you want to try mine, head to www.claireturnbull.co.nz/feelgood for my free planning tool that you can print.

BACK-UP MEALS

As well as my plan, I have a back-up list of quick and easy meals that I know I can throw together in five minutes from things I always have a stock of at home. An omelette, fresh pasta with a quick homemade tomato sauce and some frozen veggies or prawn Thai green curry made with frozen veggies and rice are the most common quick meals in our house.

Eat at the right time for you

SO MANY THEORIES – WHAT REALLY MATTERS?

Ask five people the question 'How many times should I eat each day?' and you will no doubt get five different answers. The truth is, there isn't an absolute right answer and what people tell you will be based on their opinion and what works for them. Your job is to work out what works for you or to get advice from a qualified professional who knows you and your body and can help you work it out.

We all get up at different times, go to bed at different times, and when we are active in the day will vary, depending on whether you are a morning workout person, like to go for a run at lunchtime or after work, or maybe you aren't that active at all – an area to work on, maybe?

Whoever you are and whatever way your life rolls, find what works for you. I have worked with people who very successfully live on three meals a day, no snacks and are fit as fiddles. By the same token I have met people who eat six times a day, little and often, and you know what? That works for them. When people stay with me, I encourage them to do the same. There is no exact right and wrong. When we work with clients at my nutrition clinic Mission Nutrition (www.missionnutrition.co.nz) we spend a lot of time working out what is right for that person, their life, their timetable and what will get them results.

I personally find that eating three meals and one to two snacks works well for me most days, but my snacks are absolute nutrition powerhouses and are not a time to reach for what we commonly call snacks, such as muffins, sweet cereal bars or cookies. A snack is a mini meal, so if you decide to go down the meals and snacks road, make sure you keep this in mind. Check out my healthy snack suggestions on pages 148–9 and the recipes at the back of this book (see page 252–61).

I choose to include snacks in my day as that works for me, but because of this I do have to make a conscious effort to make sure my meals aren't too energy-dense (too many kilojoules/calories) and that I don't end up overeating because I am eating every few hours. Overeating is an error I see many people make when they decide to eat more regularly. If you just add snacks to your day that you never used to have, it is likely you will gain weight as you are simply putting more food in that you aren't burning off – so if you decide to experiment with more-regular eating, please keep this in mind.

My challenge to you is to experiment, to find out what suits you. My only word of caution is that you don't try to eat less than three times a day; it is very tricky to get the nutrients you need in just two meals unless you are some kind of nutritional genius. People I have worked with who just eat breakfast, skip lunch and then have a massive dinner and pick all evening often don't look good for it, I can tell you. Eating regularly and for the right reasons is definitely the way to go.

However many times a day you decide to eat, my advice is to spread these eating episodes out evenly so that you aren't going without food for hours then having a meal plus a snack plus another meal all in one go. You also need to learn to eat in tune with your body's natural messages about feeling hungry and then stop when you are full if you can. This is a skill many of us need to learn.

ORDER OF EATING

It is very easy to get stuck in the mind-set that breakfast or the first meal of the day needs to be cereal, toast or a smoothie, lunch is something like a salad or sandwich and dinner is always a cooked meal and something hearty. Snacks then fit in around this and are often sweet treats, a latte or a piece of fruit. That's the way things roll for most people I meet.

Sometimes, first thing in the morning it might work for you to have a small snack – maybe a boiled egg, piece of fruit or yoghurt. Then you might choose to have your cereal and milk mid-morning, a hearty meal at lunchtime and a light meal, like salad with meat or fish, for dinner. This works well if you are really busy and active during the day, and you could maybe exercise mid-morning or before lunch.

Others of you may enjoy a super-hearty breakfast after a morning walk or workout, a healthy smoothie mid-morning, a light salad for lunch, a hearty afternoon tea and a light dinner.

As long as you get the nutrition you need each day, the order in which you eat your meals and snacks comes down to what is right for you. For some of you, I totally understand that your job will have a huge amount of influence on when you can and can't eat. I absolutely get that. I travel frequently for work, have meetings all over the country and speak at lunchtime mostly, so there can be very little regularity in my day – but I don't use that as an excuse. I sort out what I am going to eat during the day and then eat it in whatever order I can. You can work round things if you want to and plan to. You just have to make it a priority, taking the time to figure it out and getting support and guidance if you need to.

Time to tune in!

What changes do you need to make to the timing of your meals and snacks to make things work better for you? Maybe add an extra snack and have a smaller dinner? Plan your meals each week and always pack a healthy snack for work? Write whatever comes to mind.

Meals that make you feel good

FEEL-GOOD BREAKFASTS

Start your day the right way with a super-healthy breakfast packed with all the nutrients you need to help you get the most out of your morning! Here is what you are looking for:

Foods to include	Options and varieties	The benefits
Fruit and/or veggies	Fresh, frozen, canned, stewed fruit – you name it, you can include it. Spinach, mushrooms and tomatoes are some great veggies to have at breakfast – and there are so many more options, too.	Packed with fibre, which is helpful to 'keep things moving', as well as plenty of vitamins and minerals to help your body work at its best!
Protein-rich foods	Milk, yoghurt, eggs, tofu.	Having more protein at breakfast is a good idea to help you feel fuller for longer.
Healthy fats	Nuts, seeds, ground LSA, avocado.	Nuts and seeds provide fibre, which is great for a healthy digestive system, and they are also packed with essential fatty acids as well as vitamins A, D, E and K – great for skin, hair and nails. Avocado also provides a surprisingly good amount of fibre as well as these vitamins.
Healthy whole grains	Oats, brown rice, buckwheat, quinoa, millet and amaranth are all wonderful to include.	Rich in soluble and insoluble fibre and help give you the energy you need to power through your morning.

Here are some fabulous ideas for you to try:

Cold breakfasts

- Homemade muesli (made with a mixture of whole grains, nuts and seeds – see recipe on page 214) with low-fat milk and chopped apple/pear or any fruit of your choice.
- Bircher muesli with low-fat yoghurt and berries or grated apple/pear.
- Unsweetened natural yoghurt with a few tablespoons of stewed apple/pear/rhubarb/plums, a tablespoon of oats and a tablespoon of ground LSA.
- Overnight oats – oats soaked overnight in low-fat milk, yoghurt and fruit, and topped with nuts and seeds (see recipe on page 212).
- Smoothies – there are so many good combos you can try (see my smoothie recipes on pages 216–21).

Hot breakfasts

- You can make porridge with oats, brown rice, quinoa or buckwheat very successfully. Have a play around. Make it with milk to keep the protein up and serve with some nuts/seeds and grated or chopped fruit, dried fruit or some cooked berries.
- Poached eggs on wholegrain toast with grilled/pan-fried mushrooms, tomatoes and some wilted spinach – amazing! Have a slice of avocado, too, for a little healthy fat.
- Whip yourself up an omelette with some onion, tomatoes, mushrooms, capsicum, courgette, corn or whatever takes your fancy. Serve with some seeds on top or a slice of avocado and an optional slice of grainy toast.

FABULOUS LUNCHES

Years ago when I first started working, I never used to look forward to lunch – a boring sandwich, same old salad or the healthiest thing I could find on the run, which was never that good. These days, with a little up-skilling, experimentation and a degree of trial and error, I have to say, I absolutely love lunch! It's just about embracing new ideas, making the most of leftovers and getting into a routine that means making lunches is quick and easy, especially on weekdays if you take your lunch to work with you. Here is what you are looking for:

Foods to include	Options and varieties	The benefits
Veggies and lots of them	Ideally 2+ handfuls of veggies – lettuce, cabbage, spinach, baby kale, tomatoes, carrots, cucumber, capsicum, corn, peas, beans – the options are endless.	A great step towards making sure you are getting all the veggies you need in a day. As we know, veggies are good for you in every way!
Protein-rich food	Lean meat, chicken, fish, prawns, eggs, tofu, pulses (chickpeas/kidney beans/lentils), cheese, cottage cheese.	Much like breakfast, having enough protein for lunch is helpful for keeping you full all afternoon.
Healthy fats	Nuts, seeds, avocado, oil as part of a dressing.	A great source of healthy fat to keep your body looking fabulous.
Healthy starch	This could be whole-grain bread, crackers, rice, quinoa or any of the other whole grains (see pages 91–92). As I have previously mentioned, pulses like lentils, chickpeas and kidney beans are also considered starchy, so if you have a good serving of these as part of your lunch that will count as your healthy starch.	For energy at lunch-time and to get you through the afternoon, plus fibre to help stabilise your blood sugar levels and keep your digestive system healthy.

Salads

Now there are salads, and there are salads. I often see people heading into a deli or café and choosing the 'salad' option thinking it is healthy, but if you are going for a potato salad covered in mayo or a rice salad dripping in oil with very few veggies and little protein, that isn't the ideal.

For healthy, balanced salad ideas, check out the section on boosting your veggies (pages 72–3) and the recipes at the back of the book (pages 222–31).

Soups

In the cooler months, soups can be a wonderful, quick, satisfying lunch. Here are some great ideas:

- Carrot and lentil soup
- Tomato soup with wholegrain toast and cottage cheese
- Chicken and corn soup with a low-fat yoghurt
- Vegetable soup with peanut butter – yes, you read that right! (See recipe on page 233.)

For a complete meal, try to have a soup that is not only packed with veggies, but also has lentils or other pulses in it, too. This way the soup itself will fill you up without having to have half a loaf of bread with it!

Sandwiches/wraps/pita bread

I personally tend to opt for a salad- or soup-based lunch rather than a sandwich as it is far easier to get your veggies in that way, but if you do like a good sandwich, then here is how to make it a healthy version.

THE BREAD

In an ideal world the only types of bread we would eat would be those made from very minimally processed grains similar to those traditionally eaten in Scandinavia. You can find some of these breads in health food stores so it is worth checking them out. Pumpernickel is an option that is readily available at many supermarkets and also at health food stores, and this is a wonderful, very dense rye bread. You don't need much, though, as it is so dense and heavy.

When choosing more-widely available bread, your best bet is to always go with a dense, dark, wholegrain, high-fibre loaf. Be mindful that a soft loaf with the odd grain through it is not what I mean by this. A reminder that just because a loaf has the word 'grains' written on it, this doesn't mean it has that many whole grains in it.

If you are using wraps or pita bread, go for the wholemeal or high-fibre varieties. They can add variety and interest to your diet and they are a lot easier to stuff with salad veggies than bread, but please be aware that they are still heavily processed.

UP THE SALAD

Where you can, aim to have two handfuls of salad veggies in your sandwich, wrap or pita bread. If it is just impossible to do that because you literally can't pick up your sandwich, then you may need to have some extra veggies on the side or a cup of vegetable soup. There are lots of ideas in the boost your veggies section (see page 75).

WATCH THOSE SPREADS AND DRESSINGS

While a little healthy fat is vital for good health, going heavy on a spread or the mayo, aioli or any other creamy dressings may end up being a disaster for your waistline. Be aware that a level tablespoon of a standard mayo has the same number of kilojoules/calories as a piece of bread. So, spread thinly. Avocado or hummus as a spread on bread works well.

PORTION CAUTION

If you buy a sandwich from a bakery or café, you will probably be aware by now that, often, it might not be a healthy choice. Massive hunks of white bread, ciabatta or focaccia with creamy dressings, high-fat meats and a token bit of salad aren't everyday choices. So, if you are buying a ready-made sandwich, try to go for wholegrain bread with a healthy protein-rich filling and lots of salad. Two slices of bread will be fine for most of you – triple deckers are too big!

Crackers

I sometimes really enjoy having crackers as part of my lunch. I will often top them with something tasty and delicious alongside a salad, soup or some extra veggies to snack on.

When it comes to crackers, much like bread, look for the wholegrain varieties. Check the labels and for an everyday cracker go for one with less than 10 grams of fat per 100 grams (the lower in saturated fat, the better) and more than 5 grams of fibre per 100 grams, but the more fibre the better, really. There are corn crackers available which, although not brown, are still technically wholegrain (the whole corn kernel), and they are a good option to add variety and are helpful for those of you who need to follow a gluten-free diet.

Do be aware that crackers often come hand in hand with a lot of sodium – it is a good idea to check what you are buying. You are looking to keep your total sodium intake each day to less than 2300 milligrams. Fabulous cracker toppings:

- Cottage cheese and sliced tomato or chutney
- Extra-light cream cheese and smoked/canned salmon with lemon juice
- Sardines mashed with a teaspoon of mayonnaise, lemon juice and black pepper
- Peanut butter and sliced banana
- Hummus and sliced tomato
- Ricotta cheese and chutney
- Avocado and sliced tomato
- Mashed egg
- Horseradish or mustard and cold sliced lean meat
- Kidney bean dip (see page 252) with a slice of avocado and a teaspoon of salsa
- Tzatziki (yoghurt and mint dip)

Leftovers

Leftovers can make a great lunch. You can simply take a portion of whatever meal you have prepared (e.g. lasagne, curry or quinoa salad) and have it as it is the next day or, as I do more often, use one or two parts of the meal you have made and then create something completely new!

Nine times out of ten I will base my next day's lunch on part of what I had for dinner the night before. I deliberately cook an extra little bit of something which I can then get a little bit creative with. When you are cooking an extra serving for your lunch the next day or an extra piece of chicken or more roasted veggies, the key is to serve the extra portion onto a separate plate or into a container *before you serve everyone for dinner, otherwise there might not be any leftovers!*

Below are a few ideas of things you can do to make a great lunch from last night's dinner.

LEAFY SALADS

This almost breaks the leftover rule, but is still relevant here. When I make a salad as part of our dinner meal (lettuce, spinach, tomato, capsicum, avocado, alfalfa sprouts and so on), I always make a separate mini salad with all the delicious ingredients that I have put into the big salad to put into a lunch container for the next day. I then just add extra protein/starch/ healthy fat to make it a nutritionally balanced meal.

If you rely on using the 'leftover salad' from what has been in a bowl in the middle of the table, a) you might not get any left (I would secretly be hoping that's the case because it was so yummy everyone ate it all) or b) you end up with the scrappy bits that no one else wanted. More commonly these days, I serve salad straight onto our plates before other parts of the meal are added; that way, everyone ends up eating more of the salad goodness and we don't get any left!

A ROAST DINNER

- Some roasted veggies (like kumara, pumpkin, carrot, parsnip, onion) along with a little shredded meat and a handful of baby spinach, rocket or other salad leaves is a winning combination. Add a dollop of chutney or a splash of your favourite healthy dressing and you are away. I often add a few nuts in there, too. Cashews or a few peanuts always seem to go nicely.
- Roasted starchy veggies with a large handful of salad greens and a handful of cooked chickpeas with some cashew nuts and a lemon-mustard dressing – delicious!
- Leftover roast beef, lamb, pork or chicken (with all fat removed) can be made into a delicious sandwich, wrap or pita pocket with hummus, chutney and as many salad ingredients as possible.

CURRY

- If I make a dhal as part of an Indian-inspired dinner, I thin down the leftovers with water and enjoy it as a soup for lunch the next day.
- Leftover beef, chicken or lamb curry (if it is quite dry or without too much sauce) is delicious as part of a salad with some added nuts and seeds or in a sandwich/wrap/pita bread with plenty of salad veggies.
- I often bake chicken that has been marinated in tandoori paste and unsweetened yoghurt – it is just delicious with rice and I serve it with a coleslaw. For lunch the next day, I have a huge handful of the coleslaw (I pop a little dressing on before I leave the house in the morning) and enjoy it with some leftover baked chicken – yum!

PATTIES

Meat patties, lentil patties and vegetable patties make a great healthy dinner and are great to have for lunch the next day, too. You can have them whole or break them up into a sandwich, wrap, pita bread or on some salad greens with avocado and some nuts and seeds.

DELICIOUS DINNERS

A healthy dinner is really the same as a healthy lunch (see page 142): two or more handfuls of veggies, a palm-sized serving of protein-rich foods, a little healthy starch and some healthy fats. Here are some ideas to help you make some everyday meals fit this healthy balance:

Barbecue-style meals

The good old staple steak, potatoes and salad never fails for a quick summer meal, but to get the balance right your meat or fish serving needs to be about the size of the palm of your hand. Mix it up, too – steak might be an obvious option, but maybe try mussels, squid or prawns. Mix up your salads, too – try some of the recipes at the back of this book (pages 222–31) and in my other book *Lose Weight for Life* for more ideas.

As a change from potatoes, make a salad with some alternative healthy starchy vegetables, like the edamame and chickpea salad on page 231 or a brown rice or quinoa salad.

Spaghetti Bolognese

Rather than having half a plate of pasta and a big scoop of mince, we need to tip the balance by adding more veggies and downsizing other parts of the meal. Ideally, serve with a large mixed-leaf salad with a little avocado and nuts and/or seeds for a little healthy fat. When it comes to the spaghetti, try wholemeal. For the Bolognese, aim to use 100 grams or less of mince per person; remember you can add some cooked red lentils (this will help keep the meat portion down and make it cheaper, too) and finely chopped veggies. You can apply the same principle to other mince dishes like chilli con carne or meatballs, for example. Serve with brown rice and up the veggies big-time.

Curry

Curries come in all shapes and sizes, but to make curries healthier, add veggies – carrots, beans, broccoli or two cans of tomatoes rather than one. The type of veggies you add will very much depend on the recipe and whether it is a green curry or a tikka masala. If the curry doesn't lend itself to many veggies being added, then think about what veggies you can have on the side. Spinach and silver beet and other leafy greens go very well with Indian curries, as does cauliflower.

Stews and casseroles

These are such wonderful winter staples and they can be nutritionally so good. The great thing is that you can use super-cheap cuts of meat (as long as the fat has been well trimmed) and when you cook them slowly and for a long time, they taste just delicious. Add extra veggies and try serving with brown rice.

If a stew has starchy veggies in it, like potato or kumara, or maybe lentils, chickpeas or pearl barley, I will often just serve it with lots of green veggies rather than having extra starch with it, too – only very active people need to be doing that.

Risotto and other rice dishes

There are some fantastic one-pot rice dishes that you can make, risotto and paella being two of my favourites. These can be super healthy or very fatty, unbalanced meals – it all depends on how they are made.

If you make a risotto, find a way to add more veggies – in *Lose Weight for Life* (page 244), my recipe has onions, leeks and peas in it. The other thing to do is always serve a risotto with a salad, aiming for the salad to cover half your plate.

When I make paella I use less chorizo than most recipes suggest, add more onion and capsicum, use a reduced-salt stock, add extra peas and there you go. I also often serve it with salad or green beans.

Fish and chips

When I have fish and chips, I either just pan-fry my fish as it is, or dip it in cornflour, then in beaten egg and back in cornflour then into the pan – yum! My chips are oven-baked potatoes or kumara slices with a tiny bit of oil and are delicious. The big thing often missing with this meal is veggies, of course. I always have peas and steamed carrots myself, nothing too fancy, but the perfect match. Mmm, I love peas.

Stir-fry

Stir-fries are easy to make healthy with lean meat, skinless chicken, prawns or tofu and lots and lots of veggies. Be mindful that many ready-made sauces and soy sauce are very high in sodium, though, so use sparingly. I often flavour my stir-fries with grated ginger, lots of garlic, fresh chilli and a tiny splash of reduced-salt soy sauce. Serve with brown rice ideally.

SENSATIONAL SNACKS

A snack is a mini meal in my mind and an opportunity to get in some extra goodness rather than a whack of sugar and fat. Here are some ideas:

- Fresh fruit and ¼ cup of unsalted nuts or seeds
- A peeled frozen banana – it is like ice cream, but seriously good for you!
- Mini health shake – blend a handful of frozen berries, 1 tablespoon of vanilla or chocolate protein powder and 1–2 cups of chilled water or low-fat milk
- Green smoothie or juice – check out my recipes on pages 216–21

- Unsweetened, low-fat yoghurt with 1 tablespoon of muesli or other breakfast cereal stirred through
- Raw veggies with a healthy dip – check out my homemade dip recipes (see pages 252–6); if you buy dip, go for a hummus, or a veggie- or yoghurt-based dip rather than one based on cream cheese or sour cream
- Edamame beans
- A boiled egg
- A cup of veggie soup
- A handful of home-popped corn
- Chopped apple, pear or banana and 2 tablespoons of cottage cheese
- Wholegrain crackers with cottage cheese, tuna, salmon or hummus
- A handful of a healthy cereal – bite-sized Mini-Wheats or Minibix are ideal, filling and fibre-rich
- Homemade energy balls or a homemade cereal bar – check out my recipe for Biba bliss balls on page 260
- Snack pack of sushi – check out the range at St Pierre's, they are delicious!

Or try making your own snacking combos with dried fruit, nuts and seeds:
- 3 Brazil nuts and 3 dried figs – a great dose of selenium and fibre
- 4 walnuts, 2 dried apricots and 1 tablespoon of pumpkin seeds
- 6 raw cashews, 1 tablespoon of dried cranberries and 1 tablespoon of pumpkin seeds
- 8–10 almonds, 2 figs and 1 tablespoon of sunflower seeds
- 8 almonds, 2 Brazils, 1 tablespoon of Goji berries and 1 tablespoon of raw cocoa beans or cocoa nibs or a little 80 per cent cocoa chocolate for a treat!

These portions are just a rough guide; the amount you personally need will vary. If you are watching your waistline, though, aim to keep the total portion to about ¼–⅓ cup or a small handful.

Boost your nutrition – done!

Hopefully, you now have a really good grasp of what to eat and when, to help you look good and feel amazing! The next step in your journey is looking at the role of keeping fit and active when it comes to being the happiest, healthiest you.

What are we waiting for?! Let's get to it.

6

Move your body

Do you find it hard to get the time to exercise? Are you frustrated that you aren't getting the results you want from your workouts? Do you wish you could be as fit as you used to be? Well, help is here.

Being physically active is good for your body in every way possible, and when it comes to looking good and having amazing energy, it is absolutely essential. My aim throughout this chapter is to help you create an active life that you love and that is easy to fit in, whatever else you have going on.

For me, fitness has become an integral part of my life. Without walks, runs, gym sessions, yoga classes and bike rides I know that I would not be anywhere near as positive and optimistic as I am. I personally make exercise a priority because without it I can end up dipping into a dark hole and feeling sad and blue. Having struggled with depression in the past, I know exercise can make the entire difference to how well I cope day in day out. I also love exercise because it keeps your body toned and strong, and it helps you sleep better, too.

Where to start

Doing at least 30 minutes of activity each and every day (and by that I mean activity that is intense enough to get you huffing and puffing) is a good start, and when that becomes a breeze, build on it. Aiming for an hour of activity each day is a good long-term goal. That is certainly what I aim for.

If you are nowhere near that at the moment, start with 10 minutes a day and over a few weeks build it up. If you are totally new to exercise and/or have any health conditions like heart disease, diabetes or any joint problems, then be sure to consult your GP or another qualified health professional who knows you and your body before embarking on a new programme.

The most important thing is just to get started. Unless you are a gym bunny or planning to run a half marathon sometime soon, just set the intention to do more than you are doing now. As I have mentioned, my personal goal is to spend an hour doing something physically active each and every day. Sometimes that is a gym session, other times a run and some good stretching or it might be a yoga class. When things get super crazy it might just be three 20-minute walks as part of what I am already doing that day. I like to mix it up as much as possible, as that works for me. You will need to find what works for you. Some days it doesn't happen, but that is the exception rather than the rule.

Mix it up

Ideally, for optimal health and wellbeing, my advice is to mix up cardio, resistance training, stretching and some breathing/relaxation as part and parcel of what you do each week rather than just doing one type of activity.

CARDIO

Cardiovascular exercise is exercise that gets your heart rate up, is likely to make you get a sweat on and is great to strengthen your heart, improve your circulation and lower your blood pressure.

This includes: running, walking, power walking, cycling, swimming, rowing, tennis, squash, netball, rugby, football, athletics, boxing, hiking, gymnastics, dance and other similar activities.

I really enjoy including short, sharp bursts of high-intensity cardio (which is often combined with some resistance) in my workouts – running up and down stairs as fast as possible, star jumps, jumping on and off steps, burpees and sprints – think boot-camp-style.

STRENGTH AND RESISTANCE TRAINING

Never underestimate the importance of this type of exercise – you can get some great results and get great tone and shape. Resistance training helps you to build and strengthen your muscles – and, no, that doesn't mean you have to get big and bulky if you are doing it right. The more muscle you carry on your body, the more metabolically active you are. This means that you will be efficient at burning off kilojoules/calories – something we all want, right?

Strength and resistance training includes: free weights (at the gym or home if you have some), fixed weight machines at the gym, pump gym classes, press-ups, squats, lunges, triceps dips and chin-ups. Some yoga classes which are more intense can also fit into this category.

FLEXIBILITY AND STRETCH

You might be fit and strong, but if you aren't flexible and don't do any stretching it can lead to injuries as well as having poor posture. Yoga, Pilates and stretching all help with general flexibility.

Make it happen!

Remember to mix it up. This is what I personally aim for each week with some examples of how I do it. This might give you some ideas to help you set a goal for yourself:

- Cardio 3–4 times a week – sometimes this is on its own, sometimes combined with a resistance training session
- Resistance training 2–3 times a week
- Stretching/yoga class once a week – this is sometimes at home and sometimes a class. I also do stretching after each of my cardio and resistance sessions

You can also combine exercise too, like doing cardio at the gym and then weights or vice versa. Some types of exercise will also naturally combine different types of movement. A full-on yoga class, for example, counts as both stretching and resistance training.

My message overall is just to mix it up and look for variety. The exact combination that works for you will be something you can work out yourself or seek individualised advice on.

Progress it

Once you have got a good mix going on, I really want you to remember three words: progression, change and variety. When you start a new exercise regimen that is outside your normal comfort zone and tougher than you are used to – provided you are eating right, sleeping right and recovering properly – you will get results. The thing is, though, your body adapts, it gets used to what you do to it, used to your normal running route, the same level yoga class and walking at a particular speed. If you want to continually get good results, you need to progress your workout to make it more challenging; change it, whether it's the route you run or the type of boxing class you go to, and then mix it up – add variety. Some of you will love swimming and that's all you like to do. If that's you, that's okay, but swim in the pool, the sea, at difference paces, using different strokes, add fast and slow intervals that will not only help you maintain and improve your fitness level but make it more interesting.

I am a natural mix-it-up person (only because I get bored easily) and I will try some yoga for a few months, then another type of yoga class or boot camp. At other times, I am more gym focused, but I change my programme every 8–12 weeks and add variety.

If you are working towards a goal like running a marathon, you will obviously need to focus on running as your primary activity – but yoga, Pilates or some swimming mixed in every week might also help. The same applies if you play a team sport or are focused and passionate about one thing.

It is all individual and depends on where you are at and where you want to go. When I was working as a personal trainer I spent a lot of time making sure I was planning a training programme that was right for each individual person. The main thing is to start somewhere, but remember that to continue to get results over time you need to change and progress. If you have always done the same workout at the gym and wonder why one year later nothing has improved, it is because you need a change! If you do what you always do, you will get what you always got. As for variety, well, it is the spice of life.

Do you feel like exercise is a chore?

This is a question I asked you upfront at the very beginning of this book in the 'How are you?' section. What did you answer?

Some of you will love exercise; others might feel keeping fit is a chore that you would like to delegate. If you are not in the exercise-loving camp and tend to get demotivated quickly, I have something I would like you to try, and that is changing the way you think and speak about exercise.

I so often hear people say, 'I have to go to the gym or I will get fat', 'I should go for a run to burn off my large lunch', 'I need to work out because otherwise I will never look good'. I used to be the same. These words, though, are all very negative. Things you 'have to do', 'should do' and 'need to do' make it feel like you don't have a choice and you are being forced to do it. No one can force you to do anything. Even if you have been told to do exercise by your doctor to improve your health and to live longer, if you have this negative attitude towards it, you are likely to only move more for a week or so and then your drive will drop and, without meaning to be, you are back to your sedentary life again.

The words 'have to', 'should' and 'need' will often be coming from an unhelpful internal conversation that you are having with yourself, based on some kind of standard or goal you feel you have to reach in order to be good enough/fit in/be accepted/ accept yourself. While these negative words can indeed work as motivation (and, boy, do I know what that's like – I used the fact that I hated myself and my body as a motivator to exercise for years!), it really isn't good for your mind or soul. It is like running because you are being chased by a blazing fire. I would rather you were led by a beautiful light in front of you that is guiding you forwards, seeing exercise and keeping fit as an act of self-love, appreciation and choosing to be your best, not running away from a part of yourself that you don't like. That way, it is far more likely to last.

If you have a negative attitude before you even put your workout gear on, it is unlikely that you will enjoy your exercise sessions as much as you would if your head was in a better space.

Time to tune in – let's play a little game!

1. Think about the types of exercise or 'active movement', let's call it, that you enjoy the most – walking, swimming, yoga, boxing, dancing – and, if you made the time, which of these activities you would do each week and how often you would do them (be as specific as you can), e.g. yoga 1 x per week, walk 3 x per week, weights at home 1 x per week.

   Write down what you would like to do here:

   _____
   _____
   _____
   _____
   _____
   _____
   _____
   _____
   _____
   _____
   _____
   _____
   _____

2. I would like you to come up with at least three statements about why you want to move your body, keep active and work out. If you can, add details about the types of exercise you will be doing and how often, based on what you have written.

The rules when you are writing your statements are:

a. Your statements have to start with the words:
   • I choose to exercise/do yoga/run because . . .
   • or I am doing yoga/boxing/swimming because . . .

   These are words that imply you are already doing these things. The statements also start in the present tense and they are about you making a conscious decision to do things rather than being chased by an old programmed thought in your mind about what you 'should' do.

b. You can't use the words fat, weight or size. We focus on these things far too much. So many of us believe having less fat, being thinner or being smaller will make us happy – in part it might, but not always. Being happy is far more to do with how you feel about yourself regardless of your shape and size.

Here are some sample statements:
• I choose to walk every morning because it helps me be more productive during the day.
• I do weights at the gym on a Monday and a Wednesday because it helps me feel strong and confident.
• I choose to meet my friends for a walk or yoga class rather than for a glass of wine as it helps me relax and feel more positive afterwards.

Write your statements here:

1. _____

2. _____

3. _____

Build healthy habits and make them happen

WHAT COULD YOU DO EACH WEEK TO KEEP YOURSELF FIT AND HEALTHY?

Having looked at what you would like to do and thought about the reasons why keeping fit is important to you, it is time to make some commitments! I would like you to think about what you can do each week from here on and write it down – make the commitment to yourself, you are worth it.

I personally think it is best to plan something for every day, even if it is just a 20-minute walk. If you plan to be active only three days a week, it is all too easy to say 'oh, I am too busy today, I will do it tomorrow' and then never get round to it. Instead, commit to something each and every day – then you can just swap things round each week if you need to, based on how your week goes. Just sit down at the start of each week and plan your activity – make it happen, make the commitment to take care of yourself because you deserve to feel good. It is important to make active living a priority and part of your 'new normal' so it is just something that happens as part of your everyday life without thinking about it.

There may be some rearranging you need to do, some support you need to ask for, something you need to give up to make this happen – but you can do it. If you have kids, it might be that you need to combine activity with play, or when they go to swimming lessons you go for a walk or to the gym. You will need to think outside the box and overcome the excuses and barriers that will no doubt pop up. There is always a solution, though.

Each week I intend to:

Monday   _____
_____

Tuesday   _____
_____

Wednesday   _____
_____

Thursday   _____
_____

Friday   _____
_____

Saturday   _____
_____
_____

Sunday   _____
_____
_____

There is no denying that it can be easier to include all three types of training if you belong to a gym or are able to get to some classes or a boot camp, if that style of training works for you; but if you can't or don't want to, for whatever reason, there are some great DVDs, books and programmes that can help. When I was pregnant, especially in those initial stages, I was so sick that I totally lost my normal routine with the gym and other formal classes. Instead, I got into walking, weights at home and stretching in my lounge – you can do some great exercise in and around your own home if you need to.

Lose Weight for Life **has some exercise plans included in the book, and on my website you will also find some diagrams which go alongside these plans. Check out www.claireturnbull.co.nz to find out more.**

KEEP MOTIVATED

- Overcome barriers – there are always going to be reasons why you can't exercise: work, kids, deadlines, I know, I really do. Identify the things that are holding you back and come up with ways to work round them.
- Get a cheerleading squad or supporters, or someone else to do the exercise with you. This can be a fabulous idea if you find the right person or a total disaster if you get someone who quits on you. The radio producer on my Newstalk ZB health and fitness show recently started his own fitness journey with another guy he knows. Unfortunately, though, this friend was a quitter and was full of excuses so only ended up holding my producer back. Make sure the person you plan to train with is as committed as you are; and remember, the people who you surround yourself with can make all the difference to you reaching your goals.
- Enter a race, set your goal on a competition or do something as a team. I find having a goal to work towards really helpful. I am not a team sport player (mostly because my skills are just so terrible and I am not patient enough), but I am the kind of person to enter a running race or a mud fun run and that will keep me motivated. Others of you may be more motivated by joining a sports team, getting others cheering for you or exercising with others; go with what works for you.

FITTING IN ACTIVITY WHEN TIME IS TIGHT

There is just so much to fit into 24 hours, isn't there? Work, study, cooking, cleaning . . . it is endless! When life gets busy, one of the first things to fall off the list can be exercise. If this sounds like you, there are a couple of things you need to do. First, check in with your priorities: no one gets any more time than anyone else, we all have the same number of hours each day – what matters is how we use them. Second, see if you can find ways to weave activity into the things you already have going on, or work out where you can fit exercise in around what you are currently doing. Here are some things you can try:

- Back to basics – always take the stairs when there is that option; don't fall into the trap of using lifts just because everyone else does or because you have to look a bit harder to find the stairs. If you do that every day, everywhere you go it really can make a difference.
- Start 'walking meetings' at work. If there is something important to discuss, organise a meeting at a time when you can get your trainers on and walk and talk. You will be amazed by the ideas you come up with when you are outside in the fresh air!

- Keep fit at home – there are a huge number of online fitness programmes, videos and computer games that you can find to do in your own home. You will need to schedule this in, though, or it will become one of those things you never get round to.
- Get to bed earlier and wake up earlier – it can be tempting to stay up late, watch TV and chill on the sofa after a busy day, but if you are able to go to bed a bit earlier, you can then get up a bit earlier and could fit in some exercise at home first thing or go for a brisk walk before you start the day.
- Healthy catch ups – catch up with friends to do something healthy rather than for a wine or beer! More on this coming up on pages 184–5.

Time to tune in and take action!

Keeping active is good for your body, mind and soul and leads to you feeling better, happier and healthier. So, my challenge to you is – what are you going to do differently from now on? Write your thoughts down:

ACTIVE ADVENTURES

Keeping fit and healthy doesn't just have to be about running, the gym and yoga. If you are an outdoorsy person, or think you might like to be, then you can embrace some of the amazing opportunities this country has to offer. Wherever you go in New Zealand there are long beaches to walk or run along, hills to climb, walking tracks to explore – you just have to find them. There are bike trails, too, and if you live near the water, you have a free swimming pool right there – if it gets a bit chilly, then a wetsuit it is. There are things you can do for free to keep fit. Look them up, then create a list of things you want to do, schedule them in, get someone to go with you if you need to, and make it happen!

If you need a little more team spirit and group motivation, then see what clubs you can join; a swimming group, a boot camp, a bike race, a mud run – there are so many awesome things going on if you look. Keeping fit and healthy is good for you, your family and your friends, so be the one to embrace an active lifestyle and take others with you on the journey.

How to eat for maximum energy

Getting your eating and drinking right before, during and after exercise is something I feel a lot of people trip up on. If you don't have enough fuel for your fire, you aren't well hydrated and you don't recover properly after a workout, not only are you less likely to get the results you are looking for, but also exercising can end up being a lot harder and more painful than it needs to be and we don't need that, do we? We are here to feel good.

First and foremost, when it comes to eating and exercise, you need to get the total overall balance of your diet in check; making sure you get the foundation right is vital.

WHAT TO EAT AND DRINK BEFORE EXERCISE

Whether you choose to eat before exercise is up to you; it is an individual thing, as are many things in sports nutrition. If you are exercising at a moderate to high intensity (which is what I would be hoping you will be doing most days), your body is more likely to be burning carbohydrate as its primary fuel source. The good news is, if you have recovered from your previous workout or exercise session properly (as I outline below), you will have enough stored carbohydrate in your body to power you through a workout of 60–90 minutes. This stored carbohydrate source is called glycogen and is stored in your muscles and liver.

Morning workouts

If you are doing a workout in the morning you don't have to eat before; I never do. Having said that, many people I have worked with really do feel they perform better, are able to push themselves harder and feel less fatigued if they have something to eat before a workout and, like I said, if that is you, then embrace that and listen to your body.

If you are going to eat before exercise in the morning, the timing is important. Unless you are willing to get up 2–3 hours before your morning workout and have your eggs on toast or porridge, you are much better to go for a light snack such as a banana, yoghurt or small smoothie instead. If you have a full-on breakfast before a workout, it will take several hours to be digested and actually supply you with the fuel you need. If you don't allow enough time, then you will end up with food being left in your stomach when you start the workout and this will be no help to you at all. If you have a small light snack, as long as you have it at least 30 minutes before you start exercising, it will have enough time to be broken down and actually be useful to you during your exercise. It is all trial and error and finding what works for you, but if you have a massive meal and then go for a run straight away and don't feel too flash, now you know why!

Day time, afternoon and evening workouts

During the day, as you will be eating anyway, try to plan your food around your workout time where practical. That doesn't mean you have to start making things super complicated; more that you aim to eat your meals and snacks in a slightly different order. For example, if you are exercising after work (say 6 p.m.), it might mean that you have a light lunch (like a salad with some chicken, avocado and nuts/seeds) and then mid-afternoon you have a really substantial afternoon tea like a bowl of cereal with milk or a mini pita pocket stuffed with hummus and salad or maybe four pieces of sushi as your pre-training mini meal.

Having this 'mini meal' or 'substantial snack' (a healthy one, that is) with both carbohydrate and protein a few hours before a workout can be really helpful to power you through your workout. The error I see a lot of people make is having a big lunch, at say midday, then nothing all afternoon, or maybe just an apple or similar, and then hitting the gym or going for a mega walk after work and just feeling like they have nothing in them and they want to give up. If this sounds like you, you simply need to change what you eat slightly, not eat more; this isn't a time to add snacks and meals (unless you need to gain weight), but more a time to re-jig things.

Before all workouts, the best thing you can do for your body is to start well hydrated. First thing in the morning that can be a little trickier, but do have a glass or two of water before you start exercising and, if practical, take a bottle of water with you. For afternoon workouts, aim to have nice 'pale pee' before you start your exercise. That means that throughout the day you will have been topping up on your water and again, take a water bottle with you to exercise where you can.

DURING EXERCISE

Most of the time, if you are exercising at a recreational level for under 90 minutes, water will be all you need during a workout. If you are doing more full-on training, preparing for a marathon, or playing touch or netball for hours on end, you could be a candidate for using a sports drink.

Sports drinks are specially designed to enhance rehydration and help refuel the body, but they contain 14 teaspoons of sugar per 750ml bottle and as many kilojoules as a chocolate bar, so you really need to have a reason to use them. Some drinks on the market now do have less or no sugar in them and just electrolytes, and you can also buy electrolyte tablets to add to water which can be helpful if you do a lot of training and you sweat heavily.

If you are doing regular, high-intensity, long training sessions or are training for a specific event, it is a really good idea to seek individual advice about what to eat and drink before, during and after exercise.

I have amazing sports dietitians and nutritionists who work with me at Mission Nutrition, so speak to them or contact them at www.missionnutrition.co.nz

AFTER EXERCISE – RECOVERY TIME

This is make or break time. Recovering properly from exercise is vital to help make sure you are refuelled and rehydrated and to help your body to repair so that it can be ready and raring to go for your workout the next day. If you don't recover properly after exercise you can end up depleting your glycogen stores, getting run-down and by the end of the week just feeling like you have no energy and nothing to give. It is probably the most common mistake I see people make.

After exercise (we are talking a good intense workout here, not just a 10-minute walk round the block), aim to have your next meal or a snack containing both carbohydrate and protein as soon as possible, within about half an hour is ideal. Along with some water, this combination will help you refuel, repair your muscles and rehydrate – bingo!

So, in practical terms, how does this work?

If you exercise in the morning, have your breakfast as soon as possible afterwards. If that isn't practical, then you can try having some part of your breakfast or a small snack immediately after exercise, say a banana or a glass of low-fat milk, and then have the rest of your breakfast, maybe cereal, a smoothie or omelette when you can after that. The thing to remember, especially if you are watching your waistline, is not to add extra food into your day when you do this; you are simply shuffling food around, you don't want to end up eating more than you need.

If you are exercising after work, then try to have your dinner as soon as possible afterwards. Again, if it is going to be an hour or more before dinner, have a yoghurt, glass of milk or piece of fruit straight after and then a slightly smaller dinner to compensate for this extra mini snack.

If it is going to be hours before your next meal, you can just make one of your snacks for the day your recovery snack.

Here are some good ideas:

- Smoothie: banana and/or berries, low-fat milk, yoghurt, honey
- Yoghurt with chopped fresh fruit
- Cottage cheese and sliced apple/pear
- Cottage cheese on corn thins with sliced tomato
- Frozen banana (peel it before freezing) or fresh banana and glass of low-fat milk
- Small bowl/handful of cereal and low-fat milk
- Unsweetened (or naturally sweetened) protein powder made into a shake with water and/or milk; you can make this into a smoothie with some fruit or have the fruit on the side

Again, hydration is important to consider after exercise. Have water to hand and keep topping up on fluids after your workout – aim for that 'pale pee' again.

Note: this advice is all based on exercising at a recreational level. If you are doing intense training for more than 60–90 minutes a day, then it is best to seek individual advice to tailor your nutrition to you and your goals.

7

Have fun while keeping healthy

It's a common belief that when you are being 'healthy' you are at risk of becoming, well, a little boring. I hear it all the time when a conversation ends up on the topic of wanting to 'get in shape'. A huge concern that people seem to have is that they think they won't be able to be sociable or have fun anymore. My friends and family will be able to assure you that living a healthy life is anything but boring. All you need are some strategies for healthier socialising and to be absolutely confident and comfortable to make decisions about what you want to eat and drink without feeling like you need to overindulge or rely on alcohol as your only source of entertainment. This is your life – own it and make it fabulous.

Striking the magic balance

Some people go so far down the 'healthy living' path that they end up not seeing their friends or really doing anything remotely fun because they don't feel like they can eat or drink with others anymore. One particular friend of mine back in the UK went down this path. She ended up staying at home on her own, eating only salads and exercising obsessively, and regardless of how fit and toned she looked, she became miserable (her own words, not mine) and no one really wanted to call her anymore because she had become negative and had isolated herself. If you want to get healthier, that's not the way to do it, guys!

As well as those who isolate themselves, there are also those who become super obsessive and the whole world ends up knowing about it! They are the ones who get on the healthy wagon and start commenting on what everyone else is eating every five minutes. Or, they tell you constantly how much training they are doing and post 'selfies' of themselves at the gym, or go on about how well they are eating by being 'super disciplined and strict'. Their new-found passion soon turns into an obsession and if they miss the gym one day they feel so bad they can't sleep. I totally understand how this happens but, in my personal opinion, it is not really 'healthy' when you consider the true sense of that word – even if they have a ripped six-pack and killer toned arms. If I am honest, the 'obsessive' behaviours that some people develop around eating and exercise are often driven by insecurity and the need to 'look' a certain way or be a specific weight to gain a sense of acceptance more than anything else, but that's another story . . .

Overall, my message is that becoming boring, antisocial or obsessive in your quest for a healthier body and a happier life is not what I want for you. Sure, there are some changes that you will need to make, but the attitude you carry with you on this journey is the make or break as to whether you have fun along the way or not! You can absolutely still eat out, head to social functions and enjoy fun times with your friends; you may just need to make better choices about what you eat and drink – coming up are lots of great ideas to help you manage this.

What is important is deciding what is right for you and spending more time with people who help you live an awesome, healthy life. The kind of people I love and seek to spend time with as much as I can nowadays are those who embrace healthy living with a balanced approach. They genuinely love their healthy life, it is part of who they are and, more important than anything else, their motivation to eat well and take care of themselves comes from a place of self-love rather than a need to be, look or eat a certain way to receive acknowledgement or feel acceptance from others.

Those with a healthy, balanced approach are fun to be around and are proud of the way they live because it is right for them. They aren't pushy, preachy or boring, but positive balls of energy who make you feel good just by being with them. If you are going to be any type of healthy, be this type. On your journey to happier, healthier living, have the right attitude, be aware of yourself and the way you do things, and choose to make positive changes.

Make changes to the way you eat, exercise and live as a sign of respect for yourself, appreciation for the amazing body that you have been given and from a calm and loving place. If your motivation is to change so that you can fit in, feel acceptance from someone else or get more attention – there are deeper issues which you might need to address.

Be an awesome kind of healthy

Over the years, I have come up with a theory I would like to share with you – that is, that there are four different types of people when it comes health and eating. Which type are you?

- Sally – motivation ground zero. Poor Sally, she has unhealthy habits – doesn't eat well, can't find the time to be active and she has just got used to this way of being. No motivation – it's all a bit too hard. I am sure there aren't too many 'Sally's' reading this book – but if you know a Sally, she might just need a little help getting back on track! Get Sally a copy of this book.
- Tina – irritation central. Ah, there are so many Tina's out there – healthy Monday to . . . Wednesday, sometimes Thursday, but it all gets a bit too hard sometimes, especially when the weekend rolls round. Tina eats super

healthily most of the time, but might have the odd binge, eats emotionally and feels a bit like she's between a rock and a hard place!

- Laura – pressure cooker. This is becoming an increasingly common type. Living by strict rules when it comes to eating and exercise, Laura is terrified of being 'out of control' and, quite frankly, she has become a little obsessive and irritating to hang round with because she talks about what she eats all the time, and posts on Facebook every day about how good she has been. She is technically super healthly, but very hard on herself. It might get her results, but there is often some kind of control issue hiding under there.
- Chloe – in the zone. She has got it sussed – she is so in the zone. 'Healthy and happy' is easy for her. She eats great, nourishing food most of the time and finds it easy. She has the odd glass of wine and cake if she feels like it, but she doesn't feel guilty because it's so infrequent. She also sits down, eats her treats consciously and really enjoys them. She doesn't eat when she is bored, tired or angry, but instead is able to choose foods based on what her body needs with no emotions attached. Go Chloe!

So, who are you most like? You may totally fit into one 'type', or be a little bit of all or a few of them. My intention is to help you move to be more like Chloe – the awesome kind of healthy!

I have been all the other types in my life, the worst being Laura – I thought that was so good at the time but it turned out to be a nightmare. I am now like Chloe most of the time; of course, I have days like the others, but it is all about making those less frequent.

Make healthy happen!

HEADING OUT

I love spending time with friends and family, I enjoy going to restaurants, trying a delicious cocktail and sampling new food. Sometimes it might be a few times in a week (although that is increasingly rare with my baby to deal with), other times, not for a few months. My goal is always to enjoy myself but also to have nourished my body as well as I could and not to overeat and feel like I need to go to the gym for six hours the next day! Restaurant food is often a lot richer and higher in kilojoules/calories and fat than it would be in your own home, but you can work around that to a degree with a little know-how.

Let's first recap on the basic goals for eating well that we discussed in Chapter 4 (pages 62–129) and see how you can apply this to eating out.

- Boost your non-starchy veggies – the more the better and ideally not covered in butter or creamy sauces. Salads are often a good choice and sometimes I get a small main or a substantial starter with a side of veggies and sometimes a side of salad, too. Soup can be good, provided it is full of veggies rather than just stock or the odd mushroom and cream; it pays to check.
- Pulse power – lentils, chickpeas, kidney beans, split peas – I think you all know how much I love these now, right?! Salad bars and Indian restaurants are probably the most common places these goodies hang out, so look out for them!
- Go the healthy fats – nuts, seeds, avocado and oily fish are the winners as part of a healthy dish.
- Go wholegrain – where there is the option, embrace it! Often when you are eating out there will be bread involved, so go for the grainy option rather than white. Sometimes you might get the option of brown rice over white; it depends where you are eating.
- Cut the sugar – it will mainly be the dessert part of the menu where you will fall into the sugar trap, so this can easily be avoided. I very rarely have dessert when I go out and, on the occasions that I do, I eat it with awareness and enjoy every mouthful with no guilt – real 'joy' eating. I no longer eat dessert out of habit or because I can't say 'no'.
- Get high on hydration – keep up the water as well as whatever else you are drinking!

When it comes to healthier eating out, the place where you end up eating can have a lot to do with how well you will be able to make good choices.

If we aren't going somewhere specific and my friends or family are just looking for suggestions, I will often look for Japanese, Thai, Vietnamese or other fresh-style Asian food where it can be easy to order salads, fish or stir-fries with plenty of veggies. Alternatively, I would look for somewhere where you can easily order meat or fish and veggies or salad. I often go online to have a quick peek at the menu before I make a suggestion and there can often be a healthier choice. I love Mexican, Spanish and Turkish food and if you find the right place, you can certainly get a veggie-packed meal with pulses and healthy fats galore.

After the selection has been made and the restaurant is booked, remember these tips to help you manage a little better when you get there:

- Don't arrive so hungry that you are distracted and just wolf down everything in sight. If dinner is at 7 p.m., have a snack at 4 p.m. because you might not eat until 8 p.m., by which time you might feel like double helpings.
- Order water for the table and have some before any alcohol gets consumed.
- Unless you order a veggie-packed meal, opt for some side salads and veggies to share, and if you are eating somewhere where you are sharing dishes like at an Indian restaurant or tapas bar, be sure to order some vegetable dishes, too.

Making great choices in restaurants

The reality is that food varies hugely from restaurant to restaurant. Be it a pizza, butter chicken or salad, how healthy or unhealthy it actually is will depend on how it is made. I certainly know some Indian restaurants, for example, that serve curries that are a lot less oily than at other places I have been to. You will find it will end up being a little bit of trial and error.

Below I have outlined some of the better options in different types of restaurants and some not so good choices, but sometimes it is helpful to have a little look around when you walk in to see if you can get a feel for what the food is like! Big portions? No veggies in sight? Deep-fried food everywhere? Don't be afraid to ask the waiter either, if you want to know a bit more.

Even with the 'good options', be mindful that how much you eat still matters. Big portions, even of healthier options, aren't helpful for your body. Many places will allow you to take home what you haven't eaten so that might be something to consider. We tend to have the mentality that we have paid for it, therefore we must eat it all – but if you are eating more than you need, you are just treating your body like a rubbish bin.

You are better than that. It is a learnt behaviour, a habit as I talked about in Chapter 2 (pages 36–45), and it needs addressing!

PUB FOOD

Good options:

- Chicken or lean beef would be great plus a nice big salad with the dressing on the side; I tend to skip the fries and ask for extra salad
- Grilled fish or meat with veggies if they have that as an option
- Soup and grainy bread

Not so good:

- Battered and deep-fried options – sadly these seem to be very common pub food
- Fish and chips or pie and chips

ITALIAN

Good options:

- Salad or seafood starter, ideally without a heavy creamy dressing
- Lean meat, fish or seafood as a main with a side of veggies or salad is the way to go
- Pasta in a tomato-based sauce with a big salad on the side
- Thin-crust pizza with vegetable toppings and shredded chicken or prawns

Not so good:

- Risotto – this tends to be a heavy dish made with butter, cream, cheese and other very high-fat ingredients
- Creamy pasta dishes like carbonara – enough said
- Deep-crust/cheese-crust pizza with high-fat meat toppings, like salami, pepperoni and bacon

INDIAN

Good options:

- Chicken tikka (this is a drier dish without a sauce)
- Curries with vegetables and pulses
- Saag (spinach curry)
- Dhal
- Plain boiled rice

Not so good:

- Onion bhajis, samosas
- Creamy curries like butter chicken, tikka masala, korma
- Dishes with deep-fried meat/fish/seafood/vegetables
- Fried rice
- Naan bread

THAI

Good options:
- Grilled lean meat/fish/seafood kebabs with a little peanut dipping sauce
- Lean meat, fish, prawns or tofu stir-fried with vegetables and nuts with boiled rice
- Larb gai – minced chicken salad or Thai beef salad

Not so good:
- Curry puffs, spring rolls
- Thai green/red/yellow curry made with coconut milk or cream, very high in kilojoules/calories and saturated fat
- Pad Thai – in many cases this can be very oily, although there are some restaurants where it is made with very little oil and a good amount of vegetables, in which case it would be a suitable option
- Fried rice dishes

MEXICAN

Good options:
- Burritos with lean meat/chicken/vegetables – ask for less cheese and more salad
- Mexican-style salads
- Grilled fish/lean meat dishes with salad
- Fajitas – this gives you the option of building your own! Portions can be big though, so watch out for that

Not so good:
- Corn chips, nachos and tacos
- Enchiladas and quesadillas – often packed with cheese
- Extra cheese and sour cream

JAPANESE

Good options:
- Edamame beans
- Salads
- Sushi (without deep-fried fillings and mayo on top)
- Sashimi, beef tataki
- Grilled lean meat/fish/seafood
- Stir-fried/grilled lean meat and veggies with rice
- Soups with noodles and lean meat/fish and vegetables

Not so good:
- Tempura and other deep-fried meat/fish/seafood
- Japanese mayonnaise
- Too much soy sauce – it is very salty

OFF TO SEE FRIENDS OR FAMILY

It is one thing to be able to make a healthy choice when you are eating out at a café or restaurant and you can choose from the menu yourself, but it can be a whole lot more challenging when you go to someone else's place and they have laid on a feast!

So what can do you? Well, even before we get into the food-solution side of things, I want to remind you about the conversation we had earlier about eating for the right reasons in Chapter 2 (see pages 36–45). Sure, it can be difficult to make healthy choices if there's only chippies and cheese on offer, but to be honest, the biggest things that will affect what and how much you end up eating are likely to have nothing to do with the food at all.

These are some of the non-food factors that could lead you off track:

Non-food factors

1. YOUR ABILITY TO SAY 'NO, THANKS'

One of the main reasons I see people eating or drinking more than they want or eating foods that they know are leading them away from their goals is that they can't say 'no' to someone who offers them something. I totally understand that you don't want to be rude, seem ungrateful or be impolite, but if someone takes offence to you politely saying 'no, thanks' to food, it is their issue not yours.

Your job in this world is not to manage the way other people think and feel. You can only do that for yourself. Sure, there will still be occasions when you might have to suck it up and eat something you ordinarily wouldn't, but these need only be few and far between. One example I remember myself was when I went to visit my granny in the UK. I arrived to find that she had spent all week planning and preparing a huge afternoon tea for us – it was quite an achievement given that she is nearly 90 and very immobile. On this occasion, you know what? I ate what she had made, cream and all, and I decided to enjoy it without a scrap of guilt attached.

If every weekend or at every dinner with your in-laws, you find yourself eating things that deep down you really don't want just because you don't feel you can say 'no' – it's time to ask yourself who you are really helping. Not yourself, that's for sure! By eating again and again when someone offers you something that you don't want, you are only reinforcing the fact that you will eat whatever is given to you.

You don't need to start being rude or unkind, that is not what I am after, but I really just want you to find your own nice way to say 'no, thanks' when these occasions arise. In time, this can become your 'new normal' – you choose what you eat with no pressure from others.

2. MINDLESS EATING

You are enjoying a great conversation with a friend over a wine while sitting next to a bowl of chippies and a cheese board . . . next minute, you have eaten half of a Brie and nearly a whole bag of chippies! Yikes. Ever happened to you? It sure used to happen to me – a lot!

When you are out of your home environment and you are surrounded by food it can be very easy just to pick away without really realising what is going in your mouth. It might be because you are really hungry and just need to eat something – anything to take the hunger pangs away. Or, it might just be 'because it's there' and, well, it tastes nice.

Now, if that happens a couple of times a year, it is no big deal, but if every time you go to someone's place you end up sitting in the car on the way home thinking, *Oh, why did I eat all those chippies?* then you really have to ask yourself, was it worth it? Did your 'eating type' default to 'habit and haze' as we discussed in Chapter 2 (see pages 40–2)? If so, then you weren't really eating for the right reasons, were you?

Being aware of what you are doing is the first step in the process of change. From here you can work on some solutions to change this behaviour so you end up eating what you genuinely want to, not what you eat out of habit.

3. REACTIVE MUNCHING

Have you ever arrived at a party after a horrible day at work or sat down for dinner with friends after the kids have been driving you batty and screaming all day for no reason? No wonder you feel like knocking back a bottle of wine and having second or third helpings of dessert! Food and booze are certainly an easy answer to coping with your feelings. The problem is, when you wake up with a hangover every Saturday morning after dealing with your work issues by drinking wine on a Friday night, or you feel gross after you overindulge at a dinner party, you haven't really solved your problems at all – you have just masked them.

I am not saying a wine and a chat with friends doesn't help you process a challenging day and make you feel better, but my point is that sometimes we can get into a habit where we use food and booze to cope with our feelings and it often doesn't really help in the long-term and certainly leads us away from our goal of looking and feeling our best! So, just be aware. If you find yourself repeatedly drinking and eating more than deep down you know you really want to when you are out and about, stop to ask why. What are you trying to deal with? There will be a better way to manage it, one that helps you look and feel good.

Food-related factors

Okay, so now we have looked at the non-food side of things, let's get into the practical things you can do food-wise when it comes to eating well when you go to other people's homes, barbecues or parties.

1. If it is a 'bring and share' party, dinner or barbecue, then be the one to take something healthy and delicious. Challenge the concept that healthy is boring – it is so not! Take a fabulous Thai salad, a healthy dessert, some homemade healthy dips with veggies and wholegrain crackers. We often default to the high-fat cheese, dips and chippies options because we know they will get eaten, but I can assure you, all the healthy delicious food I ever serve or that I take to other people's places gets wolfed down before anything else. Prepping healthy food doesn't have to take you a long time, either; with the right recipe and a bit of practice, you will be onto it no problems.

2. If you take booze, take something non-alcoholic, too. If we are going out for dinner, we will often take a bottle of wine and some sparkling water; it reminds us all to stay well hydrated.

3. Always have a couple of glasses of water before you leave home. Top up on your hydration so you don't feel the need to guzzle down drinks as soon as you arrive – be that cocktails, wine, beer or whatever is on offer!

4. Depending on the occasion, it might work sometimes to have a snack before you go out. If I am going somewhere where I know there will be endless amounts of chippies and cheese, and dinner is likely to be several hours away, I will often have a small bowl of cereal, some fruit and yoghurt, some veggie soup (in winter) or another substantial healthy snack before I go.

5. Keep away from temptation. If you stand or sit right next to the drinks table or the cheese board, you are asking for trouble! If you are going to have some of the snacks on offer, then take just a few and then relocate yourself away from the food.

6. For 'serve yourself' dinners, barbecues or other social eating events, start by half filling your plate with salad or veggies, if they are available, then select a little bit of the other things you like and just keep it to one helping. Remember it takes 20 minutes for your brain to register that you have eaten, so if you are wanting seconds and you have eaten in less than 20 minutes (which most people do), be mindful that your body hasn't had a chance to register the food you have already eaten. Another thing to remember is that you will see food again. There will be other meals, other dinners, other barbecues; you don't have to eat like you are never going to eat again, even if your mind tells you that's what you need to do.

7. If food is served out to you, please know that it is okay to leave something on your plate if you are full. As I have said before, don't use your body as a rubbish bin. Please treat your body more kindly than that. If you know your host serves large portions and you find it hard to leave food or say 'no' (which you will get better at, won't you?) just ask for a smaller portion to start with.
8. If you need to take a gift, rather than wine or chocolates take a healthy gift. See my ideas on page 185.

ENTERTAINING AND EATING IN

I love, love, love entertaining! There is nothing better than having people that you adore in your home, sharing great food and great conversation. The question is: 'How can you entertain the healthy way?'

Here are my ideas for you.

1. If you are going to do nibbles, make that your 'starter' and serve some delicious healthy things. You could try:
   • Vegetable-, pulse- or yoghurt-based dips with chunks of veggies to dip in and wholegrain crackers or wholemeal pita bread cut into wedges and baked
   • Wholemeal pikelets or courgette fritters topped with extra-light cream cheese or 'lite' sour cream and salmon
   • Mini pinwheel wrap bites
   • Sushi rolls
   • Mini chicken or prawn kebabs with a chilli dipping sauce
   • Falafels (pan-fried) with yoghurt dip (tzatziki)
2. Have water on the table as well as alcohol to help make sure your guests stay well hydrated. Have full water glasses on the table when people sit down; you will notice that most people will then drink the water throughout the meal. If the glasses aren't there, your guests might not ask or think to ask.
3. If you are having a sit-down meal, just have a bowl of raw nuts and maybe some olives out for people to nibble while they have a drink, then aim to sit down soon-ish and tuck into the delicious meal you have prepared. Often when you do too many nibbles, once people sit down to eat your food they don't enjoy it nearly as much and by the time you reach dessert, everyone is too stuffed to enjoy it.
4. Veg it up! Making sure there are lots of veggies on offer is the way to go. You can make veggie-based dips, salads to go with your dishes, some roasted non-starchy veggies (like onion, garlic, capsicum, courgette, tomatoes and so on), or look at making a vegetable-based dish as part of your meal. Ideally, if the total amount of veggies served up

to everyone is equivalent to about half of their plate, you are onto a winner. Show everyone how good healthy food can be.

5. If you are throwing a good old Kiwi barbecue then look beyond the sausages, steak, potato salad and Kiwi dip for inspiration. Mussels, prawns and squid are great on the barbecue. Make kebabs with both meat and veggies on the same stick to encourage your guests to have some goodness with their meat fix. Choose leaner cuts of meat to put on the barbecue and make sure that the meat is well cooked and nothing is burnt. Burnt food is not good for you at all and is considered to be a contributing factor in some cancers. Serve some delicious big salads, too.

6. Opt for a healthier dessert. Check out my ideas on pages 258–61.

Healthy nibbles/platters

I really enjoy sharing food with others and a delicious platter is the epitome of that, I reckon. The problem is that many of the foods you commonly find on a snacking platter are really not that healthy. High-fat dips, creamy cheeses, salty crackers, white bread and fatty meats. Then there are those more 'bar style' platters with deep-fried everything: chips, crumbed fish bites, chicken wings and so on.

Most people don't realise that if they share a platter in a bar before dinner, it is possible to eat more kilojoules/calories and fat than you need for not just one, but possibly two of your complete meals! Here is an example:

- 6 Sesameal crackers (over 30 per cent fat) each with slices of Brie on top
- 4 slices of salami
- 2 cocktail sausages
- Handful of chips with Kiwi dip

Total = 4540 kilojoules (1135 kcals) and 84 grams fat

So, if you love sharing nibbles and platters, make them healthier. Here are my ideas of what you can put on a healthier platter.

VEGGIES
- Cherry tomatoes
- Snow peas
- Carrot
- Celery
- Raw or blanched and cooled broccoli and cauliflower
- Capsicum
- Courgette sticks

FRUIT
- Bunch of grapes
- Strawberries
- Blueberries
- Wedges of orange or kiwifruit

HEALTHY PROTEIN
- Cold lean sliced meat
- Smoked salmon
- Shredded chicken chunks
- Chicken kebabs
- Lean meatballs with tomato chutney
- Micro-mini frittatas

HEALTHY FATS
- Raw nuts and seeds
- Olives

EXTRAS
- Gherkins
- Sundried tomatoes
- Edamame beans

Any of the ideas on page 178 will work well, too.

Healthy takeaways

Do you always seem to end up at the pizza shop on a Friday night? Or get to the point every week where you are just over it, so you head to the Chinese or Thai takeaways, or maybe a burger bar? I totally understand that days can go to custard and at the end of the week things all seem to get a bit too hard. The odd takeaway every couple of weeks can be part of a healthy balance but if you find yourself heading for fast food every week for dinner, it might be something that is leading you away from a healthy life and may be an area on which to focus some attention. You first need to understand why it is that you are reaching for takeaways because therein lies the solution!

1. IS IT BECAUSE THERE IS NOTHING IN THE HOUSE TO COOK?

If so, this could be solved by having done a weekly food plan, which I do religiously, even when I go away, or if I am coming back from overseas, or when I am all over the show with work. Without my plan I would be lost. It is a flexible plan, though, ideas and a guide. It never becomes a point of obsession, more of a healthy helpful habit that means there is always something I can prep quickly when needed. Everyone who has stayed with me always ends up planning their meals as an ongoing healthy habit – it just makes life so much easier. To recap on planning, check out pages 135–6.

2. IS IT BECAUSE YOU DON'T HAVE A CLUE WHAT TO COOK THAT ONLY TAKES 10 MINUTES TO MAKE?

You only have to watch Jamie Oliver in action to realise that if you know how, you can make some amazing food super fast. I love a show he did once about his cooking classes in the UK where he made an amazing three-course dinner in less time than it took for a pizza he ordered to arrive.

If lack of inspiration is the problem, then see my ideas over the page. On days when you do have a little more time, experiment by trying some new speedy recipes so that when you do need to whip up a dish in next to no time, you know how to.

3. IS IT BECAUSE YOU HAVE HAD A DAY FROM HELL, CAN'T BE BOTHERED COOKING OR JUST DON'T FEEL LIKE YOU HAVE THE ENERGY?

I get that, I know those long hard days. Hopefully they aren't too plentiful, or it is time to reassess your priorities. Anyway, there are a few solutions here: have a back-up meal in the freezer that you can whack in the oven; have a good idea of what meals you can make in just 5 minutes; or, if it comes to it and you have been on a 24-hour flight or worked 14 days straight with virtually no sleep, just try to make a takeaway choice that at least does some good for your body – a healthy stir-fry with lots of veggies and a small portion of boiled rice from an Asian-style takeaway shop or restaurant; maybe a stuffed pita pocket with loads of salad and lean meat or fish; or a chicken kebab on rice with yoghurt dressing and extra salad.

4. IS IT BECAUSE YOU JUST REALLY LIKE BURGERS, PIZZA AND OTHER TAKEAWAY FOODS?

The solution here, if you love this kind of food, is to make your own healthier version. Homemade pizzas are super easy to make. You can either use pre-made pizza bases or use wholemeal pita breads or even make your own cauliflower pizza base (see recipe on page 240) if you are being more adventurous. Add healthy toppings of your choice and a sprinkle of cheese and they are done. Serve with salad to up those veggie serves.

Homemade burgers are a regular feature in my house. My husband has homemade meat patties in wholemeal bread buns with lettuce, grated carrot, beetroot and a slice of cheese; I opt for a plate of salad (lettuce, cucumber, grated carrot, tomato, sliced beetroot, lightly fried onions) with my lovely homemade pattie on top – delicious.

There are lots of great recipes around for other takeaways. Why not make Friday your homemade healthy takeaway night? Mix it up each week and get each person in your flat or family to make a suggestion about what they would like to make that week. If you live on your own or it is just two of you, make a list of all the things you would like to try to make a healthier version of and tick them off one week at a time. Put the option you decide to make on your weekly planner, make sure you buy everything you need, and job done.

Growing up, we never really had takeaways. My mum had some fab solutions for quick and easy meals – she needed to, working full-time with three kids. I guess I have just learnt from her. I very rarely eat takeaways now either, maybe a couple of times a year max, and that is purely down to the fact that I have never had to. I plan things every week and have a list of back-up meals which are actually faster to make than the time it would take for me to dial a pizza. For me, takeaways are the harder option.

QUICK AND EASY IDEAS
- Omelette – you can use any veggies you have in the fridge or freezer.
- Fresh filled pasta – we always have this at home. Boil the kettle, add water to the pot and pop the pasta in for a few minutes – done. I serve it with some frozen veggies which I steam on the side or, if even that seems too hard, you can just cook them in with the pasta in one pot.
- Baked potato or kumara – wash or scrub and prick them, and microwave for 5 minutes or until they start to soften while you are waiting for the oven to heat up. Then pop into the oven (ideally with a metal skewer through them to help them cook in the middle more quickly) and serve with baked beans or cottage cheese and, ideally, some salad, too, if you have some.
- When you make soups, casseroles, lasagne, Bolognese, mince, curries or any other dish that freezes well and is quick and easy to heat up, be sure to make extra to freeze – then you can have a stock of dinners ready to go in the freezer. Each week I try to do this at least once.

ALTERNATIVES TO ALCOHOL

One thing that many people need to work on is reducing their alcohol intake. Alcohol not only hammers the liver but when it comes to increasing your cancer risk, alcohol has a lot to answer for.

Alcohol also affects your weight, compromises the quality of your sleep so you wake up not feeling rested and also has a significant effect on how you feel. It is a depressant. Drinking alcohol can also very much fit into the 'habit and haze' or 'reactive response' type of eating/drinking.

Drinking alcohol can become a vicious cycle – you have a few drinks to unwind, don't get good-quality sleep, wake up feeling not rested, can't get to sleep at the end of the day because there is so much on your mind, you have a drink to make you feel sleepy and round it goes.

Whether you are a big drinker, have a glass of wine each night or just drink at the weekends, I encourage you to go for a period of time without drinking – a good couple of weeks, ideally a month or two – and see how you feel. If you instantly think *I can't possibly* then I would really question why you are drinking. What does alcohol mean to you? What does it offer you that you feel you can't get in other ways?

We are a society that commonly uses alcohol to cope with the way we are feeling: to unwind at the end of the day, as an escape from the things that are worrying us, or as social glue to help us fit in. I have certainly fallen into that trap myself. If you felt all parts of your body saying 'no way, I can't' to my suggestion of taking a break from booze, I would really like you to take a good long look at yourself and ask: What role does alcohol play in my life?

There is a very big difference between the odd glass of wine with dinner or a couple of beers while you watch the rugby and having half a bottle or more every night after work, or not feeling like you can go out and be sociable without an alcoholic drink. I want to help you be the happiest, healthiest version of yourself and I know from my own experience, having worked with thousands of people, that regardless of what you initially think about how much you drink, neither myself nor one person I have ever worked with hasn't felt better in multiple aspects of their life after a good break from booze. It is not until you take a break that you realise how good you can feel. Even if you start by just cutting back, start somewhere. I would love to know how you get on.

For some great reading on the impact of alcohol on your body and tips to cut down, check out www.alcohol.org.nz

Recommendations from the experts to reduce your long-term health risks

- Women – no more than two standard drinks a day, no more than 10 units a week and at least two alcohol-free days a week. More than four standard drinks on a single occasion is considered binge drinking.
- Men – no more than three standard drinks a day, no more than 15 units a week and at least two alcohol-free days a week. More than five standard drinks on a single occasion is considered binge drinking.[13]

A standard drink has 10 grams of alcohol. Below are examples of one standard drink:

- 330ml of beer (4% alcohol)
- 100ml of wine (12.5% alcohol)
- 160ml of RTD (8% alcohol)

If you are ready to reduce your drinking and look for some healthier non-alcoholic alternatives that are more interesting than water, here are some ideas you can try:

- Homemade (without added sugar) chilled iced teas – these are very easy to make.
- Homemade lemonade or limeade – squeeze the juice of a lemon or lime into a glass and top up with sparkling or soda water. If you want a sweeter taste you can add a tiny amount of stevia, a natural sweetener.
- Coconut water.
- Mojo-hito (yes, that is a name I made up) – lime juice, crushed mint leaves and soda water. If you want it a little sweeter you can add stevia or some diet lemonade.
- Spicy tomato juice – this is probably my favourite! Lots of ice, tomato juice, black pepper and Tabasco sauce – so good.
- Non-alcoholic wine – I came across this when I was pregnant – marvellous stuff! Far lower in kilojoules/calories than regular wine, that's for sure.
- Still or sparkling water with sliced cucumber and/or lemon/lime.
- Dilute cranberry juice with soda water or sparkling water. One-third juice to two-thirds water is a good combo.

HEALTHY CATCH-UPS

It is so easy when you catch up with friends to polish off a bottle or two of wine while debating your relationships, marriages, break-ups, family dramas, children, job changes and sad moments. But there are other great ways to catch up with your friends that don't have to revolve around food and booze. There are so many ways you can have a good chat, and have an amazing time without having to ditch your healthy habits in the process. Here are some ideas of things you can do:

- Go to a yoga class, then head to a super-affordable Asian restaurant – order a stir-fry with double the veggies, half the rice and opt for water or green tea.
- Go for a walk and then head to a café for a healthy brunch or cup of herbal tea.
- Head to an exercise class at the gym – chat on the way there and back.

- Why not try ice skating or bowling – go back to your childhood roots. Pack healthy snacks, too.

When it comes to fun adventures with family and friends, here are some other ideas:
- Go on a day adventure – pack a picnic and go for a walk.
- Organise a themed dinner with friends and make part of the challenge for everyone to bring a 'healthy plate'.
- In the summer, head to the beach for a walk and a picnic.
- Organise to meet at a farmers' market and check out delicious healthy food as you chat away.
- Meet for a family 'brunch' instead of dinner – no booze required then, I hope?

HEALTHY GIFTS

Recently, someone who stayed with us for a while bought us a little lemon tree for our back garden. She said, 'I know you wouldn't want chocolates or a cake, so I thought this was a good idea instead.' I love that.

It made me think, *You know what? There are some healthy gifts you can give.* So when it comes to birthdays, house warmings or Christmas, see if you can give a healthy gift! Here are some suggestions:
- Small lemon, lime, orange or fig tree
- Pots of herbs – I was gifted some beautiful pots once which I treasure
- Homemade chutneys or nut and seed balls nicely gift-wrapped (see recipe on page 260)
- Plant – maybe a nice orchid
- Magazine subscription – try *Healthy Food Guide* or *Green Ideas*
- Healthy cookbook or an inspirational book
- Apron or cooking utensils
- Yoga mat or a Swiss ball
- Healthy cooking class voucher (I run these, too)
- Blender or a juicer
- Popcorn maker
- Ice block maker – for healthy homemade ice blocks
- Pizza stone to make healthy homemade pizzas
- Massage voucher
- Workout gear – top, shorts, pants, cap, towel
- Tea pot and herbal tea
- Coffee plunger with some beautiful Swiss Water® decaffeinated coffee

See . . . it's as easy as that!

8

Get your body
in balance

Now that we have had a really good look at how what you eat and how much you move affects how you feel, it is time for us to complete the picture and talk about sleep, rest and relaxation – all of which are vital when it comes to nourishing your body and feeling good for life!

Sleep time

We all need sleep. It is our body's time to take over, rest and recover on a deep level. Unfortunately, though, inadequate and poor-quality sleep is one of the biggest issues I come across with people these days and it goes hand in hand with low energy levels and generally not feeling good.

With so many of us having busy, full-on lives it is no surprise that our sleep is suffering. Excess stress hormones being pumped round your body, an extra coffee to help you push through the afternoon, the reliance on alcohol to help you get to sleep – it is really just a recipe for disaster. These things all have a negative impact on the quality of your sleep and end up creating a vicous cycle. Hello grumpy mornings, fatigue and no energy!

If you feel like sleep is a part of your life that needs some attention, here are a few things for you to consider:

- Most people need at least seven hours sleep each night and some of you will naturally seem to need a bit more – especially if you do lots of exercise. If you don't get anywhere near this much, identify the reasons why and find a solution. There will always be other things you feel you need to do before you go to bed and there is always more work that can be done, but sleep and sanity make everything a whole lot easier in the long run so be ruthless and prioritise. If you are spending half an hour on Facebook every evening or watching TV late at night, you have to really ask yourself what's more important. When you really, honestly look at it, there is always something you can do if you are willing.
- There are some times when it can be impossible to sleep for seven hours: for instance, if you have a new-born baby, do shift work, or have a sick family member to care for. If this is the case then napping is your friend.
- When you nap, ideally set your alarm for either 15–20 minutes or 90 minutes. The shorter nap will allow you to get a little energy boost, but in this short time you are less likely to go into the deep sleep phase. If you nap for an hour say, as many people do, you are likely to wake up in the middle of a deep sleep and you will probably feel groggy (almost hung over!), and you often feel worse before you feel

better. If you have longer, a 90-minute nap is ideal as that is roughly the length of one complete sleep cycle. You will go into and out of a deep sleep during this time and feel really good when you wake up!

For more on sleep and sleep cycles, check out *Lose Weight for Life* where this is covered in greater detail.

- Allow yourself time to be away from your computer, phone or TV before bed to disconnect and unwind and get yourself into a good sleeping routine.
- Limit the amount of caffeinated drinks you have during the day; they can have a far bigger impact on your sleep than you may realise, as I mentioned on pages 127–9.
- Alcohol has a very similar effect on sleep to caffeine and even though your wine, beer or vodka may have knocked you out and made you fall asleep, when you are asleep, deep sleep is compromised and usually you have a restless night. Even if you do manage to sleep for nine hours you are likely to not be feeling that special when you wake up.

If you really struggle with sleep, seek expert advice. Dr Alex Bartle is fantastic, you can find out more about his work at www.sleepwellclinic.co.nz.

Get outside

I was recently talking about health and happiness to the editor of *Green Ideas* (a fabulous magazine about sustainable living), and during our conversation about the various reasons that people can feel unhappy, he said to me, 'You know what Claire; I think people are suffering from a serious case of nature-deficit disorder.' I love his theory.

I absolutely believe that many of us suffer from a 'nature deficit' – not spending enough time outside in the fresh air and natural daylight, simply walking through the trees, playing on the grass and running barefoot in the sand. Connecting with nature, the real beautiful world in which we live, is very powerful and allows us to connect with what is really important, and that's not money, things or stuff.

EXPOSE YOUR EYES

There is another great reason to get outside, too. Exposing your eyes to light is important to regulate one of the major hormones that affects your mood, serotonin. When you experience the mid-afternoon energy dip where you just want to fall asleep or grab a coffee and a sugary treat, what you really need is some exposure to natural light! It will certainly help you feel good, make you feel less sleepy and, combined with a glass of water and maybe a piece of fruit or a few raw nuts for a little energy, you will be good to go. No caffeine or sugar rush required.

As well as boosting your mood during the day, exposure to light also plays a vital role in helping to regulate another hormone called melatonin which helps you sleep. You know why you sleep well after a day outside? It's not the fresh air; it's that you have seen lots of light. Blue and green light (from trees, the sea, grassy areas and so on) are particularly good.

My suggestion is to make sure you get outside every day and expose your eyes to the light. If you go on an early-morning walk, head out of the office at lunchtime or are pottering around outside mid-afternoon and it's not super bright and the light isn't glaring, take your sunglasses off and allow your eyes to see the light. Some people are so reliant on their sunnies as a fashion accessory that come rain or shine their glasses will be on and it's really not a good thing! Protecting your eyes from harsh light with good-quality lenses is vital: virtually never seeing the light of day because you are a sunglasses addict is a total disaster.

VITAMIN D

Yet another important reason to make sure you are getting enough exposure to light is to help your body make vitamin D. When your skin is exposed to sunlight it is able to make this vitamin which is super important for bone health and has been shown to have a positive effect on your immunity, heart health and so many other aspects of your health and wellbeing. By the end of winter, many people in New Zealand will be deficient in vitamin D because of their lack of exposure to sunlight. Those at particular risk all year round are those who spend a lot of time inside, older people, people with darker skin and those who cover up for cultural reasons.

So the simple message here is to make sure you get outside and expose yourself to light – you need it. Of course, I support the recommendations to use sunscreen and stay out of the sun during burning times, but there is still room for sensible exposure to sun within these recommendations. For more detailed information, check out the information on vitamin D on the Ministry of Health website www.health.govt.nz.

Vitamin D supplementation certainly has a place in high-risk groups and for those of you who don't get enough sun exposure. Talk to your GP or my team at Mission Nutrition if you think you might be falling short (as most people are) of this vitamin.

MAKE IT HAPPEN!

- Wear sunglasses only when they are needed, i.e. when it is sunny, super bright or there is glaring light.
- Plan to get outside each and every day for at least 20–30 minutes. This could be walking to work, going outside on your lunch break or going for a walk when you get home from work.
- At the weekends or your days off from work, get outside. Go for a bike ride, walk through the forests or head to the beach. Exploring the great outdoors is an ideal way to spend time with people you love and cherish. Write a list of places you can go and things you can do outside and put it on your fridge, aim to tick everything off, and then repeat. Put the times in your diary and just make it happen. You will feel much better for it.

What action will you take to make sure you are getting enough light and don't suffer from nature-deficit disorder?

_____
_____
_____
_____

Disconnect, rest and relax

If there is one thing I have learnt in the last few years it is that a little down time and rest makes you a million times more productive. Your body isn't designed to be constantly on the go; it needs to switch off and rest and it is your job to find a way to make it happen, however challenging that is.

DISCONNECT

Technology is fantastic on so many levels, but the one massive down-side of phones, texts, emails and being accessible 24/7 is that it has become virtually impossible to disconnect yourself from work, status updates and news feeds. In my personal opinion, that's damaging. So many of us are so over-stimulated that we become anxious when we are off email or have no cell phone coverage – how sad is that? I totally fall into that trap from time to time and I constantly try to be aware of how unhealthy it is for me. I have to put strategies into place to help me disconnect.

Having mental space is the most basic form of rest and is vital for you to be able to feel good. You might hands down tell me that you simply cannot and do not have time for 15 minutes to yourself a day (which with a young baby myself, I totally understand), but you do have many, many opportunities to quieten your mind and create virtual space – even if it is just a few moments during the day. Mental space allows you to be clearer, more productive and creative.

It is so easy to think that by reading more, knowing more and being more connected that things will be better, but I don't believe that is necessarily true. Albert Einstein said something very wise: 'Imagination is more important than knowledge.' He is bang on, I say. In the space of a peaceful and quiet mind, amazing things can be created. You just need to allow yourself the opportunity to disconnect and create that space.

Here are some ways you can disconnect:

- Avoid checking your phone or emails first thing in the morning. There aren't many things in life that are genuinely life or death – you may have just learnt to believe there are. If you can't avoid the temptation (I fall into that camp), then have an alarm clock which is not your phone and leave your phone charging in another room. The first thing to do when you get up in the morning is to visualise a fabulous day, set an intention for yourself, think about how you want to feel and acknowledge something you are grateful for. If that feels like a step too far right now, then at least say good morning to your partner, your kids, your flatmates, your dog or even just to the world before you start worrying about how much you have to do. There is always stuff to do – worrying doesn't help it get done, but being in a healthy frame of mind does.
- When you are driving, on the bus or walking somewhere, rather than having loud music blaring from your iPod or radio, choose to enjoy the peace and quiet, or play some relaxing and calming music, or listen to an inspiring or motivating audio book. It is really frustrating when you first do it; I couldn't stand the silence, it made me agitated, but that just showed me how much I needed it. Create space. You need it for your sanity.
- Try to check your emails only two to three times a day – again, this can be very tricky, particularly if you have trained people to expect you to reply in less than a minute. If it is practical in your job to do this, make it happen. You can set an out of office email saying: 'Thanks for your email, I check my Inbox at 8 a.m., 12 p.m. and 4 p.m. so will be back in touch as soon as I read your email – have a

wonderful day.' Job done! When I am working on a deadline, I always do it – it is far too distracting to get the 'new email sound' or see the little envelope icon pop up.

- Take some slow deep breaths. Learning to breathe correctly, in my opinion, is one of the most powerful things you can ever do. Slow, gentle diaphragmatic breathing slows your heart rate down, reduces your stress hormones and helps clear your mind. When you have too many stress hormones pumping round your body all day every day, not only does it wear you out, but for some of you it will be affecting your weight and body fat levels, too, and not in a good way, so keep that in mind!

- Where you are sitting now, without changing your breathing (which I know is very hard to do when I have asked you not to), time the number of times you breathe in and out in a minute (with each in and out being counted as one breath). How many was it? If it was more than 15 you certainly need to slow your breathing down. (Normal breathing is considered 10–14 breaths per minute.) For all of you, regardless of the number of breaths, it is well worth learning to breathe properly. It honestly has such a big impact on your health and how you feel. I had no idea until I learnt myself.

REST AND RELAX

Allowing yourself time just to sit and 'be' is powerful – often tricky to do if you have an active and full-on life, live with other people and have a busy workplace, but it is not impossible. Rest and relaxation allows your body and mind to slow down and creates space for your true self to be present. Letting the stress go and allowing your body to return to a state of calm is energising and rejuvenating for every part of you.

If possible, take time each day to relax, whether it's by having a warm bath or a long shower, or flicking through a light-hearted magazine, lighting a candle or painting your nails. Just take a few minutes, and more if you can, to turn the music down, the TV off and be away from distractions to focus on the moment and enjoy just being you.

If you find it hard to do this or it just seems to never happen, then doing something structured is the way to go. Yoga, a gentle swim, tai chi, a meditation class – whatever works for you. Just try, see how you go and don't give up the first time. If you have never taken time out before or can't remember the last time you did, then like me, the first time you try, you might hate it – but that means you need it more than ever.

9

Feed your mind and soul

Welcome to the final stage of our journey together! Up to now we have really focused on all the amazing things you can do for your body to help make sure you wake up in the morning and feel good (oh, and have fun at the same time, of course), but that isn't the full picture. For amazing health and happiness, as well as nourishing your body you need to nourish your mind and soul, and that is what this next chapter is all about.

Body, mind and soul

There are an endless number of ways to describe the body, mind and soul but let's keep things super simple:

- Your *body* is your human form which you need to nourish with great food, look after by keeping fit, and let rest and sleep. Through this book so far we have covered hundreds of hints and tips to help you get on top of this.
- Your *mind*, in the most basic of terms, is what you think and making sure you feed yourself healthy thoughts is essential for a healthy, happy life! We are going to look at this next.
- Your *soul* is the core of who you are; your essence, your being. It doesn't have a location as such, you can't see it – it just 'is'. It is your internal guidance system and tuning into it will be the most powerful thing you can ever do. More on this coming up on pages 200–1.

It is my belief that when you consider all three parts of yourself together the real magic can happen and you will truly be able to live your healthiest, happiest life.

Feed your mind

In the same way that many of us get into the habit of using food or alcohol to cope with difficult times, eating something sweet after dinner or finishing everything on our plate, our minds learn to think in a certain way and repeat certain thoughts – just out of habit. One of my very best friends, Louise Thompson, who works in the health-coaching world, always tells me that if people really want true health and happiness, there is no point in them feeding their bodies green smoothies and going to the gym every day if they are feeding their minds deep-fried chicken all day long! She is seriously onto something.

YOU GET TO CHOOSE

Whether you believe it now or not, you do have a choice about what you do every day and how happy you allow yourself to be. We all get 24 hours a day and you do get to choose how to use it. You may think: *Well, no I don't. I have to work 14 hours a day, I have to live in this place, I have to make my family dinner every night*. Well, you don't have to, you choose to.

You don't actually *have* to do anything. Sometimes, if you want something like better health, more time or more space, it is not that you can't have it – it is just that you don't think you can.

Your mind tells you that you can't based on its conditioning, but that's just your mind, it's not reality. To get the things you want, sure, you will have to drastically re-prioritise, things will change and you may have to say 'no' to things. You might also have to get used to not being the person who does everything for everyone all the time, you may earn less money, you may need to live on your own or move – but you do get to choose. Sometimes it is just about having the courage to face the change.

I never used to believe this; I thought that life was just what came and depended on your background and education but, now, after a lot of self-work, I realise this is so far from the truth. So many people go through their entire lives without knowing who they really are and live their lives based on fear, other people's expectations and worrying about what other people think. That is madness.

If you want to look and feel good, you have to believe you deserve it and think thoughts that help you head in the direction of happier and healthier living, rather than pulling you away from it.

For healthier, happier living, you need to learn to feed your mind nourishing thoughts and replace the default negative thoughts that you have picked up throughout your life, like *I am not good enough*, *I will never be able to do that* or *It's too hard*, with ones that help you get where you want to go and help you to live a life that is in alignment with the goals of your soul. Let me assure you, too, that you are good enough and you deserve to be happy, regardless of what your thoughts tell you sometimes.

MANAGE YOUR THOUGHTS AND BELIEFS

This is a huge topic and deserves its own book, but here are the basics of managing your thoughts in three easy steps.

1. Become aware of what you think. This means noticing your thoughts, writing them down and just seeing them for what they are. Not judging them, just observing. Just because you think something, it doesn't mean it is true or real. It is just what you have 'learnt to think' based on what you have been through in your life so far.

2. Replace negative or unhelpful thoughts with positive or neutral ones, which actually help you get where you want to go.
3. Practice and repeat, repeat, repeat.

Time to tune in and take action!

Take charge of your thoughts
Step 1: Over the next three days identify one unhelpful or negative thought that seems to crop up repeatedly, and write it down below.
Step 2: It is now time to 're-frame your thought' and replace it with a more positive one, or even a neutral one to start with. Every time you find the negative thought coming up, notice it and say your new helpful thought to yourself instead.

Here is an example:
Current recurring negative thought:
- *Eating well is hard work and takes too long.*

New alternative thoughts you could try:
- *Eating well helps me feel good and allows me to be more productive; I choose to make this a priority today.*

Write your notes here:

Current recurring negative thought:
_____
_____
_____

New alternative thought:
_____
_____
_____

Work on one thought at a time; you can come back to this at any stage and repeat it as many times as you need. If you find that you have a lot of negative thoughts cropping up, check out Louise's work at www.louisethompson.com. She has some amazing ideas and resources that can help get to the bottom of negative thought patterns.

You are worth it

To look and feel your best each and every day, one of the first things I want you to know is that it is okay to put yourself first sometimes. It is okay to say 'no' to people, too. Of course, some things you say 'yes' to so that you don't lose your job and to ensure that you are pulling your weight with household chores, for example. However, there is a difference between saying 'yes' to things that you know are important for you to be doing, versus simply saying 'yes' to extra tasks, drinks or jobs because you feel you aren't strong enough, or find it too hard to say 'no'.

When you become a 'yes' person all the time, you are likely to be making other people's priorities bigger than yours and even though it might feel 'normal' for you to do this, the most common reason why we find it hard to say 'no' is that we don't want to feel rejected, to upset others or to feel like another person won't like us as much. It has nothing to do with you really wanting to take on that extra thing at all.

All you ever need to do is learn to accept yourself – you don't have to run round like a headless chicken pleasing other people to feel like you are good enough. You are good enough as you are and you are worth it. It is okay to say 'no' sometimes and if you don't currently do it, it is time to start practising. You don't need to be aggressive or feel like you have to make up a million excuses as to why you are saying 'no', either. A simple 'no, thanks' to that top-up of wine, 'thanks for the invite, but I won't be able to make it' or 'I won't be able to get that done by the time you need it so I am going to have to say no'. If you have always been a 'yes' person, people will no doubt try to talk you round, give you more time, say something to put the pressure on – but stay firm and simply say, 'I am sorry but no' and then move on. I cannot tell you how much this simple thing has totally changed my life as well as so many people I have worked with.

Self-care and looking after yourself is not selfish. It is an essential part of survival which allows you to do more in the world as well as be there for others. Too many people feel guilty about doing something for themselves, taking time on their own or even feeling happy – what madness have we created for things to be like this? Looking after yourself helps you to be much more productive and certainly helps you to be there for other people more completely than ever before.

When it comes to making changes to the things I outlined in the questionnaire at the start of this book (pages 18–21) – food, alcohol, exercise, sleep, stress and being able to say 'no' to most of the questions I asked – it takes some dramatic re-prioritisation, getting over your limiting beliefs and ditching the drama – it is all possible.

These changes will take time, you will need to work on things little by little. Treat this process like a journey. There is no such thing as an overnight success, regardless of what some people will have you believe. Good things take time and you are worth the investment – after all, there will never be another you who walks on this earth. The world needs you and everything you have to offer.

Connect with your soul

Who are you? Boy, that's a big question when you are nearing the end of the book. I hope you are sitting down.

You might initially think: *Well, I know exactly who I am, thanks. I am a daughter, parent, caregiver, business owner, hard worker, supporter, a fitness fan, a shopaholic* – the list is endless and it's true you could be many of these things and no doubt a lot more.

The reality is, though, if we look a little bit closer at this, these are actually all roles that you play. You may play these roles very well and be okay with that, but they aren't who you 'are'. There is a difference.

Getting to know who you really 'are' is getting to know the core of you. Your essence. Your soul. Who you 'are' has absolutely nothing to do with your job, how much money you have, what car you drive, where you live or how many people you know. You are not your things, you are not your roles and nor, in fact, are you your thoughts.

So, why does this even matter? Well, because true peace and happiness doesn't come from having things or doing things, but more from being – being who you were meant to be, who you really are. If you take away everything you have, everything you do and all the roles you play, what is left is who you 'are'. It is a scary thought, isn't it? Without all those things most people feel lost, hopeless, empty, but you still have you; it's just that most people don't know what that is.

When you are connected with your soul, your inner-self, your sense of 'being' (i.e. who you 'are'), then you are able to make decisions about your life, how you choose to spend your time and the people you surround yourself with based on what is right for you – not what is right for the person you think you should be or who you have learnt to be over the course of your life so far.

So, how on earth do you get to know the real you? Well, that is a book (or really thousands of books) in itself, so my advice if you are interested in this is to seek out the wisdom of the geniuses in this area and explore their endless resources – Eckhart Tolle, Deepak Chopra, Martha Beck, Wayne Dyer, the Dalai Lama and Debbie Ford are some of my favourites.

The essence of all of their work is that to be able to connect with who we really are at the core, we need to find a way to disconnect from the constant chatter in our heads and to separate ourselves from our thoughts and conditioning.

So many of us have deeply unhelpful thoughts and beliefs that control our lives day in and day out without us even realising that it's happening. When you can quieten your mind and detach from your thoughts you will find the space that is you, who you really are, and be present. When you learn to tap into this you will be able to make clear decisions in your life about what you truly want and what will really make you happy. The geniuses I have mentioned above all have their own way to help you do this – it's just about finding a way that resonates and works for you. It will help you feel good on a totally different level.

USING YOUR SOUL AS A COMPASS IN YOUR LIFE

A few years ago I stumbled across the concept of living your life based not on what you want to 'have' or what you should 'achieve' but instead focusing on how you want to feel day in, day out – using my soul as a compass rather than my mind. This simple thing changed my whole life and is one of the reasons I decided to write this book and include this message as part of it.

When we make goals in our lives about how much money we want to earn, how much weight we need to lose or what car we want to drive we think that when we get these things (the money, the skinny jeans, the car) we will be happy. The reality often is, though, when we get the thing we have always wanted, the outcome isn't as life-changing or amazing as we thought it might be and we don't always feel as good as we thought we would. Then, we move on to the next thing; there is always more you can do, buy and have – the question is, does it actually make you any happier?

I am sure you all know someone who seems to have 'everything' but isn't as happy on the inside as you think they would be. The things they are surrounded by might make them feel powerful, in control and safe, but it doesn't make them feel loved, supported or treasured, which deep down is what so many of us really want. Happiness is far more to do with how you feel on the inside than what you have to show on the outside. Happiness in my mind is an inside job.

CREATING YOUR JOURNEY

You no doubt picked up this book because you wanted to look and feel good and, hopefully, what you have read so far has helped you get on the right track. To make sure you are able to keep things going as the weeks and months pass by, it is important to have a clear vision of where you want to go in the future and to create a road map of how you are going to get there. Having a clear picture in your mind of how you would like things to be is really very powerful when it comes to your day-to-day choices. The content of this book so far is packed with 'how to make it happen' guidance, but to keep things going and to keep yourself motivated, your drive to be healthy and happy needs to come from the core part of who you really are and help you feel how you want to feel.

When you make decisions about what you eat, drink, how much you sleep and what exercise you do as well as what you say 'yes' and 'no' to based on how you want to 'feel' about those things, you will be amazed by the results. You will be able to shift the kilos, complete the bike race, spend more time with your friends and family or whatever it is you really want. When you focus on feelings first, it means that your motivation comes from a positive place.

Often, when we set goals and write lists of things we 'should do' to get there, the motivation is actually coming from a negative place, a place of fear or not wanting to let yourself or other people down. I find that self-sabotage can creep in a lot more when this is the case.

Time for a little tune-in session

Please, please don't skip this exercise. I know what it is like when you are reading a book and you are nearing the end, you just want to get to the next page – but this is super important! If it is not a good time to do this now, put a star at the top of the page and make sure you come back to it – it really will help you.

Step 1: What does feeling good really mean to me?

Okay, so . . . first up, close your eyes and take 10 slow, deep breaths.

Now, visualise yourself waking up in the morning in your favourite place. You have your favourite people and things around you. You are looking how you want to look, you are doing what you want to be doing and there is absolutely nothing to worry about at all. You feel really good.

Take a few minutes to look around, notice where you are, what is happening and just observe your surroundings. Then start to notice, what does good really feel like? Give yourself a good few minutes just to see what words come up. Write down any words that spring to mind about how you feel in this place below.

Please don't rush this – take as long as you need.

What feelings came up?

_____
_____
_____
_____
_____
_____
_____
_____
_____

There are hundreds of words to describe your feelings – peaceful, calm, clear, open, relaxed, present, energised, radiant, powerful, strong, open, bold, grateful, courageous, excited, confident . . . the list goes on and on.

What I want you to do now is pick four or five of the words that you really feel you connect with. You might want to use a dictionary or thesaurus alongside what you have written down to make sure that the words you choose really do align with what feeling good means to you.

You may find it helpful to repeat this exercise several times, once a week, every day for a fortnight – whatever feels right for you, but see if you can tap into four or five words that really make your face light up and your heart sing because you know that they truly represent how you want to feel each and every day about yourself and your life.

How do you want to feel? List your top five words.

1. _____
2. _____
3. _____
4. _____
5. _____

Step 2: What choices can you make to help you feel how you want to feel?

Now you have figured out how you want to feel each and every day, I want you to think about the things you need to take action on to help you feel this way. When you do these things (like go to the gym, say 'no' to dessert, etc.), rather than thinking *I am doing this to lose weight because I have to fit into my bikini*, think *I am doing this because I want to feel energised, radiant and strong*. That's being motivated from a positive place and it's powerful.

On the page opposite, write down the choices you can make in each area of your life which will help you feel how you want to feel based on your four or five top feelings. You may want to recap on notes you have made throughout the book so far to think about some of the things you really want to do to that will help you feel the way you want to feel.

To help you, here is an example:

Marie wants to feel inspired, energised, connected, creative and authentic.

So as an example, these are things Marie might want to do:

Food and drink
- Make one new recipe every Wednesday night to help me feel *inspired*
- Have vegetables at lunch and afternoon tea every day to feel *energised*

Exercise
- Go to boot camp three times a week to feel *energised*
- Enter a half marathon to feel *inspired*

Sleep and rest
- Turn off my computer and the TV at 9.30 p.m. and be in bed by 10 p.m. so I wake up feeling *energised*

Time out
- Walk in the forest or on the beach every weekend to feel *connected* to nature
- Read a book on healthy cooking to feel *creative*

Social time
- Turn my phone on silent when I am with friends/family to feel *connected*
- Practise saying 'no, thanks' to food and drink I don't want, to feel *authentic*. I am making decisions for me based on what I really want

Work
- Leave work on time every Thursday so I can go to yoga with my friend to feel *connected*

Now it is your turn:

Food and drink

Exercise

Sleep and rest

Time out

Social time

Work

Nice work! This is a really good start and an important process to go through to help get you on the right track when it comes to applying the 'feel good for life' principles. Re-visit this part of the book as often as you can to remind yourself of what you need to do to feel how you want to feel.

SURROUND YOURSELF WITH GREAT ENERGY

Last but not least, a few pieces of advice to help make sure you create a healthy, happy life that lasts.

- Surround yourself with visual reminders, quotes and pictures that reinforce your goals, how you truly want to feel, live and be.
- Change your screen saver to a place you want to visit, or somewhere beautiful that you have been, a photo of yourself looking and feeling amazing or a collage of images that encapsulate the life you know you will live someday.
- Write down your four or five words describing how you want to feel in your diary or somewhere you will be able to see them several times a day. Maybe on the screen saver on your phone or a Post-It note on your mirror.
- Write down a list of things you love doing that make you feel good. I know winning the lotto and a luxury holiday might be the first things that come to mind, but I am talking about free or very low-cost things. Having flowers in your lounge, baking for your friends, watching a

comedy. Focus on some of the little things. How good it feels to give someone a gift, call a friend or try something new. Every day plan to do at least one thing that you know makes you feel good.

- Spend time with people who support you and lift you up. As I have said before, you become like the people with whom you spend the most time and they will influence who you become. Choose wisely. Spend more time with the right people. There are times when you can't always choose who you spend time with: at work, for example, or the members of your family. You can, however, choose how much they affect the way you think.
- Find some role models – who really inspires you? Jamie Oliver and Hugh Fearnley-Whittingstall are two of mine. They are real, have true passion and they make a difference. Look for role models who reflect your values and who inspire you to be the best you. If you choose the right role models, it can be really helpful, when you feel a bit stuck or lost, to ask yourself 'what would they do right now?'.

Time to tune in and take action!

What will you do to surround yourself with positive energy?

In summary

Well, my lovely friends, our time together has come to an end. It has been a fun journey and I hope you have enjoyed it. Now it is time to hand over the reins to you so you can make it happen! Here are a few recaps and reminders for you as you head off on your own.

- Include more plant food each and every day
- Reduce your reliance on heavily processed food and added sugars
- Boost your healthy fats and whole grains
- Keep yourself well hydrated
- Plan, plan, plan – it is the key to making healthy happen
- Adapt your meals to make them healthier
- Eat at the right time for you
- Understand your eating habits and behaviours
- Move your body each and every day
- Learn how to breathe correctly
- Do whatever it takes to get good-quality sleep
- Manage your thoughts
- Feed your body, mind and soul
- Make decisions based on how you want to feel
- Surround yourself with people who make you feel good

For ongoing support and guidance from me, just sign up for my updates at www.claireturnbull.co.nz. I am here to help you be the happiest, healthiest version of yourself day by day.

I look forward to seeing you soon at one of my events or cooking classes and if you are keen to have me to speak at an event or conference then just let me know, it would be great to meet you.

With love and healthy thoughts,

Claire
X

Recipes

Morning magic

Awesome overnight oats *(serves 1)*

This is a quick and easy breakfast or snack that you can enjoy at any time of the day.

⅓ cup oats
⅓ cup low-fat milk
⅓ cup low-fat
  unsweetened
  yoghurt
½ cup frozen or fresh
  berries
1 tbsp ground
  flaxseed or LSA
2 drops vanilla extract

Mix all the ingredients together in a container with a sealable lid or a clean (and empty) jam jar.

Seal and leave to soak overnight in the refrigerator.

In the morning you can serve with extra yoghurt, a few chopped nuts, a sprinkle of seeds or even a teaspoon of a nut butter of your choice.

Adapt it
• Swap the berries for ½ mashed banana and add a pinch of cinnamon or mixed spice.
• Replace the berries with 1 tablespoon of chopped dried fruit – sultanas, dates, figs and apricots all work well.
• Swap the ground flaxseed or LSA for 2 teaspoons of chia seeds, or any seeds you like, really.
• Add 1 teaspoon runny honey for a little sweetness.

Top tip
• LSA is ground linseed (flaxseed), sunflower seed and almond mixed together. You can find it in most supermarkets and health stores. It is best stored in the refrigerator.

Nutrition information per serve					
kJ = 982	kcals = 234	Carbs = 37g	Protein = 12g	Fat = 6g	Fibre = 8g

For Claire's health kick bircher muesli recipe check out
www.claireturnbull.co.nz/feelgood.

Raw muesli mix *(32 serves)*

Get up and glow! It is super easy to make your own raw muesli mix, plus you get to make it however you like it. It is time to start experimenting. Here is one of my favourite combos.

5 cups wholegrain (chunky) oats

5 cups rolled oats

1 cup pumpkin seeds

1 cup raw almonds or walnuts

1 cup sunflower seeds

½ cup each Brazil nuts, sesame seeds, flaxseeds (linseeds), chia seeds

1 cup dried figs, chopped

Mix all the ingredients together in a large mixing bowl.

Store in an airtight container.

To serve, measure about ½ cup into a bowl and serve with low-fat milk or low-fat unsweetened yoghurt, or soak it overnight in low-fat milk for a softer Bircher-style muesli.

Adapt it
- You can toast the sesame seeds before adding, if you like, as it makes them taste nuttier. Simply heat them in a dry frying-pan for 1–2 minutes until lightly browned, and cool before adding to the rest of the ingredients.
- You can also toast the oats in the oven, if you prefer them to be crunchier, but it is totally fine to eat them raw as I have suggested.
- Either enjoy your nuts whole or, if you prefer, chop them up.
- Instead of figs, try sultanas, dates or dried cranberries.

Top tips
- The type of oats you buy will affect the texture of the muesli. Some are harder than others so just play around and see what works best for you.
- Choose figs that are dry rather than moist or everything will stick together!

Nutrition information per serve (½ cup)

kJ = 1256	kcals = 314	Carbs = 31g	Protein = 12g	Fat = 15g	Fibre = 9g

For Claire's health kick bircher muesli recipe check out
www.claireturnbull.co.nz/feelgood.

Nutty apple crumble *(serves 1)*

Crumble, for breakfast?! Well, yes! This is not your average crumble, though, to be honest. It is a super healthy version and it is so tasty you won't believe that it is so good for you.

¾ cup low-fat
   unsweetened
   yoghurt
1 apple, washed and
   grated (skin on)
1 tbsp rolled oats
1 tbsp ground
   flaxseed or LSA
1 tsp ground
   cinnamon
2–3 walnuts or raw
   almonds, chopped
1 tsp runny honey
   (optional)

Spoon the yoghurt into a bowl and place the grated apple on top.

Sprinkle the oats, ground flaxseed or LSA and cinnamon over.

Add the chopped nuts and optional drizzle of honey.

Stir it all together or eat it as is – however you prefer.

Adapt it
* Try grated pear instead of grated apple.
* Try stewed apple or pear instead of grated.
* Swap the oats for 1 tablespoon of pumpkin seeds, or use both.

Top tip
* LSA is ground linseed (flaxseed), sunflower seed and almond mixed together. You can find it in most supermarkets and health stores. It is best stored in the refrigerator.

Nutrition information per serve

kJ = 1000   kcals = 238   Carbs = 28g   Protein = 12g   Fat = 10g   Fibre = 10g

For more delicious recipes, including healthy cooked breakfasts, omelettes, porridge and toasted mueslis, check out *Lose Weight for Life* (available at www.claireturnbull.co.nz).

Smoothies

Green goodness *(serves 1)*

This fresh green smoothie will help you feel energised in no time at all!

2 handfuls spinach, well washed
1½ cups chilled water or coconut water
1 small banana, peeled and chopped into small pieces (ideally frozen)
Juice of ½ lemon
2 sprigs parsley (optional)

In a blender or food processor, blend the spinach and chilled water or coconut water thoroughly.

Add the chopped banana, lemon juice and, if you are up for it, some parsley.

Blend until smooth. Add more water if you like.

Serve with ice.

Adapt it
• Swap the banana for a chopped apple, pear or peach or use ½ banana and ½ apple.

Top tip
• If your green juice is lumpy, it might be a sign that you need a more powerful blender or food processor.

Nutrition information per serve					
kJ = 473	kcals = 113	Carbs = 25g	Protein = 2g	Fat = <1g	Fibre = 4g

Green kiwi *(serves 1)*

A refreshing smoothie packed with the goodness of greens and a good dose of vitamin C to boost your immune system.

2 handfuls spinach, well washed
1½ cups chilled water or coconut water
½ banana, peeled and chopped into small pieces (ideally frozen)
1–2 kiwifruit, peeled and chopped

In a blender or food processor, blend the spinach and chilled water or coconut water thoroughly.

Add the chopped banana and kiwifruit.

Blend until smooth. Add more water if you like.

Serve with ice.

Top tip
• You can use green or golden kiwifruit in this recipe.

Nutrition information per serve

kJ = 601   kcals = 144   Carbs = 32g   Protein = 3g   Fat = <1g   Fibre = 6g

Monkey shake *(serves 1)*

How can something so tasty be so good for you? You have to make this shake!

1 banana, peeled and chopped (ideally frozen)

1½ cups low-fat milk

1 tbsp peanut or almond butter

1 tsp cocoa powder (optional)

In a blender or food processor, blend the chopped banana, milk and peanut or almond butter thoroughly.

Sprinkle over the cocoa powder, if using, and enjoy.

Adapt it

• If you are dairy free, use the milk alternative of your choice.
• You can add 1 tablespoon of oats or LSA if you want a thicker, nuttier shake.
• Add 1 tablespoon of cocoa powder before blending, for a chocolate monkey shake.

Top tip

• For a rich, chocolatey taste, use raw Dutch cocoa – you can buy it at some supermarkets, health stores and specialty food stores.

Nutrition information per serve					
kJ = 1470	kcals = 350	Carbs = 43g	Protein = 18g	Fat = 12g	Fibre = 3g

Berry green *(serves 1)*

This smoothie makes a great breakfast or snack any time of the day.

1 handful spinach,
    well washed
½ cup chilled water
1 large handful frozen
    berries
1 cup low-fat milk
1 tbsp ground LSA
2 tbsp low-fat
    unsweetened
    yoghurt
1 tsp vanilla extract

In a blender or food processor, blend the spinach and chilled water thoroughly.

Add the frozen berries and blend again.

Add the milk, LSA, yoghurt and vanilla extract.

Blend until smooth, and serve.

Adapt it

• Replace the unsweetened yoghurt and vanilla extract with vanilla yoghurt, or 1–2 tablespoons of vanilla protein powder if you want to have a little extra protein.
• If you are dairy free, use the milk alternative of your choice and leave out the yoghurt.
• You can add a drizzle of honey for a little sweetness.

Nutrition information per serve

kJ = 1110	kcals = 264	Carbs = 27g	Protein = 14g	Fat = 11g	Fibre = 5g

Chocolate health shake *(serves 1)*

A thick and creamy shake that is packed with goodness!

4 chopped dates
1 frozen banana, skin
    removed
Flesh of ¼ avocado
1 tbsp pumpkin seeds
2 tbsp cocoa powder
1 tsp vanilla extract
1 cup low-fat milk or
    water

Soak the chopped dates in a few tablespoons of boiling water and allow them to soften for a few minutes while you prepare the rest of the ingredients.

Chop the banana into a few chunks and pop into a blender or food processor.

Add the remaining ingredients, including the soaked dates, and blend thoroughly before serving.

Adapt it

• This smoothie has a slightly coarse texture because of the seeds and dates. If you prefer to have a smooth shake then replace the pumpkin seeds with peanut or almond butter and soak the dates for a little longer before adding them.

Top tip

• For a rich chocolate taste, try using raw Dutch cocoa. You can buy it at some supermarkets, health stores and specialty food stores.

Nutrition information per serve (with water)					
kJ = 1694	kcals = 403	Carbs = 47g	Protein = 10g	Fat = 20g	Fibre = 11g

Nutrition information per serve (with milk)					
kJ = 2191	kcals = 522	Carbs = 50g	Protein = 19g	Fat = 24g	Fibre = 11g

Salads, soups and light meals

Lebanese brown rice salad
(serves 4–6 as a main or 8–10 as a side)

Ellie, one of the dietitians who used to work with us at Mission Nutrition, brought this salad to one of our 'bring and share' lunches and I have been making it ever since. I just love it!

¼ pumpkin (approx. 600g), peeled and cut into cubes
1 tbsp olive oil
1 tbsp brown sugar (optional)
2–3 tsp ground cumin
2 cloves garlic, peeled and crushed
3 cups cooked and cooled brown rice
1 punnet cherry tomatoes (approx. 200g), cut in half
½ cup sunflower seeds
½ cup pumpkin seeds
1 red onion, very finely sliced
1 handful coriander or parsley, chopped
Flesh of 1 avocado, cut into chunks

Dressing
Juice of 2 large lemons
2 tbsp extra virgin olive oil

Preheat oven to 180°C. Line a baking tray with baking paper.

Lay out the chopped pumpkin on the tray and sprinkle with olive oil, brown sugar (if using), cumin and crushed garlic.

Roast in the oven for 20–30 minutes or until soft (the time will depend on the size of your pumpkin pieces). When the pumpkin is cooked, remove from the oven and cool.

Meanwhile, in a large bowl, place the brown rice, tomato halves, seeds, red onion and herbs. Mix together and put to one side.

To make the dressing, simply place the lemon juice and olive oil in a clean jam jar, put the lid on and shake.

Add the cooled pumpkin to the brown rice mix and stir through. Add the chopped avocado and pour over the dressing.

Serve with a plain green salad. For extra protein, add a boiled or poached egg, shredded chicken or fish.

Adapt it
• You can use cooked quinoa, buckwheat or bulgar wheat as an alternative to brown rice, if you prefer.
• Add extra lemon juice, if you like.

Nutrition information per serve (based on 6 serves)

| kJ = 2392 | kcals = 570 | Carbs = 58g | Protein = 15g | Fat = 31g | Fibre = 5g |

Tomato and basil salad *(serves 4 as a side)*

This is a fresh, delicious summer salad that is super easy to make, colourful and tastes delicious!

4–6 large ripe
   tomatoes
1 medium cucumber,
   peeled
50g reduced-fat feta
   cheese
1 handful basil leaves
Black pepper

Dressing
4 tbsp balsamic
   vinegar
1 tbsp extra virgin
   olive oil

Slice the tomatoes and cucumber. Layer them on a plate or in a wide bowl.

Place the dressing ingredients in a jam jar, put the lid on, shake and pour over the salad.

Crumble the feta cheese over.

Tear up the basil leaves and sprinkle over (tearing is better than slicing as it will release more flavour).

Season with black pepper, eat and enjoy!

Adapt it

- You can also use parsley or coriander instead of basil, if you like. If you don't have any herbs to hand, you can still make the salad without them. Just add more black pepper and maybe a few slices of avocado, too.
- Try mozzarella or a few dollops of ricotta cheese instead of feta.

Nutrition information per serve					
kJ = 275	kcals = 65	Carbs = 7g	Protein = 4g	Fat = 2g	Fibre = 3g

Tabbouleh *(serves 4 as a main or 8 as a side)*

This is a family recipe that I have been enjoying for years! I eat this most of the time with homemade lamb or beef meatballs, a crunchy green salad and a yoghurt dressing like tzatziki (yoghurt, mint, cucumber, garlic).

1 cup bulgar wheat, thoroughly rinsed
8 spring onions, finely sliced
4 large tomatoes, finely chopped
1–2 cups finely chopped parsley
½ cup finely chopped mint
½ tsp mixed spice
¼ cup lemon juice
2 tbsp extra virgin olive oil
Black pepper

Soak the bulgar wheat in warm water for about 10 minutes or until it is soft but still has a bite to it. Rinse, drain thoroughly and place in a mixing bowl.

Add the spring onions, tomatoes, chopped herbs and mixed spice. Stir together.

Add lemon juice and olive oil, and season with plenty of black pepper.

Chill before serving. Enjoy as a side dish with fish, chicken or meat and a green salad.

Adapt it

- If you are short on time, you can use hot water to soak the bulgar wheat and it will only take 5 minutes to soften. It can go very soft, though, so keep checking as it is soaking to make sure it doesn't go mushy; it still needs to have a 'bite' to it.
- You can use cooked brown rice, buckwheat or quinoa for a gluten-free version.

Nutrition information per serve (based on 4 serves)

kJ = 1240   kcals = 295   Carbs = 44g   Protein = 10g   Fat = 9g   Fibre = 4g

Asian-style slaw *(serves 4 as a main or 8 as a side)*

Healthy, crunchy and delicious.

2 cups shredded red
  cabbage
2 cups shredded
  white cabbage
2 cups grated carrot
1 red capsicum, finely
  sliced
1 cup shelled, cooked
  and cooled
  edamame beans
4 spring onions, finely
  sliced
½ cup peanuts (may
  be chopped)
1 handful coriander,
  chopped

Dressing
4 tbsp rice wine vinegar
  or sushi vinegar
1 tbsp neutral-
  flavoured oil
  (e.g. canola)
2 tbsp runny honey
1 tbsp reduced-salt
  soy sauce
1 tsp sesame oil
1 tbsp smooth peanut
  butter
1 chilli, finely chopped
1 clove garlic, peeled
  and crushed

In a large bowl, mix together the cabbage, carrot, capsicum, beans, spring onion, peanuts and coriander.

To make the dressing, simply mix all the ingredients together in a bowl or put them in a clean jam jar, put the lid on and shake thoroughly until the peanut butter is completely mixed in.

Pour the dressing over the salad.

Perfect served with grilled or shredded chicken, tofu or fish. Add an extra sprinkle of nuts before serving, if you like!

Adapt it
• You can use white wine vinegar if you don't have sushi or rice vinegar.
• If you want to take some to work the next day, don't add dressing to the whole mixture. It is best to add the dressing just before you serve it.

Top tip
• You can buy edamame beans from the frozen section of most supermarkets – ideally choose those which have already had the shells removed.

Nutrition information per serve (slaw without dressing, based on 4 serves)

kJ = 457	kcals = 109	Carbs = 9g	Protein = 10g	Fat = 4g	Fibre = 8g

Nutrition information per serve (dressing only, based on 4 serves)

kJ = 391	kcals = 93	Carbs = 9g	Protein = 1g	Fat = 6g	Fibre = <1g

Spinach, feta and mint frittata *(serves 4)*

This fantastic frittata is perfect for a snack, lunch or light dinner.

2 tsp oil
1 large onion, peeled
   and finely chopped
4 cups spinach (baby
   spinach works
   well), well washed
8 eggs
4 tbsp milk or water
1 cup frozen peas,
   defrosted
50g reduced-fat feta
   cheese
1 handful mint leaves,
   finely chopped
Salt and black pepper

Preheat oven to 200°C. Grease and line a 20cm square baking tin.

Heat the oil in a frying-pan over a medium heat and add the chopped onion. Cook for 2–3 minutes or until soft.

Add the spinach to the frying-pan for 30–60 seconds or until it wilts very slightly.

Remove from the heat and allow to cool.

In a large mixing bowl, beat the eggs and add the milk or water.

Add the remaining ingredients to the eggs, including the cooked onion and spinach, and stir through.

Pour into the prepared tin. Bake for 20–30 minutes or until set and golden brown.

Serve with a mixed green salad and chutney.

Adapt it

• You can add so many different types of veggies to a frittata. Make the recipe above and replace the peas with chopped cherry tomatoes or slices of courgette and use parsley instead of mint. Have a play around with different combinations of veggies and see how you get on!

Nutrition information per serve

| kJ = 951 | kcals = 226 | Carbs = 6g | Protein = 18g | Fat = 15g | Fibre = 4g |

Rainbow power salad
(serves 4-6 as a main, 8-10 as a side)

A fresh, colourful salad packed with goodness.

2 medium beetroot, peeled and grated
3 large carrots, peeled and grated
2 courgettes, grated
½ punnet cherry tomatoes (approx. 100g), cut in half
¼ cup pumpkin seeds
¼ cup sunflower seeds
1 handful parsley, finely chopped

Dressing
¼ cup balsamic vinegar
2 tbsp runny honey
Juice of 1 large orange
1 tsp sesame oil

On a large platter or plate, lay out the grated beetroot. Sprinkle the grated carrot on top to create a layer that is slightly smaller than the first. Add a layer of grated courgette – again, making it smaller than the carrot layer so you can see the rainbow effect.

Place the sliced tomatoes on the top and sprinkle with seeds and parsley.

To make the dressing, simply mix all the ingredients together and serve with the salad.

Mix the salad up just before you eat it, if you like, or leave it all layered up; whatever works for you!

Enjoy as a main for lunch or dinner with grilled chicken, lean meat, fish, tofu, a boiled egg or pulses, or serve as a side salad with a main meal.

Nutrition information per serve (without dressing, based on 6 serves)

kJ = 518	kcals = 123	Carbs = 7g	Protein = 6g	Fat = 8g	Fibre = 4g

Nutrition information per serve (dressing only, based on 6 serves)

kJ = 183	kcals = 44	Carbs = 9g	Protein = <1g	Fat = 1g	Fibre = <1g

Mexican salad *(serves 4 as a side)*

This is a super quick, delicious and filling salad that is packed with flavour.

1 cup cooked black beans

1 cup cooked corn (cooled)

2–3 large tomatoes, chopped

2 spring onions, sliced

Chopped jalapeños (as many as you like)

Juice of 1 lime

1 handful coriander, chopped

Mix all the ingredients together, chill and serve.

Great for lunch with some crunchy iceberg lettuce, or serve for dinner with healthy homemade meatballs, salsa, guacamole and lettuce.

Adapt it
• Use kidney beans instead of (or as well as) black beans.
• If you don't have jalapeños, you can use red chilli or chilli flakes.

Top tips
• Soak and cook the black beans yourself or use a canned variety.
• You can use fresh or frozen corn. If you use frozen corn, you don't need to cook it first; simply defrost it and use as is.

Nutrition information per serve					
kJ = 551	kcals = 131	Carbs = 22g	Protein = 7g	Fat = 2g	Fibre = 6g

Edamame bean salad *(serves 4-6)*

Need a new idea for a tasty lunch? Look no further. This salad is an absolute winner! This is a salad my fabulous friend (another fellow dietitian) Caroline shared with me and I love it – you will too.

1½ cups cooked chickpeas

1½ cups shelled edamame beans (can buy frozen, then just defrost) or broad beans

1 cup frozen green peas, defrosted

2–3 large handfuls baby spinach

50g reduced-fat feta cheese

Dressing

Juice of 1 large or 2 small lemons

Zest of 1 lemon

2 tbsp olive oil

1 tbsp runny honey

2 tbsp white wine vinegar

2 tsp Dijon mustard

Salt and black pepper

In a large bowl, mix the chickpeas, edamame or broad beans, peas and spinach together.

Crumble the feta cheese over.

In a small jug or clean jam jar, mix the ingredients for the dressing together then pour over the salad.

Chill if required and serve.

This salad makes a great lunch – you can add extra protein by having it with a boiled egg or some tuna, if you like. It is also great served for dinner with grilled meat, chicken or fish.

Top tips

• You can either soak then cook the chickpeas yourself (see page 84) or use a canned variety, which you can use straight from the can after rinsing. One can, drained, is approximately 1½ cups.

• You can use fresh peas if you grow them or can get your hands on them!

Nutrition information per serve (without dressing, based on 4 serves)

kJ = 710   kcals = 170   Carbs = 10g   Protein = 16g   Fat = 7g   Fibre = 11g

Nutrition information per serve (dressing only, based on 4 serves)

kJ = 170   kcals = 40   Carbs = 5g   Protein = <1g   Fat = 2g   Fibre = <1g

Green pea power soup *(serves 8)*

A delicious thick soup that makes a perfect lunch, snack or light dinner.

2 tsp oil
1 large onion, peeled and finely chopped
2 large cloves garlic, peeled and crushed
2 stalks celery, diced
2 carrots, peeled and diced
2 tsp ground cumin
1 tsp chilli powder (more if you like)
4 cups vegetable or chicken stock
2 cups boiling water
1½ cups red lentils, rinsed
4 cups frozen peas, defrosted
Black pepper

Heat oil in a large saucepan, add onion and garlic and cook for 4–5 minutes until soft.

Add celery, carrot, cumin and chilli to the pan and cook for another 4–5 minutes.

Pour stock, water and lentils into the pan. Bring to the boil, then reduce heat to a simmer and cook for 20–25 minutes.

Add defrosted peas and cook for another 5 minutes, adding extra water if needed.

Season with black pepper.

Either enjoy the soup with the chunky vegetables or blend it up before serving with a dollop of natural yoghurt or lite sour cream.

Top tip

• Ideally use a homemade stock; if you use ready-made, opt for a reduced-salt variety.

Nutrition information per serve					
kJ = 450	kcals = 107	Carbs = 13g	Protein = 7g	Fat = 3g	Fibre = 10g

Savoury oaty loaf *(serves 8)*

This is my Aunty Karen's recipe and it is a regular feature in our house – perfect for a lunch, picnic or snack. Do not be put off by the list of ingredients, which seems a very odd combination. I promise you won't be disappointed. It tastes a bit like stuffing – yum!

250g cottage cheese
2 tsp Marmite or
    Vegemite
⅓ cup oil
4 large or 5 medium
    eggs, lightly
    beaten
2 cups rolled oats
2 tsp dried sage
2 tsp reduced-salt soy
    sauce
1 onion, peeled and
    finely chopped
Black pepper

Preheat oven to 160°C. Grease and line a 21cm x 11cm loaf tin.

Place cottage cheese in a large mixing bowl. Stir through Marmite or Vegemite until it is evenly distributed.

Add the remaining ingredients and mix together.

Spoon the mixture into the prepared tin. Bake for 40–45 minutes or until firm to the touch.

Allow to cool, then slice and serve. Enjoy a slice or two with a large salad.

This can be stored in the refrigerator for 1–2 days.

Nutrition information per serve

kJ = 913	kcals = 217	Carbs = 15g	Protein = 10g	Fat = 13g	Fibre = 3g

Veggie deluxe soup with nut butter
(serves 8)

Another one of my fabulous nutritionists at Mission Nutrition introduced me to this recipe – thanks Dominique, it is a winner!

5 large carrots, peeled and roughly chopped

3 large parsnips, peeled and roughly chopped

¼ large pumpkin (approx. 600g), peeled and roughly chopped

1 large kumara (approx. 400g), peeled and roughly chopped

8 cups vegetable or chicken stock

1 large bunch spinach, well washed

4 tbsp smooth peanut butter

Place the carrots, parsnips, pumpkin and kumara in a large pan and cover with the stock.

Bring to the boil and then reduce heat to a simmer. Cook for approximately 40 minutes or until vegetables are very soft and starting to break up.

Add the spinach and cook for another 5 minutes.

Remove from the heat, add the peanut butter and blend – yes, sounds odd but it is essential and tastes *amazing*!

Serve with a dollop of natural yoghurt and a sprinkle of freshly chopped parsley.

Top tips
• This is a low FODMAP soup, which is great for those with Irritable Bowel Syndrome.
• Ideally use a homemade stock; if you use ready-made, opt for a reduced-salt variety.

Nutrition information per serve
kJ = 495   kcals = 118   Carbs = 15g   Protein = 6g   Fat = 4g   Fibre = 6g

Magical main meals

Salmon salad cups *(serves 4)*

This is a deliciously light and fresh dish and the perfect way to get a dose of omega-3, whole grains and veggies all in one!

Cooked brown rice (approx. 1 cup dry rice cooked with 2 cups water)

500g skinless, boneless fresh NZ king salmon, sliced into pieces 1cm thick

1 iceberg lettuce, cut into quarters

Salsa

½ large cucumber, peeled, seeds removed and finely diced

4 large tomatoes, finely diced

Flesh of 1 avocado, finely diced

1 red onion, very finely diced

1 red chilli, very finely diced (deseeding optional)

2 tbsp coriander, chopped

Juice of ½ lemon or 1 lime

Black pepper

First, cook your brown rice – it will take about 20–25 minutes.

While the rice is cooking, prepare the salsa. Mix the cucumber, tomato, avocado, red onion, chilli, coriander and lemon or lime juice together in a small bowl. Add black pepper to taste. Transfer to a bowl suitable for serving at the table and pop it into the refrigerator.

When the rice is nearly cooked, heat a frying-pan over a high heat and add the sliced salmon. Cook each piece for 30–60 seconds on each side or until cooked to your liking. Remove from the pan, drain on a paper towel if required and place on a serving dish (ideally pre-warmed so the salmon stays warm, too!).

Transfer the brown rice to a serving dish and then lay everything out on the table (lettuce, salmon, rice and salsa) and dig in.

This is a 'make your own' kind of meal. The iceberg lettuce can be used like a 'cup'. Into the 'cup' add a spoonful of the cooked brown rice, a couple of pieces of salmon and top with salsa. Then eat with your hands.

If you like things hot, try it with some extra-hot chilli sauce or for a little sweetness, try sweet chilli sauce.

Adapt it
- If you prefer, don't cook the salmon – eat it raw (sashimi style).
- Replace the salmon with white fish, chicken or finely sliced beef.
- Replace the tomato in the salsa with fresh or canned mango and add a few teaspoons of sweet chilli sauce.

Top tip
- Dice the cucumber, tomato and avocado to the same size (5mm cubes are good) to make it easy to eat.

Nutrition information per serve (with rice)

kJ = 1982   kcals = 471   Carbs = 23g   Protein = 31g   Fat = 28g   Fibre = 7g

Nutrition information per serve (without rice)

kJ = 1633   kcals = 388   Carbs = 8g   Protein = 30g   Fat = 27g   Fibre = 6g

Curried chickpea patties *(makes 8 large patties)*

These patties are packed with flavour and make an ideal lunch or dinner.

2 x 400g cans
  chickpeas or
  3 cups cooked
  chickpeas
2 tsp oil
1 medium onion,
  peeled and finely
  chopped
2 cloves garlic, peeled
  and crushed
1 large carrot, grated
1 tsp ground cumin
1 tsp ground
  coriander
½ tsp turmeric
2 tbsp tomato paste
1 egg, beaten
1 large handful freshly
  chopped parsley or
  coriander
Extra oil for frying

Place the chickpeas in a food processor and blend for a few seconds until broken down but not completely smooth. Alternatively, you can mash them. Transfer to a mixing bowl.

In a frying-pan, heat the oil over a medium heat, then add the onion, garlic and carrot. Cook for 2–3 minutes or until they start to soften. Add the spices and cook for another 2 minutes.

Mix the tomato paste with 1 tablespoon of boiling water and add this to the carrot mix. Cook over a low heat for 1–2 minutes. Remove from the heat and add to the chickpeas.

Add the beaten egg and chopped herbs to the mixing bowl and combine everything together.

Chill for 30 minutes (if you have time) to allow mixture to firm up; or just use immediately.

Divide the mixture into 8 patties or, if you like, 16 mini patties.

Place a clean frying-pan with a little oil over a medium heat and cook the patties for 3–4 minutes on each side until golden brown and hot through.

Serve with salad and natural yoghurt, tzatziki, hummus and/or chutney.

Adapt it
- You can use curry paste as an alternative to the three spices and tomato paste.
- If you prefer a firmer patty, add 1–2 tablespoons of rolled oats or breadcrumbs.

Nutrition information per serve (1 pattie)					
kJ = 391	kcals = 93	Carbs = 8g	Protein = 5g	Fat = 5g	Fibre = 6g

Lentil bake *(serves 6)*

Growing up, this was a staple meal in our house. It was the only way my mum could get us to eat veggies without realising, and it totally worked.

250g red lentils, rinsed

2 large onions, peeled and chopped into quarters

3 large carrots, peeled and roughly chopped

2 bay leaves

2 cups chicken or vegetable stock

¾ cup boiling water

1 large head broccoli

100g cheese, grated

3 tsp dried dill or 2 tbsp fresh dill, chopped

¾ cup wholegrain breadcrumbs

In a large saucepan, put the lentils, onion, carrot, bay leaves, stock and water. Bring to the boil, then reduce the heat to low, cover and simmer for 30 minutes until the vegetables are very soft and the lentils are well cooked. Be sure to check and stir the pan every few minutes to prevent the lentils sticking and burning on the bottom of the pan. Add a little extra water if needed.

Remove the bay leaves.

Preheat oven to 180°C. Grease an ovenproof dish (8-cup capacity).

Remove the florets from the broccoli. Trim the tough outer edges of the broccoli stalk and discard, keep the soft inner flesh – add this with the florets to the saucepan and simmer for a further 10 minutes.

Take the pan off the heat and blend the mixture with a stick whizz or in a food processor. Stir through the dill and half of the cheese. Pour the mixture into the well-greased ovenproof dish.

Top with breadcrumbs and remaining grated cheese and pop into the oven for 15–20 minutes or until the top is golden brown.

Delicious served with green veggies or salad and homemade potato/kumara wedges.

Adapt it
• You can add extra veggies if you like. Courgettes work well.
• Add an extra cup of stock and one of water to make this into a soup.

Top tip
• Make a double batch and freeze half.

Nutrition information per serve

| kJ = 770 | kcals = 183 | Carbs = 19g | Protein = 12g | Fat = 7g | Fibre = 7g |

Cauliflower base pizza *(serves 2)*

Using a vegetable as the base of a pizza – this recipe is so clever! It works so much better than you might imagine and tastes really, really good.

Base
½ head cauliflower
   (about 2 cups
   grated)
1 clove garlic, peeled
   and crushed
⅓ cup grated
   mozzarella cheese
2 eggs, beaten
1 tsp dried or fresh
   oregano

Topping
2 tbsp tomato purée
   or paste
A selection of sliced
   vegetables of
   your choice, e.g.
   tomato, capsicum,
   corn, courgette
⅓ cup grated
   mozzarella cheese

Preheat oven to 200°C. Line a baking tray with baking paper.

Remove the stems and leaves from your cauliflower and coarsely grate the florets (alternatively, you can use a food processor to do this).

Pop the cauliflower in a microwave-proof bowl and cook on High for 2 minutes. Remove from the microwave, stir and pop it back in for another 2 minutes. Repeat again if required but be very careful not to burn the cauliflower. It is likely to take 6–8 minutes in total, depending on the power of your microwave. You want the cauliflower to be very soft. (Alternatively you can steam it in a pot.)

Add garlic, cheese, eggs and oregano to the cauliflower and stir through to create a dough.

Spread the dough out evenly on the baking paper (about 5mm thick). The pizza should be about 20–25cm in diameter.

Bake for 15–20 minutes or until the crust is golden, crispy on the edges and cooked through the middle. Remove from the oven.

Top with tomato purée or paste, sliced vegetables (avoid adding too many heavy toppings) and cheese.

Return to the oven for about 5 minutes or until toppings are hot and cheese is melted.

Serve with a large salad with nuts and seeds and a delicious, healthy dressing.

Nutrition information per serve					
kJ = 973	kcals = 232	Carbs = 8g	Protein = 22g	Fat = 13g	Fibre = 4g

Garlic, chilli and prawn stir-fry *(serves 4)*

The perfect quick and easy mid-week meal.

2–4 tsp oil for stir-frying
400g raw prawns, tails removed (defrosted)
2 cloves garlic, peeled and crushed
1–2 red chillies (depending on how hot you like it! Deseeding optional)
1 tbsp freshly grated ginger
1 large red onion, sliced
8 cups vegetables, finely sliced (e.g. capsicum, broccoli, carrot, snow peas, sugar snap peas, mushrooms, courgettes)

Sauce
2 tsp cornflour
3 tbsp water
2 tbsp reduced-salt soy sauce
1 tbsp runny honey
1 tbsp rice wine or white wine vinegar

First make the stir-fry sauce. Mix the cornflour with the water in a mug or small jug until all the lumps have gone. Add the soy sauce, honey and vinegar, and put to one side.

Heat 1–2 teaspoons of oil in a wok or large frying-pan over a high heat, add the prawns and cook through for 3–4 minutes until they turn pink. Remove from the heat and put to one side in a bowl.

Heat another 1–2 teaspoons of oil in the wok/pan over a high heat, add the garlic, chilli, ginger and red onion, and stir-fry for 1 minute.

Add the vegetables and stir-fry for 4–5 minutes. You can add 1–2 tablespoons of water if needed during this stir-fry process to create a bit of steam to soften the vegetables (this is helpful if you are using lots of hard veggies like carrots/broccoli/green beans).

Add the stir-fry sauce and return the prawns to the wok/pan. Cook for another 2–3 minutes to allow cornflour to cook out and prawns to heat through.

Delicious served with rice.

Adapt it
• Instead of prawns use chicken or tofu – cook it first until done and then add it back in after stir-frying the veggies.

Nutrition information per serve					
kJ = 1037	kcals = 247	Carbs = 30g	Protein = 22g	Fat = 5g	Fibre = 12g

Beef and chickpea casserole *(serves 6)*

A wonderful winter recipe that uses pulses and plenty of veggies for extra goodness.

500g beef rump, fat removed and cut into chunks

2 tbsp flour

1 tbsp oil

1 large onion, peeled and chopped

1 tbsp dried sage or small handful fresh sage leaves

2 medium carrots, peeled and chopped

1 large or 2 small parsnips, peeled and chopped

¼ large pumpkin (600g), peeled and chopped

2 x 400g cans chopped tomatoes

2 tbsp tomato paste

1 cup reduced-salt beef stock

1½ cups cooked chickpeas (1 x 400g can, drained)

1 cup peas (frozen is fine)

2–3 large handfuls spinach, well washed

Zest of 1 large lemon

Coat the beef chunks in the flour and put to one side.

Heat the oil in a large pan and add the onion and sage. Cook over a medium heat for 5 minutes or until onion is soft.

Add the beef to the pan and brown very slightly for five minutes, then add the carrot, parsnip, pumpkin, canned tomatoes, tomato paste and stock. Bring to the boil, then reduce to a simmer. Cook over a low heat with a lid on for 1½–2 hours or until meat is soft and vegetables are well cooked. Check and stir every 20 minutes or so and add an extra splash of water if needed.

Add chickpeas, peas and spinach and cook for another 5–10 minutes.

Add lemon zest and stir through.

Serve with brown rice, mashed kumara or potato, mashed beans (e.g. butter beans) and lots of green veggies.

Adapt it

- Use lamb instead of beef.
- If you are gluten free, leave the flour out. If you want, you can thicken the casserole towards the end of cooking with cornflour (mix 1 tablespoon of cornflour with 3 tablespoons of cold water to make a paste, add in and stir quickly through, cooking for a good 10 minutes before serving).

Top tips

- The vegetables need to be chunky for this.
- As odd as the lemon zest might sound, don't miss it out – it is really essential for flavour balance!
- This dish freezes well.

Nutrition information per serve (without rice/veggies)

kJ = 1335   kcals = 318   Carbs = 23g   Protein = 30g   Fat = 12g   Fibre = 12g

Sensational sides and vegetable dishes

Butter bean mash *(serves 4)*

This is a tasty mash that is a great alternative to mashed potato.

2 tsp extra virgin
   olive oil
1 clove garlic, peeled
   and crushed
Sprig of rosemary
   (optional)
Zest of 1 lemon
2 x 400g cans butter
   beans, drained and
   rinsed (or 3 cups
   cooked butter
   beans)
2 tbsp low-fat milk,
   low-fat yoghurt or
   lite sour cream
Salt and black pepper

Heat the olive oil in a saucepan. Reduce the heat right down and add the garlic, sprig of rosemary (if using) and lemon zest. Warm through then remove the rosemary and discard.

Add the beans to the pan and heat through. Remove from the heat and add the milk, yoghurt or sour cream.

Mash roughly or blitz completely with a stick whizz or food processor, depending on your preference.

Season with salt and pepper and serve. Sprinkle with finely chopped parsley before serving, if wished.

Adapt it
- Instead of butter beans try cannellini or haricot beans.
- Mix this bean mash 50:50 with potato mash – super tasty and a great way to slowly introduce your family to more beans!
- As well as garlic you can also use finely chopped onion or shallot.

Top tip
- You can soak and cook the beans yourself or just used the canned variety if time is an issue. If you use canned beans, be sure to thoroughly wash and drain them before adding.

Nutrition information per serve					
kJ = 1026	kcals = 244	Carbs = 34g	Protein = 12g	Fat = 4g	Fibre = 13g

Smashed swede and carrot *(serves 6)*

This is a favourite family recipe that is perfect with a roast dinner or to accompany any meal where extra veggies are required.

2 large onions
3 large carrots
1 medium swede
Black pepper

Peel and roughly chop the onions, carrot and swede.

Steam the vegetables for 20 minutes or until very soft.

Using a stick blender or a food processor, blend the vegetables together and season with black pepper.

A perfect side dish for a healthy roast!

Adapt it
- Add parsnip too, if you like.
- If you don't have a steamer, boil the vegetables in hot water and drain.
- If you prefer a chunkier mix, mash with a potato masher instead of blending.

Nutrition information per serve
kJ = 76   kcals = 18   Carbs = 4g   Protein = <1g   Fat = <1g   Fibre = 2g

Spinach saag *(serves 4–6 as a side)*

A perfect vegetable side dish to accompany a meat, chicken, fish or prawn curry along with steamed rice. It can also be enjoyed as a meal by itself.

2 tbsp oil
1 onion, peeled and chopped
4 cloves garlic, peeled and chopped
1 tbsp freshly grated ginger
2 tsp ground coriander
½ tsp turmeric
1 red chilli roughly chopped (deseeding optional)
500g spinach, frozen and defrosted or fresh
½ cup water
250g cottage cheese
Salt and black pepper

Heat the oil in a large frying-pan over a medium heat. Add the onion and garlic, and cook for 3–4 minutes until soft and translucent.

Add the ginger, coriander, turmeric and chilli (if using) and cook for a further 2–3 minutes.

Stir in the spinach and water, and bring to a boil. Reduce heat to low and simmer for another 10–15 minutes. Remove from heat and allow to cool slightly.

Using a stick blender or food processor, quickly blitz the spinach mix until it breaks down a little but isn't completely puréed.

Return the spinach mix to the pan and add the cottage cheese. Stir and simmer for 5–10 minutes.

Season with salt and pepper and serve.

Adapt it
- Add cooked shredded chicken to this dish to make a complete dish.
- Leave out the cottage cheese if you are dairy free.
- Lite cottage cheese works as well as regular cottage cheese.
- You can use silver beet or other leafy greens if you prefer, or use a mixture.

Nutrition information per serve (based on 4 serves)					
kJ = 344	kcals = 82	Carbs =4g	Protein = 6g	Fat = 5g	Fibre = 8g

Zesty greens *(serves 4 as a side)*

A simple way to enjoy green veggies with the added zing of citrus.

Zest and juice of
   1 lemon
1 tbsp olive oil
1 large head of
   broccoli
500g leafy greens
   e.g. spinach, silver
   beet, kale
Black pepper

In a jam jar, cup or small bowl, mix the lemon zest and juice and olive oil together, then put to one side.

Wash the vegetables thoroughly.

Remove the broccoli florets and slice them each in half or quarters depending on their size.

Remove the hard outer layer from the broccoli stalk to reveal the soft inner flesh. Slice it into 5mm-thick pieces.

Remove any hard stems from the leafy greens and then roughly chop.

Steam the vegetables for 3–4 minutes. Remove from the heat, drain off any excess water and transfer to a serving dish.

Pour over the lemon and olive oil mix and season with black pepper.

Adapt it:
• You can use any green veggies you like. Green beans, snow peas, asparagus, savoy cabbage, sliced courgettes all work well – experiment!

Nutrition information per serve

kJ = 213   kcals = 51   Carbs = 3g   Protein = 5g   Fat = 2g   Fibre = 8g

Delicious dressings and nut butters

Wasabi mayo *(makes 4 serves)*

Great on coleslaw or perfect with any salad, especially if you are planning to serve the salad with fish.

4 tbsp mayonnaise
4–5 tbsp boiling water
1 large squeeze wasabi paste

In a clean jam jar, combine the mayonnaise and the boiling water. Whisk together with a fork to remove the lumps.

When it has cooled slightly add the wasabi paste, put the lid on the jam jar and shake vigorously.

This is a great dressing for coleslaw or a green salad and is perfect with fish.

Top tip
• I use a mayonnaise that is about 30 per cent fat made with real eggs; you can use a lower-fat version if you prefer.

Nutrition information per serve (1 tbsp/15ml)					
kJ = 155	kcals = 37	Carbs = 1g	Protein = <1g	Fat = 4g	Fibre = 0g

Simple balsamic dressing *(makes 1 cup)*

I make this in a jam jar and keep it in the refrigerator so I can use it whenever I need to.

¾ cup balsamic vinegar
¼ cup extra virgin olive oil
2 tsp wholegrain mustard
1–2 tbsp runny honey
Black pepper

Put all the ingredients in a jam jar, pop on the lid and shake.

Delicious with a green salad, poured over sliced tomatoes, coleslaw or grated vegetable salads.

Nutrition information per serve (1 tbsp/15ml)					
kJ = 184	kcals = 44	Carbs = 2g	Protein = <1g	Fat = 4g	Fibre = <1g

Avocado dressing *(makes 4 serves)*

This is a great alternative to ranch or other creamy-style dressings.

Flesh of 1 large
 avocado
2 tsp fresh lemon
 juice
½ cup low-fat
 unsweetened
 yoghurt
1 tsp hot chilli sauce
2 tbsp extra virgin
 olive oil
2 cloves garlic, peeled
 and crushed

Place all the ingredients in a food processor and blend.

Delicious with any salad or poured over pasta.

Nutrition information per serve

kJ = 704   kcals = 168   Carbs = 1g   Protein = 1g   Fat = 18g   Fibre = 2g

Tahini dressing *(makes 4 serves)*

The perfect accompaniment to a green salad.

½ cup low-fat
 unsweetened
 yoghurt
2 tbsp tahini
1 small clove garlic,
 peeled and
 crushed
1 squeeze lemon juice
Salt and black pepper

Mix everything together in a jug or clean jam jar.

Delicious with any salad.

Top tip
• For a thinner consistency, add a little water or use a yoghurt that has more of a pouring consistency.

Nutrition information per serve

kJ = 262   kcals = 62   Carbs = 2g   Protein = 3g   Fat = 5g   Fibre = 1g

Nut and seed butters *(makes 40 serves)*

Making your own nut and seed butters is much easier than you think – give it a go!

500g raw unsalted nuts and/or seeds
Neutral-flavoured oil, e.g. canola oil

Method 1

Place the nuts/seeds in a food processor and turn it to High. Blend for several minutes until they break down and start to form a thick paste or simply go into a very fine powder (it will depend on what nuts/seeds you are using).

While the food processor is still going, add 1 tablespoon of oil at a time, allowing at least 20–30 seconds before adding more oil each time.

Keep adding oil until the nut/seed butter is the consistency you desire.

Pop the seed butter into a jar (best to sterilise the jar first) and then keep in the refrigerator.

Method 2

Preheat oven to 150°C.

Lay nuts/seeds out on a baking tray and pop into preheated oven. Dry-roast for 5–10 minutes until very lightly browned, moving nuts around every 2–3 minutes.

Remove nuts/seeds from oven and allow to cool.

When nuts/seeds are completely cool, pop them in the food processor and blend with oil (as per Method 1) until a smooth paste forms.

Adapt it

- You can use any kind of nuts or seeds you like. Nuts that work really well include peanuts, almonds, walnuts, cashews and macadamias. You can also make mixed combinations like almonds, Brazils and cashews – have a play!
- The most successful seed butters I have made are those with sesame seeds (tahini), sunflower and pumpkin seeds.

Top tips

- I normally make my nut butters using Method 2 as I prefer the taste when the nuts are roasted first. It's up to you!
- I always prefer to make tahini (sesame seed butter) with toasted sesame seeds as it has a much nuttier, fuller flavour (5 cups sesame seeds needs about 1 cup oil to blend).
- It is likely that the oil and nuts/seeds will separate when you leave it for a while so just stir together before using.
- The key to making nut butter is having a really grunty and powerful food processor; it will give you a much better result.

Note: Nutritional information will vary depending on the nuts/seeds used and the amount of oil added.

Snacks and sweet treats

Red kidney bean dip *(makes 4 serves)*

All things hot and spicy!

1½ cups cooked
kidney beans
(1 x 400g can,
drained and
rinsed)
Juice of 1 lemon
Thumb-sized piece
fresh ginger,
peeled and finely
chopped
1–2 hot chillies (or
to your taste;
deseeding
optional)
1 small handful
parsley
1 tbsp extra virgin
olive oil
Salt and black pepper

Put all the ingredients in a food processor and blend – it's as easy as that.

Serve with chopped veggies, wholegrain crackers or wholemeal pita bread wedges.

Nutrition information per serve					
kJ = 422	kcals = 100	Carbs = 10g	Protein = 6g	Fat = 4g	Fibre = 6g

Spicy carrot and chickpea dip *(makes 6 serves)*

Ideal served with crackers or raw veggie sticks.

4 medium carrots (400g), peeled and cut into chunky pieces
1 tsp each ground cumin, coriander and medium curry powder
1½ cups cooked chickpeas (1 x 400g can, drained and rinsed)
2 tbsp water
½ cup (50g) tahini
Juice and zest of 1 medium orange

Coat the carrot with the spices and steam until tender, then cool.

Put all the ingredients into a food processor (including the carrots) and blend together, adding 1–2 tablespoons of water if required.

Serve with chopped veggies, wholegrain crackers or wholemeal pita bread wedges.

Nutrition information per serve

kJ = 499   kcals = 119   Carbs = 9g   Protein = 5g   Fat = 7g   Fibre = 7g

Pea and mint hummus *(makes 6 serves)*

This is by far one of my favourite recipes of all time.

1½ cups frozen peas
1½ cups cooked
    chickpeas
    (1 x 400g can,
    drained and
    rinsed)
1 heaped tbsp tahini
1 tbsp water
Zest and juice of
    1 lemon
1 handful mint leaves
Salt and black pepper

Put all the ingredients in a food processor and blend.

Serve with chopped veggies, wholegrain crackers or wholemeal pita bread wedges.

Top tip

- You can also add a small amount of reduced-fat feta cheese to this if you like!

Nutrition information per serve (without feta)					
kJ = 323	kcals = 77	Carbs = 6g	Protein = 5g	Fat = 4g	Fibre = 6g

Guacamole *(makes 6 serves)*

Perfect as a dip or served with chili con carne or a vegetable chili.

Flesh of 2 ripe avocados
Juice of 1 lemon
3 tbsp lite sour cream or unsweetened yoghurt
3 large ripe tomatoes, finely diced
½ red onion, very finely diced
1 red chilli, finely chopped (deseeding optional)
Salt and black pepper

In a medium-sized mixing bowl, mash the avocado flesh roughly with a fork.

Add the lemon juice and sour cream or yoghurt and mix through.

Add the tomatoes, red onion and chilli and gently fold in.

Season with salt and pepper and serve.

Lovely with chilli con carne (or a veggie version). Perfect to enjoy as a dip, too – delicious with chopped veggies, wholegrain crackers or wholemeal pita bread wedges.

Adapt it

• Replace the chopped chilli with 1 teaspoon of hot chilli sauce, 1 pinch of chilli flakes or, if you don't like it hot, 1 teaspoon of sweet chilli sauce.

Nutrition information per serve					
kJ = 507	kcals = 121	Carbs = 5g	Protein = 2g	Fat = 10g	Fibre = 4g

Beetroot hummus *(makes 6 serves)*

This colourful hummus makes a great snack and is perfect to serve when you are entertaining.

2 medium beetroot,
  cooked and cooled
  (or 1 x 400g can)
1½ cups cooked
  chickpeas
  (1 x 400g can,
  drained and
  rinsed)
1 heaped tbsp tahini
1 tbsp water
2 tsp horseradish
Salt and black pepper

Put all the ingredients in a food processor and blend.

Serve with chopped veggies, wholegrain crackers or wholemeal pita bread wedges.

Nutrition information per serve

kJ = 382   kcals = 91   Carbs = 11g   Protein = 4g   Fat = 4g   Fibre = 5g

Date and orange balls *(makes 30 balls)*

These taste just like chocolate orange truffles.

400g pitted dried dates

400g almonds, macadamias or walnuts (or any combination of these)

5 heaped tbsp cocoa powder

Juice of 1 large orange

Zest of 2 large oranges

Desiccated coconut for coating

Place dates in a bowl and cover with 1 cup very hot water (almost boiling). Leave to soak for 15 minutes.

Place nuts in a food processor and blend until they resemble fine breadcrumbs. Pour the ground nuts into a mixing bowl.

Drain the dates thoroughly and check there are no pips hiding anywhere (reserve the soaking water for later). Pop the dates into the food processor along with the cocoa powder, orange juice and zest and blend together.

Slowly add the ground nuts back into the food processor while it is still going until you have added all the nuts. If the mixture is too dry, add a little of the date soaking water you have reserved. If it is too wet, add a little desiccated coconut until the mixture becomes firm enough to roll into balls that will hold their shape.

Take heaped teaspoons of the mixture in your hands and roll into balls. Cover with coconut. Place the balls onto greaseproof paper and chill in the refrigerator until ready to eat (1–2 hours).

Adapt it
• You can also coat the balls in cocoa powder or chopped nuts.

Top tip
• These freeze well.
• Dutch cocoa gives these a really delicious dark chocolately taste.

Nutrition information per serve					
kJ = 530	kcals = 126	Carbs = 10g	Protein = 3g	Fat = 8g	Fibre = 3g

Biba bliss balls *(makes 30)*

At Biba Hair Salon (www.biba.net.nz), the hairdressers I go to, you are offered a lovely cup of herbal tea, a small handful of raw nuts and one of these amazing nut and seed bites when you arrive! They are just so delicious that I had to get the recipe and (with their love and blessings) share it with you. Enjoy!

½ cup ground LSA (linseed, sunflower seeds and almonds)
½ cup desiccated or shredded coconut
½ cup raw almonds, roughly chopped
½ cup dried cranberries
¼ cup tahini
¼ cup smooth peanut butter
¼ cup honey
Additional ½ cup desiccated or shredded coconut for coating

Put LSA, coconut, almonds and cranberries in a bowl and mix together.

In a saucepan, combine the tahini, peanut butter and honey and melt together over a low heat – do not allow to boil or it will burn the mixture.

Pour the liquid mix into the dry mix and combine with a spoon.

Take heaped teaspoons of the mixture in your hands and roll into balls. Roll in coconut and place on a piece of greaseproof paper on a plate or tray and pop into the refrigerator to chill for at least 1 hour.

Adapt it
• Replace the almonds with any nuts of your choice.
• Replace the cranberries with sultanas, figs, raisins or chopped dates.

Top tip
• Store in the refrigerator to keep them fresh.

Nutrition information per serve					
kJ = 371	kcals = 88	Carbs = 5g	Protein = 2g	Fat = 6g	Fibre = 2g

Avocado chocolate mousse *(serves 4)*

Thick, creamy and decadent! You would never believe this has avocado in it.

2 ripe avocados
2 tbsp cocoa powder
1 tbsp runny honey or
   maple syrup
1 tsp vanilla extract
1–2 tbsp water or
   coconut water

Remove the flesh from the avocados and pop it in a food processor with the cocoa powder, honey or maple syrup, vanilla extract and 1 tablespoon of water or coconut water. Blend until thick and smooth.

Add a little extra water if you like a thinner consistency.

Divide into 4 serving bowls or glasses and chill to set (ideally for at least 1–2 hours if you have time).

Adapt it
• Replace the water or coconut water and vanilla extract with the zest and juice of an orange.

Top tip
• For a delicious dark chocolate mousse, I use Dutch cocoa which you will find at health food stores and specialty food stores.

Nutrition information per serve
kJ = 970   kcals = 231   Carbs = 5g   Protein = 2g   Fat = 23g   Fibre = 5g

Thanks and acknowledgements

From the bottom of my heart, thank you to all the wonderful people who have helped me create *Feel Good for Life* and thanks to you for reading it!

To my amazing friends who encouraged me to take my ideas and put them to paper, I am so glad you did. Thanks also to Penguin for encouraging me to write a second book and to all the people behind the scenes who make the book come to life.

Mum and Dad, thanks for believing in me. You have created so many opportunities for me to grow and learn in my life, and your unquestionable support has helped me be the best I can be. Mum, a special note of thanks for getting up at the crack of dawn to help me proof my drafts, especially as I was pregnant when I wrote this book and really needed that second pair of eyes!

To those who have helped me on my own journey to feeling good, I will be forever grateful. Thank you for holding my hand, wiping away my tears and loving me beyond measure. You know who you are and I can't thank you enough.

To my husband Troy, what can I say? Since the day I met you, you have encouraged me to find strength from within and find ways to make myself feel good without needing to seek recognition from others. With you by my side, you help me to believe anything is possible.

Last but not least, to the newest addition to my life, baby Zac. Your arrival into this world has reaffirmed just how amazing and precious life is. I promise to live true to the words in this book and to be an inspiration to you each and every day.

Resources

www.glnc.org.au/legumes/

www.glnc.org.au/legumes/legumes-nutrition/

shepherdworks.com.au/disease-information/gluten-free-diet

www.nrv.gov.au/nutrients/fat.htm

www.health.govt.nz/publication/vitamin-d-status-new-zealand-adults

www.health.govt.nz/your-health/healthy-living/food-and-physical-activity/nutrition/vitamin-d

www.xyris.com.au/foodworks/download.html

Endnotes

1   Wansink, B., and Sobal, J., 'Mindless Eating: The 200 Daily Food Decisions We Overlook', *Environment and Behavior*, 2007, 39:1 (Jan), pp106–23; Chadwick *et al*, *Nutrition Bulletin*, 2003, 35:36–42.

2   *A Focus on Nutrition: Key Findings of the 2008/09 New Zealand Adult Nutrition Survey*, Ministry of Health, Wellington, 2011, p 219.

3   FoodWorks® 7, nutrient analysis software, 2012.

4   www.glnc.org.au/legumes/legumes-health/

5   World Cancer Research Fund/American Institute for Cancer Research, *Food, Nutrition, Physical Activity and the Prevention of Cancer: A Global Perspective*, AICR, Washington, DC, 2007.

6   www.glycemicindex.com

7   Sivakumaran, S., and Huffman, L., *The Concise New Zealand Food Composition Tables* (9th edition), The New Zealand Institute for Plant & Food Research Limited and Ministry of Health, Palmerston North, 2012.

8   A special thanks to Dr Laurence Eyes, specialist in fats and oils, for his expert knowledge of oils and assistance with this section. For more information about oils check out www.oilsfats.org.nz.

9   www.heartfoundation.org.nz/know-the-facts/food-and-drink/salt

10 Ros, E., 'Health Benefits of Nut Consumption', *Nutrients*, 2010, 2:652–682.

11 *A Focus on Nutrition: Key Findings of the 2008/09 New Zealand Adult Nutrition Survey*, Ministry of Health, Wellington, 2011.

12 Hammami, M. M., *et al*, 'Interaction between drug and placebo effects: A Cross-over Balanced Placebo Design Trial', *Trials*, 2010, 11:110.

13 www.alcohol.org.nz

Index

Recipes index

K

kidney beans: Red kidney bean dip 252
kiwifruit: Green kiwi 217
kumara: Veggie deluxe soup with nut
   butter 233

L

Lebanese brown rice salad 222
lemon
   Green goodness 216
   Zesty greens 247
lentils
   Green pea power soup 234
   Lentil bake 239
lettuce: Salmon salad cups 236–7
linseeds *see* flaxseeds
LSA (linseed, sunflower seed and almond
      mix); *see also* seeds
   Awesome overnight oats
   Berry green 220
   Biba bliss balls 260
   Nutty apple crumble 215

M

mash: Butter bean mash 244
Mexican salad 230
milk; *see also* milkshakes
   Awesome overnight oats 212
   Berry green 220
milkshakes
   Chocolate health shake 221
   Monkey shake 218
mint
   Pea and mint hummus 256
   Spinach, feta and mint frittata 227
Monkey shake 218
mozzarella cheese: Cauliflower base pizza
      240
muesli
   Awesome overnight oats 212
   Raw muesli mix 214

N

nuts; *see also* individual nuts
   Date and orange balls 258
   Nut and seed butters 250–1
   Nutty apple crumble 215

O

oats
   Awesome overnight oats 212

   Nutty apple crumble 215
   Raw muesli mix 214
   Savoury oaty loaf 232
onion, red
   Lebanese brown rice salad 222
   Salmon salad cups 236–7
orange: Date and orange balls 258

P

parsnip
   Beef and chickpea casserole 242–3
   Veggie deluxe soup with nut butter
      233
patties: Curried chickpea patties 238
peanut butter
   Biba bliss balls 260
   Monkey shake 218
   Veggie deluxe soup with nut butter
      233
peanuts: Asian-style slaw 226; *see also*
      peanut butter
peas
   Beef and chickpea casserole 242–3
   Edamame bean salad 231
   Green pea power soup 234
   Pea and mint hummus 256
   Spinach, feta and mint frittata 227
pizza: Cauliflower base pizza 240
prawns *see* seafood
pumpkin
   Beef and chickpea casserole 242–3
   Lebanese brown rice salad 222
   Veggie deluxe soup with nut butter
      233
pumpkin seeds
   Chocolate health shake 221
   Lebanese brown rice salad 222
   Rainbow power salad 228
   Raw muesli mix 214

R

Rainbow power salad 228
Raw muesli mix 214
Red kidney bean dip 252
rice
   Lebanese brown rice salad 222
   Salmon salad cups 236–7
rolled oats *see* oats

S

saag: Spinach saag 246